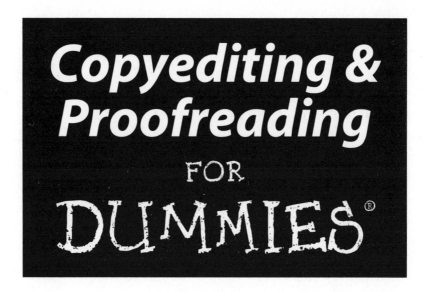

Copyediting & Proofreading FOR DUMMIES®

by Suzanne Gilad

BICENTENNIAL
1807
WILEY
2007
BICENTENNIAL

Wiley Publishing, Inc.

Copyediting & Proofreading For Dummies®

Published by
Wiley Publishing, Inc.
111 River St.
Hoboken, NJ 07030-5774
www.wiley.com

Copyright © 2007 by Wiley Publishing, Inc., Indianapolis, Indiana

Published by Wiley Publishing, Inc., Indianapolis, Indiana

Published simultaneously in Canada

For general information on our other products and services, please contact our Customer Care Department within the U.S. at 800-762-2974, outside the U.S. at 317-572-3993, or fax 317-572-4002.

For technical support, please visit www.wiley.com/techsupport.

Wiley also publishes its books in a variety of electronic formats. Some content that appears in print may not be available in electronic books.

Library of Congress Control Number: 2007924228

ISBN: 978-0-470-12171-9

Manufactured in the United States of America

10 9 8 7 6 5 4 3

WILEY

Copyediting & Proofreading For Dummies®

Cheat Sheet

Must-Have References

Much of the information in desk references can be found on the Internet, but a good copyeditor or proofreader should have hard-copy references. (You never know when your Internet connection may slow to a crawl.) Here are five you can't live without:

- ✔ **House style sheet:** You get this reference from the company you work for or, if you freelance, the person who hires you. When you question how something is presented in a document, it's the first reference you check.

- ✔ **Style manual:** Your employer or client is likely to have a favored style manual, which may be *The Chicago Manual of Style, The Associated Press Stylebook,* or *The New York Times Manual of Style and Usage.* If the house style sheet doesn't answer your question, check the style manual. And make sure you know which edition of the style manual is being used.

- ✔ **Dictionary:** Don't copyedit or proofread without one. I prefer *Merriam-Webster's Collegiate Dictionary,* 11th Edition, but you must use whatever dictionary your employer or client prefers. Get the latest edition; language changes quickly, especially in the technical realm.

- ✔ **Grammar and usage guide:** Some examples are *Garner's Modern American Usage, The Elements of Style, Words Into Type,* and *The Merriam-Webster Usage Dictionary.*

- ✔ **Specialty references:** Some books I have collected for various projects are *The Synonym Finder* by Rodale, *Merriam-Webster's Geographical Dictionary, Wired Style,* and *Bartlett's Familiar Quotations.* Depending on the types of projects you work on, your bookshelf may soon sport specialty references you never imagined needing.

Some Soon-To-Be Favorite Web Sites

Here are just a few online resources you may want to mark as favorites:

- ✔ `www.bartleby.com`: I'll let the resource speak for itself: "Bartleby.com combines the best of both contemporary and classic reference works into the most comprehensive public reference library ever published on the web."

- ✔ `www.google.com`: Google will be your gracious fact-checking workhorse.

- ✔ `www.m-w.com`: Merriam-Webster OnLine provides the 10th edition of *Merriam-Webster's Collegiate Dictionary* for free and the 11th edition for a subscription fee.

- ✔ `www.nytimes.com/navigator/`: This is *The New York Times's* Newsroom Navigator: a fact-checking launchpad for its reporters.

For Dummies: Bestselling Book Series for Beginners

Copyediting & Proofreading For Dummies®

Cheat Sheet

The Proofreading Symbols

Following are the symbols that every proofreader should know. For details about how to use them, see Chapter 9.

Core symbols

- ∧ Insert
- ℘ Delete
- ⌒ Close up
- ℮ Delete and close up
- # Space
- ⓣⓡ Transpose
- ⓢⓟ Spell out

- ⓒⓐⓟ Uppercase
- ⓛⓒ Lowercase
- ⓢⓒ Small caps
- ⓔⓠ Equal space
- ⓢⓣⓔⓣ Stet, or let it stand

Punctuation symbols

- ∧ Comma
- ⊙ Period
- ⬍ Semicolon
- ⬍ Colon
- ○/○/○ Ellipsis
- ⌓ Hyphen
- ⌃ᴺ En dash

- ⌅ᴹ Em dash
- ∨ Apostrophe
- ∨/∨ Quotation marks
- ? Question mark
- ! Exclamation point
- ⟨/⟩ Parentheses
- ⟦/⟧ Brackets

Formatting symbols

- ⓑⓕ Boldface type
- ⓘⓣⓐⓛ Italic type
- ⓤⓢ Underscore

- ⓡⓞⓜ Roman type
- ⓦⓕ Wrong font

Layout symbols

- ⌊ Move left
- ⌋ Move right
- ⌐ Move up
- ⌊⌋ Move down
- ⓒⓣⓡ Center

- ⓡⓤⓝ ⓘⓝ Run in text
- ¶ Begin paragraph
- ⓑⓡⓔⓐⓚ Break or rebreak
- ⓑⓑ Bad break

Wiley, the Wiley Publishing logo, For Dummies, the Dummies Man logo, the For Dummies Bestselling Book Series logo and all related trade dress are trademarks or registered trademarks of John Wiley & Sons, Inc. and/or its affiliates. All other trademarks are property of their respective owners.

For Dummies: Bestselling Book Series for Beginners

About the Author

Suzanne Gilad is the founder of PaidToProofread.com. Over the course of ten years, Sue proofread or copyedited over 1,200 books for Random House, Simon & Schuster, John Wiley & Sons, St. Martin's Press, Oxford University Press, and Workman Publishing, among others.

Illustrating firsthand that proofreading and copyediting can be profitable and fun while allowing additional pursuits, Sue is also a successful voice-over artist based in New York. You can hear her voice happily hawking products and playing characters on national and regional radio and television.

Thanks to some unexpected proofreading projects on personal finance a few years ago, a whole world of education in residual income opened for Sue. She wrote *The Real Estate Millionaire* (McGraw-Hill, 2005) with her husband, Boaz Gilad.

Sue currently leads seminars on multiple streams of income, and her latest passion is to teach financial freedom. Sue's next book is the story of the creation of 15 millionaires in five years. Visit www.SueGilad.com to learn more.

Author's Acknowledgments

This book is the culmination of thirteen years' experience, and many people encouraged me during the entire process. I would like to acknowledge the generous individuals who helped bring it to fruition.

To my students at PaidToProofread.com, who gave such valuable feedback on creating proofreading and copyediting careers across the country and the world. Your success stories are thrilling.

Thank you to Mike Lewis and Joyce Pepple at Wiley, and to Wendalyn Nichols who gave the manuscript such a detailed technical review. Special kudos to editor Joan Friedman.

To Michael Larsen and Elizabeth Pomada, magnificent agents of change!

To my remarkable team of business partners for their daily inspiration: Christine and Joe Abraham, Barbie Andrews, Corey Anker, Alicia Armistead, Lisa Boggs, Tracey Bonner, Tony Colombo, Bobby Creighton, Ash Curtis, Matt Daugherty, Dionne Dilks, James Donegan, Donna Drake, Kelly Drury, Sean Dugan, Jay Falzone, Niceto Festin, Kenneth Gartman, Meta Goforth, Lisa Gold,

Myles Goldin, Eric Briarley Grundy, Christopher Hadlock, Matt Hagmeier, Chris Hall, Marnee Hollis, Jessica Horstman, Kristin Huffman, Matty LaBanca, Geri and Zoe Lance, Renee Lawless, Mike Lesser, Shana Levy, Kevin Loreque, Josh Marmer, Sherry Mills, Heather Morgan, Cynthia Murray, Tony Nation, Tootsie and Jesse Olan, Gregg and Jeff Pasternack, Dara Praisler, Shira Price, Andy Reimann, Larry Rogowsky, Joe Rojas, Max Ryan, Mark Sanders, Amy Silverman, Karen Slavick, Rebecca Soler, James Stirling, Joy Styles, Jen Swiderski, Eric Thomann, Yanick Thomassaint, Veronica Vera, Heather Wahl, Jason Weston, Amanda Whitford, Elaine Williams, Tashana Williams-Moye, Lizette Yeakley, Kenneth Yim, and Stephanie Zinn.

A special thank you to Anthony Tedesco for his brilliant contributions and for keeping me on track.

Jeff Riebe, who was in my thoughts during every moment of writing. Riebe, you are a true champion.

Judy Cohen and Colette Russen, thanks to both of you for guiding me through the freelance path and for believing in me when I truly stunk at this.

To the amazing Andrew Gitzy, who spearheaded it all as my co-writer for Paid To Proofread.

Dad, you're the best for whisking the girls away to the playground every time I had a deadline to meet.

Tami Gaines is a wonderful gift. Thank you for your wisdom and guidance over the past two years. You have changed my life.

Words cannot express my gratitude to Christopher Braund Simpson and Kelly Suzan Waggoner, without whom this book could not have been completed — but if there were such words, Chris and Kelly would have written them.

Most of all, I am grateful to Boaz for being an extraordinary force in my life — best friend, cheerleader, husband. With Boaz, all things are possible. In all the romance novels I've edited, I have never found a hero who comes close to mine.

Thank you, readers, students, and colleagues, for reading, absorbing, and utilizing the principles in this book. May your wallet and intellect grow!

Dedication

For Mom, who taught me to love literature and the magic of words.

And for my greatest muses, Noa and Ella — the next generation of wordsmiths.

Publisher's Acknowledgments

We're proud of this book; please send us your comments through our Dummies online registration form located at www.dummies.com/register/.

Some of the people who helped bring this book to market include the following:

Acquisitions, Editorial, and Media Development

Project Editor: Joan Friedman

Acquisitions Editor: Michael Lewis

Technical Editor: Wendalyn Nichols

Editorial Manager: Michelle Hacker

Editorial Supervisor: Carmen Krikorian

Editorial Assistants: Erin Calligan Mooney, Joe Niesen, Leeann Harney

Cover Photos: © Daniela Richardson/ Wiley Publishing

Cartoons: Rich Tennant (www.the5thwave.com)

Composition Services

Project Coordinator: Jennifer Theriot

Layout and Graphics: Shawn Frazier, Brooke Graczyk, Denny Hager, Joyce Haughey, Barbara Moore

Anniversary Logo Design: Richard Pacifico

Proofreaders: Aptara, Dwight Ramsey

Indexer: Aptara

Special Help
Renata Butera

Publishing and Editorial for Consumer Dummies

    Diane Graves Steele, Vice President and Publisher, Consumer Dummies

    Joyce Pepple, Acquisitions Director, Consumer Dummies

    Kristin A. Cocks, Product Development Director, Consumer Dummies

    Michael Spring, Vice President and Publisher, Travel

    Kelly Regan, Editorial Director, Travel

Publishing for Technology Dummies

    Andy Cummings, Vice President and Publisher, Dummies Technology/General User

Composition Services

    Gerry Fahey, Vice President of Production Services

    Debbie Stailey, Director of Composition Services

Contents at a Glance

Table of Contents

Introduction

You read, right? Magazines, books, the back of your toothpaste tube. (Hey, we all get desperate.) How did that stuff get written? Well, people tend to think of writers, but few think about the unsung heroes who make those words look good: copyeditors and proofreaders.

Most words go through an entire process before they get printed on your toothpaste tube. Or in your magazine. Or in the juicy thriller in your backpack. In this book, I demystify the smoke and mirrors behind making writing *good* writing.

Let me be clear from the start: The grammar check function on your word-processing software does not create the kind of good writing I'm talking about. Don't get me wrong: Technology is good. But all the electronic organizers, GPS devices, and robot vacuum cleaners in the world can't do what people have been doing for thousands of years: communicate clearly and effectively through writing. That task is left to the writers, who are very much still in vogue. It can only follow that we copyeditors and proofreaders — who clean up after writers — are very much in our heyday as well.

I wrote this book for word lovers: people with an interest in becoming copyeditors or proofreaders, improving their language skills, and increasing their knowledge of the world of editing. I'm not talking about snobby word freaks here. (You know who you are, Edmund, from Freshman Composition.) I'm talking about people who love language, have a pretty solid understanding of how a sentence and a paragraph are put together, and truly enjoy the hunt for errors. If I just described you, welcome to your book! You and I are going to have a good time — promise.

About This Book

This book is meant to be used as a resource. Pick the parts that interest you most, and get what you need from them. If you want to delve in further at a later date, more will be waiting for you. You don't need to read everything in order; this is no murder mystery where each section leads to the next.

I wrote this book knowing that you may be just starting out in the career world or you may be looking to change careers. Either way, I show you how to prepare yourself to be a good copyeditor or proofreader (or both), build your résumé, hunt for paying work, and excel on the job.

Conventions Used in This Book

Because almost no book can be the only resource you need on a particular topic, I include references to lots of other helpful books and Web sites. When you come across a Web address (which appears in monofont), be aware that the page layout may have required it to break across two lines of text. If that happened, trust me that I didn't insert any extra characters (such as hyphens) to indicate the break. So just type the link into your browser like the break doesn't exist. Then cross your fingers and hope that your Internet connection is better than mine.

What You're Not to Read

I wrote every word of this book with the hope that you'd read it. But if you're strapped for time, here's a hint: Text that appears in sidebars is not critical to your understanding of copyediting and proofreading. I include that material for people who want a little more information or require a deeper explanation. If you're in a hurry, just ignore that stuff. I'll never know.

Foolish Assumptions

I'm guessing you're reading this book for one of two reasons:

- **You want to become a copyeditor or proofreader.** Perfect. This book contains lots of information you need to know to become a skilled copyeditor or proofreader — or both. Each section is designed to give you the tools and information necessary to get hired in an increasingly competitive field.

  I confess that I can't cover every topic in-depth. Most of my work experience is with book and magazine publishing, so those fields naturally get a lot of attention in the text. And much of the information applies no matter what type of publication you want to work with. However, working on a newspaper staff is very different from working with a book or magazine publisher. Most people interested in newspaper work spend at least four years and lots of dough to get a journalism degree. I simply can't give newspapers the coverage they deserve, but I can (and do) suggest resources to supplement this book if newspapers are your destination.

✔ **You want to brush up your editing skills.** Perfect. This book offers lots of juicy info that can help you improve your editing skills (and your writing skills as well). This isn't a grammar guide, but you get solid tips about how punctuation should be used, and I point out the most commonly misspelled and misused words. I discuss various methods of reading documents so you can train your eyes and your brain to catch errors and question inconsistencies. I also list lots of other references so you know where to look if you're craving more details about grammar or usage.

How This Book Is Organized

This book is divided into seven parts:

Part 1: Welcome to the Word World

Want to explore the world of publishing without having to break the door down? Here's where you get to know the major, minor, and little leagues in the prettily packaged planet of publishing. You also get the lowdown on the processes of bookmaking — the editing, production, and manufacturing steps that bump the book from conception to completion. But what if books aren't your professional destination? No problem. I also discuss other ways to turn your passion for words into a full-time or freelance salary, from working on magazines to creating corporate documents to cleaning up the information superhighway.

Part 11: Conquering Copyediting

In this part, I escort you through the gates of copyediting. I explain what copyeditors do all day and how they get it done, and I discuss the nuances of perfecting copy. You also find valuable sample sections to review so you can see copyediting techniques in action.

Part 111: Picking Up a Proofreading Career

This part offers the 4-1-1 on proofreading. I know you're already a great reader, but here I ask you to reconsider your approach so you can pick out all the things a proofreader looks for. You get a crash course in the hieroglyphics better known as proofreaders' marks and two chapters' worth of opportunities to see proofreading in action.

Part IV: Adding to Your Repertoire

Whether you want to copyedit or proofread, you need to be able to quickly identify punctuation and usage errors. I begin this part by reviewing punctuation use and highlighting some of the most commonly misspelled and misused words. Next, I offer a chapter on the anatomy of a book and magazine so you speak with authority about front matter, back matter, and all the matters in between.

I also show you how to balance rules against style and make informed judgment calls, and I explain what a style sheet is and how to use it. One of the most important chapters in the book appears here as well: one that explains how to copyedit and proofread electronic documents. (Even if your computer skills won't earn you bragging rights, you want to add this knowledge to your repository so you don't miss out on valuable job opportunities.)

Part V: Turning Your Skills into Paychecks

Here's where you get the scoop on how to hunt for full-time or freelance work. If freelancing is your goal, you can read success stories from the people who are at the top of this profession, find out how to land your first paying gig, and discover how to make that first opportunity translate into a steady stream of work.

Part VI: The Part of Tens

If you're looking for quick advice on how to make yourself stand out as a copyeditor or proofreader, this is the part for you. I offer ten tips for succeeding in each field.

Part VII: Appendixes

This part may make your life a bit easier: It contains three handy guides that you can use as references. First, I present a list of the most commonly misspelled words you'll see while reading. Next, you find a glossary of terms you can use while navigating the book or magazine publishing world. Finally, I offer a list of online resources to use for checking facts, improving your skills, or chatting with people who share your love for words.

Icons Used in This Book

To keep things around here neat and tidy, I've marked some paragraphs of this book with the following icons:

This icon indicates something that you want to keep in mind for a later time. The information may be something you're already aware of, but even so, tuck it away for future use because it's something that I think could make the difference between doing okay at copyediting and proofreading and doing some serious cranking.

This icon indicates something that I've found to be particularly useful in my career as a copyeditor and proofreader. Think of these little nuggets as tricks of the trade.

I don't use this one often — try to accentuate the positive whenever possible, right? But if I want you to avoid making a mistake that could cause some serious friction with your boss, client, or author, I highlight the suggestion with this explosive icon.

Where to Go from Here

Figuring out copyediting and proofreading is all about taking the leap and giving it the old college try (no matter how poor your skills may be at first).

If you find that you are more interested in one part of this book than another, and you want to start there, go for it. There's no reason to read each page in succession from cover to cover. By all means skip around and find the sections that are most useful to you. When you hit the ones that are closest to your heart, I have every confidence that you'll laugh, you'll cry, you'll wax grammatical.

Part I

Welcome to the Word World

The 5th Wave By Rich Tennant

"I see fashion editing in her future. She can already spell 'Guess,' 'GAP,' and 'Hilfiger.'"

In this part . . .

I help you get a general sense of what these folks called copyeditors and proofreaders do and where they do it. That way, as you prepare to join their ranks, you can develop a pretty clear picture of what your work life may look like.

You may know a lot more about copyediting and proofreading than you think. Don't agree? Flip to Chapter 1. I bet you'll be totally impresed with yourself. Er, make that *impressed.* In Chapter 2, I explore the world of book publishing, in case that's the type of job you're aiming to get. If it isn't, you may want to jump right to Chapter 3, where I touch on some of the other job opportunities available.

Chapter 1

Reading as a Job? Oh, Yes

. . . .

In This Chapter

▶ Recognizing your qualifications to proofread and copyedit

▶ Setting aside some outdated images

▶ Discovering some truths about copyediting and proofreading

▶ Considering which career path to pursue

. . . .

So you picked up this book to discover how to become a copyeditor or proofreader? I've got some news: You're probably already pretty good at it. You've been training for this career path since you first picked up A B C blocks in nursery school. Let me guess: You're the person everyone begs to review their résumés . . . college applications . . . term papers . . . doctoral theses.

Any time you improve upon someone else's writing, you take on the tasks of a copyeditor or proofreader. If you share your skills, helping people by word-smithing for them and providing them with a better finished product, you're already working in this field. The question is, are you getting paid for it? If not, I offer lots of advice in this book for turning your skills into paychecks. But let's not put the cart before the horse. Here's a little (true) tale for you.

I was bursting with pride when my friend Kevin called me on my lunch break many years ago. I had just landed my first freelance proofreading job through a temp agency, and my head was awash with the possibilities that lay ahead of me: an extra paycheck, potentially interesting material I could read in my spare time, and a flexible schedule that would allow me to have a social life. I told Kevin all about the job, adding that I had just proofread a piece for a major advertising firm.

"That's scary," he said.

I tried to reassure Kevin. "It's not scary at all. You just have to read a little more slowly than normal and keep in mind . . ."

"Actually," he interrupted, "I don't mean scary that way. I mean that, here's this big agency that feels it's so important that whatever-it-is-they-sent-you is correct, they don't trust their own people with it. So they decide it's worth it to pay an 'expert' to proof it for them . . . and then it goes to *you*, who always misspells my last name. That's scary."

Hm. For a moment, I agreed with him.

But what I didn't know then was that almost all proofreaders start out as I did — with little more than an interest in reading, access to a dictionary, and a few short lessons on style, grammar, and how to make proofer's marks. See, I didn't have to be a phenomenal speller; I just had to be able to look up words I was unfamiliar with. If I was unsure about grammar, I just had to know which reference guide to check. (And in all fairness, that guy's last name was really hard to spell. It had, like, four consonants in a row.)

It soon became clear to me that I was doing just fine. And looking back, I realize that I did so without the kind of guidance I include in this book. So if you take nothing else away from reading this text (which I sincerely hope isn't the case), know that you are indeed qualified to review the writing of others. And believe me, the more you do it, the better (and faster) you will be.

As for me, knowing that I can impart information to you that will put you way ahead of where I was when I began my proofreading career makes me so proud I could pretty much, well, burst.

Debunking Some Myths

Maybe you're carrying around some archaic images in your skull about what copyediting and proofreading entail. If you assume that taking this career path means you'll be wearing nerdy glasses while forever flipping through dusty grammar tomes and making nice white sheets of paper bleed with the markings from your red or blue pencil, think again. The resources you turn to for advice on grammar, spelling, and usage are just as likely to be Web sites as reference books. (See the resource listings in Chapter 14 and Appendix C if you want proof.) And depending on your employer, you may make all your contributions via keyboard instead of red or blue pencil (as I discuss in detail in Chapter 17).

So put your nerdy glasses away (unless you really like them, in which case, who am I to judge?). The world of professional words is full of infectiously cool creative types — writers, editors, designers, and artists. We're movers and shakers with creative ideas and (almost always) a true love of reading, which means we're pretty fascinating to talk to at parties.

Here are some other myths to strike:

- ✔ **Copyeditors and proofreaders have to be students of literature and English, classically trained by Ivy League professors.** Even if there were a million bucks in it for me, I don't think I could diagram a sentence. And reciting Shakespeare? Let's just say my exposure to good ol' William has more to do with Kenneth Branagh than I care to admit. Really. Or, um, verily.

  You don't need to know every nuance of the English language to be a copyeditor or proofreader. It helps to be an avid reader, but it doesn't matter if you fall asleep at night reading Norton anthologies or copies of *Sports Illustrated.*

- ✔ **If you read for money, you'll never enjoy reading again.** The running joke among copyeditors is that if anyone ever buys us a book, there better be some cash tucked into the table of contents or we're not going to bother reading it.

  For me, it's definitely a bonus that nowadays most of what I read is on someone else's dime. Still, there's no better thrill than putting my feet up and settling into a suspense thriller — without having to scour for errors. Chefs still enjoy tasty meals. Lifeguards still enjoy swimming. I still enjoy reading.

  If reading is pleasurable to you now, it always will be. And I encourage you to pursue jobs that allow you to read the types of materials you find most interesting; don't assume that in order to preserve your love for romance novels you'd better focus your professional efforts on scientific journals, for example. Stick with your passions, and chances are that you'll be inspired to do great work (which will lead to you getting even more jobs). See Chapters 2 and 3 for some ideas of how to fine-tune your career goals.

- ✔ **All that reading will destroy your eyes and your back.** If you choose to copyedit or proofread, you won't be reading in the dim confines of a monastic cave. You'll be reading the way you normally do — as if you're perusing the morning newspaper or your favorite Web site. The difference is that you'll be a bit more focused on the content.

  In Chapter 17, I offer lots of tips for keeping your eyes, back, and other parts healthy while doing these jobs. The harder part is keeping your brain from experiencing overload while you process hundreds of bits of information on each page!

Getting a True Picture of the Professions

So copyediting and proofreading don't require an Ivy League degree, won't destroy your love of reading, and shouldn't cause your body to deteriorate. In place of these myths, allow me to offer some truths that may help you develop a better idea of what to expect from either profession:

✔ **You can't pick copyeditors or proofreaders out of a crowd.** They're people just like you and me. Some are full-time wordsmiths, and some are stay-at-home moms and dads fitting jobs in between the kids' naps. (If you're the stay-at-home type, be sure to check out Chapters 19 and 20 for tips on constructing a freelance career.) Some make copyediting or proofreading their sole profession, and some use their language skills to supplement an unsteady (or steadily low) income.

If there's one thing that is true about copyeditors and proofreaders across the board, it's that they are all fantastically beautiful and charming. And funny.

✔ **Opportunities abound.** As literacy rates and the global population grow, so grow the markets for proofreaders and copyeditors. If the job opportunities available in the United States aren't quite vast enough, you can always market yourself to firms in countries with significant English-speaking populations. A lot of people across the globe speak English as their first language. (I could tell you how many today, but that population explosion would keep proving me wrong.)

Here's another reason you should have no trouble finding work as a copyeditor or proofreader: the World Wide Web. Before the Web came along, there were already lots of words being printed every day that needed to be copyedited and proofread. But with Web content thrown into that mix of (constantly changing) written communication, the possibilities for someone with your skills are limitless. Who knows? You could become the official copyeditor or proofreader of a Web site just by spotting an error and sending a friendly e-mail with your résumé attached (see Chapter 3 for ideas).

✔ **You get a paid education from either profession.** Tell me if this advice sounds familiar: "Get a good education so you can get a good job!" That was my dad, the proponent of higher education. Well, we editorial types have good jobs that give us *great* educations.

My job as a copyeditor and proofreader is to get educated — oftentimes, with information I never would have happened upon in a library or bookstore. Whether you want to work with books, newspapers, Web sites, magazines, corporate reports, advertising copy, or bubblegum wrappers, I can pretty much promise that you'll be introduced to information you never knew existed.

✔ **Your career can be as mobile as you need it to be.** If you're looking for full-time employment that comes with an office (or at least a cubby), mobility may not matter much to you. But if you're given to roam, you're considering the right professions.

Copyediting and proofreading can be done from anywhere in the world. If you freelance, or if you work for a company that allows telecommuting, you can work from your bedroom, on an airplane, or at the beach — no one will care as long as the job gets done well and on time. To make this happen, you may need to invest in a quality laptop computer; see Chapter 17 for my thoughts about what to look for in that piece of essential equipment.

Even if mobility isn't your key concern right now, the skills you develop as a copyeditor or proofreader can help you get work wherever you may wander during your lifetime. These days, few of us stay put for decades on end, so investing the effort in a career with this kind of portability makes a whole lot of sense.

✔ **Your hours can be as flexible as you need them to be.** Again, you may prefer (or need) a full-time schedule that comes equipped with health benefits and the other perks of a salaried position. But if you prefer (or need) a flexible work schedule, you definitely want to check out Chapters 19 and 20 where I discuss how to build a freelance career.

How flexible is flexible? Well, it's 1:22 a.m. right now, and my home office (which happens to be a few steps from my bed) is open. As a freelancer, you can copyedit or proofread at 9 a.m. or 3 a.m. — the person giving you the assignment doesn't care as long as you meet the deadline.

And another key perk of this flexibility is that you can say yes to as many or as few jobs as you can handle at any one time. If you've got other obligations that will demand a great deal of time in certain weeks or months, you have complete freedom to keep your copyediting or proofreading schedule clear during that time period. As long as you deliver quality work (on time), your contacts should be happy to hear from you when your schedule lightens and you're available to accept assignments again.

✔ **If writing is your ultimate goal, copyediting and proofreading can carry you closer to it.** Reading published work — or about-to-be-published work — can help you develop your own writing skills. Obviously, you could just read these pieces on your own and gain the same benefits. But why not get paid to do so? Besides, as I explain in Chapters 4 and 8, the process of copyediting or proofreading requires digesting text in ways that are atypical of a pleasure read. When you're hired to help make a publication as perfect as it can be, you pay some serious attention to every word on the page.

And if the on-the-job writing education isn't enough of a perk, the networking opportunities are another selling point. I wouldn't encourage you to try to sell yourself as a writer as soon as you finish the first proofreading job for a new employer, but over time, as you prove how adept you are at wielding a pronoun, you may be able to identify writing opportunities that fit your skills.

✔ **You'll have lots of fun stuff to talk about at your next class reunion.** When you bump into an old acquaintance and he asks what you've been up to, won't it be fun to rattle off the latest books, magazines, or Web sites you've worked on? This line of work makes for good conversation. Don't be surprised if people ask you how they can get into it too.

So . . . Are You a Copyeditor or Proofreader?

Even a trained eye can mistake a copyeditor for a proofreader or a proofreader for a copyeditor — they know the same marks, they carry the same tools, and they even kinda look the same. What's the difference, then?

Distinguishing between the two

The skills that a proofreader needs are probably the same ones that led you to pick up this book. You're the person who can't keep from crying out at errant apostrophes, right? And I think I heard your scream in the Italian restaurant a few weeks back — something along the lines of "How could they forget the *h* in spaghetti, for heaven's sake!" And then there's that pesky issue of which witch is which. *Nobody* gets that right but you. A proofreader examines text, discovers what's wrong, and fixes it.

A copyeditor is like a proofreader who has gone to grad school. Well, metaphorical grad school.

Here's the simplest difference between the two positions: The copyeditor gets his mitts on the text first. That's because he has responsibilities that go beyond the proofreader's. He pays close attention to grammar, punctuation, usage, and spelling, of course, but he also is charged with ensuring the consistency of voice, chronology, and fact. Plus, he checks every fact, every name, every Web site referenced to make sure the reader is getting accurate information. And he keeps meticulous notes the whole time (in a document called the *style sheet,* which I discuss in detail in Chapter 15) so he can make sure that the writing on page 203 reflects the same decisions as the writing on page 14.

Yup, good writing requires making a *lot* of decisions. Writers make them, publishers make them, production editors (whom I introduce in Chapter 2) make them, and copyeditors usually get to make them too. (At the very least, copyeditors can *query* authors and editors — ask questions and make suggestions — to highlight potential problems and suggest solutions. I spend some quality time discussing the fine art of the query in Chapter 4.) Proofreaders generally don't make a lot of decisions; their job is to make sure that every decision documented on a style sheet (or in a publisher's house style documentation — see Chapter 14) is implemented on every page of the document.

Choosing where to focus your energies

I began as a proofreader, so it's my humble opinion that the best path is the one that starts at proofreading. If you're getting into these fields because you adore reading, proofreading gives you exactly what you want: the chance to cozy up with (you hope) good writing and help to make it even better. Plus, you get to examine exactly what the copyeditor did before you got the text. If you're observant (and I know you are), you can pick up a lot of new skills that way and prepare for a future career in copyediting, if that's your goal.

But hey, if copyediting is where you want to begin, don't let me stop you. Maybe you'd go mad if you couldn't influence the bigger picture of how a book or article or annual report is put together. Maybe you've already had enough proofreading experience (paid or unpaid) to know that you're ready to dig deeper into how writing is crafted.

Want some really great news? If you want to do both jobs, you can. You may have a slightly harder time doing so in a full-time position than in a freelance capacity, but the possibility exists either way. For full-time work, you may want to focus your search on smaller organizations whose staff members may be expected to fill multiple functions during the publishing process. If freelancing is your aim, the only person who decides whether you accept a proofreading job or a copyediting job is you.

Whichever path you choose to start down, I offer lots of info in Parts II and III of this book to get you going. And I strongly encourage you to read chapters in both parts even if you're confident that you're going to search for only one type of job. If copyediting is your thing, you definitely need to know proof-reading marks and the types of errors you'll be correcting — information I detail in Part III. And if proofreading is your destination, you can certainly benefit from understanding what a copyeditor does. (The more you under-stand about that job, the better the chance that you'll avoid overstepping your bounds by questioning decisions made before you get the text.)

Preparing to Invest Yourself

This is a reference book. I don't expect that you'll read every word (I know, you're not proofreading it); I do expect that you'll turn back to certain chapters and the appendixes as you begin to establish yourself in the publishing world.

Here's something else I expect: When you get a copyediting or proofreading job (or multiple jobs, if you're freelancing), you'll discover that your employer does things just a bit differently than what I describe here. Maybe even a lot differently. The challenge of writing a book like this is that I can't possibly prepare you for every scenario; you have to do the work of adapting the information I offer to your specific work situation.

If you're looking for a hard-and-fast truth about copyediting and proofreading that won't change from job to job, here it is: To succeed in these professions, you must be persistent and patient. When you're searching for work, persistence and patience definitely pay off; you can't let rejections deter you from your goal. And when you're on the job, those attributes are crucial as well.

I'd like to promise that when you start getting paid to copyedit or proofread you'll never again have to work on documents as horrid as your college roommate's term papers. But I can't make that promise. Once in a while (I hope not too often), you're bound to find yourself staring at a manuscript or computer screen filled with text that makes absolutely no sense — and not because it's tackling a subject like quantum physics. The good news is that, as a copyeditor or proofreader, your job isn't to rewrite that gobbledygook. Your job is to politely point out its deficiencies (see Chapter 4 for wording suggestions) and nudge it as far toward publishable status as you can.

In this scenario, persistence and patience will see you through. Your best option is to try to wow the person who hired you by identifying (and, if possible, correcting) as many errors and sources of confusion as possible. If you can accomplish that while working on a truly problematic piece, I can say with confidence that you'll be rewarded with much more fun assignments as time goes by.

Chapter 2

Jobs for Bookworms

I'm betting you wouldn't drive from Rochester to San Diego without checking your map (assuming, of course, that you are not my father). For such a trip, you'd probably note your overall direction, choose the highways to take (or let an online mapping program do it for you), get a sense of what cities you'll pass through, and maybe even scope out a few possible places to sightsee or find lodging for the night. You want to know more than your destination; you want to know what's just beyond the next bend as well.

Likewise, if you're a person who's loaded up, strapped in, revving the engine, and destined to work in the publishing industry, you're probably curious about what comes next. The road ahead is dotted with publishing prospects. In this chapter and the next, I help you map them out.

I have a hunch that you may be most interested in copyediting or proofreading books. (If I'm wrong, feel free to go directly to Chapter 3, where I talk about lots of other opportunities available to you.) In this chapter, I give you ideas for getting starting on that path. For copyeditors and proofreaders, book publishing is a great industry to focus on. It can provide not only steady work but also defined standards to follow as you go about your business. Most book publishers have style guides chock-full of details you need to apply to the copy you're reading — things like whether the house uses serial commas or how to hyphenate compound modifiers and other stuff to satisfy your word-nerd heart.

In some ways, the explosion of technology and mega-media ownership has made the publishing industry easier to navigate than before. But it's still a place of bewildering stages of approvals and rejections, agents and editors, and politics and polishings to get from the writer's brain to the book's binding. If you'll allow me room to wave my wand, I'll do my best to break down the bewilderment.

Becoming a Professional Bookworm

If books are your destination, one of the best first steps you can take is to get familiar with various publishing houses and their specialties. Your goal is to find out who publishes what and then zero in on the type of stuff you're interested in reading.

Browsing the shelves

Field trip time!

Here's a field trip you can go on without even putting on your shoes: Go to the bookshelves of your personal library, and take a look-see at the spines of what's there. See a Penguin or an Oxford? How about a Vintage or a Faber & Faber? You'll probably pick up on a theme — you'll see that the same publishers keep popping up. Well, that's a pretty good indication of the publishers you want to focus on working with in the future.

Okay, now pull on a backpack (and some shoes) and walk to your local bookstore. Spend some time wandering through the aisles, maybe even traipsing to those far-reaching sections you never darken with your presence. Like children's books? Pick up your favorite, flip to the copyright page, and take note of the publisher's contact info. Enjoy New Age novels? Get a feel for who the major publishers are, and move in that direction when making your contacts.

As soon as you start identifying publishers of material you enjoy, jot down their contact information. That way, when you begin job hunting (see Chapter 18), you already have company names and addresses on hand.

Eyeing imprints

Book publishing is an industry that offers plenty of in-house copyediting and proofreading jobs — and it's prolific in offering those of the freelance variety. Like any other industry, it has gone through a number of consolidations in recent years, resulting in but a handful of conglomerate houses publishing the bulk of the novels and nonfiction marvels read each day. I can't tell you if that's great for the publishing industry, but it's great for you. Here's why: You could conceivably work within one publishing house and hit every fiction genre and nonfiction subject area through its imprints.

What are imprints? *Imprints* are ways for publishing houses to market specific groups (or, in the biz, *lines*) of books to specific segments of the population. For example, Random House's Knopf imprint is known for high-end writers with a literary bent. Vintage, part of the Knopf division, is the paperback imprint. Another Random House imprint, Doubleday, does more commercial work, and one of its paperback imprints is Bantam. Imprints are like neighborhoods that have their own character; the publishing house is the city that comprises all the neighborhoods.

Usually, imprints have their own look and feel (the biz lingo is *branding*). For instance, the Rough Guide imprint owned by Pearson publishes travel guides for lower-budget travelers, and the logo appears on everything from books to maps to phrase books and more. This branding lets a reader know the type of information, language, and style that can be expected, even before picking up a particular book.

The great thing about imprints is that many are housed within the same building of a particular publisher. After you've got a foot into one imprint, you've got at least a toe or two in the door of a sister imprint as well.

Getting to know the major publishers

So who are these publishing conglomerates? There are really only six major publishers these days, each housing the many divisions and imprints that make up the book industry. Gather 'round for the breakdown:

- ✔ **Bertelsmann AG:** Anchor, Ballantine, Bantam, Broadway Books, Crown, Dell, Dial, Doubleday, Fodor's, Golden Books, Knopf, Modern Library, Pantheon, Random House, Vintage, and others

- ✔ **Hachette Book Group USA** (until recently Time Warner Book Group): Bulfinch Press; FaithWords; Little, Brown and Company; Springboard Press; Warner Books; and others

- ✔ **Holtzbrinck:** Faber & Faber; Farrar, Straus & Giroux; Henry Holt; Let's Go; Macmillan; Metropolitan; North Point Press; Owl; St. Martin's Press; Times Books; and others

- ✔ **News Corp.:** Access Travel, Amistad, Avon, Ecco, Cliff Street, HarperCollins, HarperCollins Children's Books, Harper Perennial, William Morrow, and more

- ✔ **Pearson:** Addison-Wesley; Berkley; DK Publishing; Dutton, Grosset & Dunlap; Ladybird; Longman; Peachpit; Penguin; Penguin Putnam Young Readers; Plume; Prentice Hall; Puffin; Rough Guides; Viking; and others

- ✔ **Viacom:** Archway, Free Press, Kaplan, Pocket, Scribner, Simon & Schuster, Touchstone, and others

These are the mainstream mainstays who publish more than 100 titles per year. And this is all-important to you because this key piece of information — how many titles are published each year — helps you determine the heavy hitters who will need you (and many others like you) to copyedit and proofread everything that's produced. The production editors at these publishers are your no-brainer starting points.

Just because a certain publisher doesn't appear on this list doesn't mean you can't find work there. For example, I haven't included John Wiley & Sons in the list, and that's the company responsible for the words you're reading right now. Consider all the publishers who interest you, and check how many books they publish a year. If your chances of finding work look good, go for it.

Writer's Market (F&W Publications, Inc.) is the industry bible containing names, addresses, phone and fax numbers, and Web sites for every book, magazine, and trade journal publisher you could possibly want to know more about. (To find out how many books a publisher produces each year, this is your go-to resource.) In Chapter 18, I show you how to use *Writer's Market* as a job-hunting tool. For now, know this: If you want to work in book publishing, you need to have access to this book. Buy it, borrow it, or pay a subscription fee to access it online at www.writersmarket.com.

Another goldmine of a resource is the *Literary Market Place* (Information Today). This tome, produced for domestic as well as overseas publishers, covers books, magazines, and newspapers. It is a yearly publication about the size of a phone book. You can find it in the reference section of your local bookstore or library.

Working with the specialists

No, I'm not talking about specialists who don lab coats and sprinkle finger-print powder. Specialists are niche-market houses, academic publishers, and others. They also represent another career path for copyeditors and proofreaders.

Working at a university press is an interesting way to gain access to what's being discussed at the academic level. New poets and literary trends, recent research in the arts and sciences, studies in the geographical areas of the universities themselves — the books produced by university presses are often fascinating scholarly works written by experts in the field. If you love Wallace Stevens, you just may be able to edit somebody's academic thesis on his works!

Some of the bigger university presses include Cambridge University Press, Columbia University Press, MIT Press, New York University Press, University of California Press, University of Chicago Press, and Oxford University Press. Your handy *Writer's Market* includes these presses and more. Take a gander at the number of titles they publish annually so you have a clue as to the size and viability of each university press.

For each publisher listing in *Writer's Market,* there's a rundown of the subject areas in which the publisher specializes. Take a look at them, and contact publishers that match your own areas of interest. All that time you spent in school may give you an advantage within a specific field (unless you focused a bit too much on the underwater basket-weaving).

There are enough niches in book publishing for just about anybody to get published. Religion can include reads for Christians, Jews, Wiccans, and follows of Zoroaster. Romance encompasses books for the gay and lesbian communities, the religious communities, and the . . . ahem, slightly naughtier communities. Whatever you're interested in, you'll find something to explore in the recesses of any topic.

Some publishers produce few enough materials each year to actually count on your digits — maybe on one hand. What's great about them? Nobody's calling every minute of the day for a job. And if they're located in your hometown, you can slip in for a day or a week, maybe even take a project home, getting a good foot in the door and a few lines on your résumé. Hometown beginnings need not be so humble!

Vanity, thy name is . . .

Everybody has a book she wants to get into the grubbies of publishers, and a venue exists to meet that demand: subsidy presses. Through the average publishing process, an author submits a proposal or sample chapters to a literary agent or acquisitions editor, crossing her fingers that it will be chosen for publication. If the manuscript is chosen, the publisher pays an advance to the author and negotiates a contract that includes (one hopes) paying out royalties on the work.

In contrast, any Tom, Dick, or Mary can publish a work with a subsidy press. In fact, subsidy presses pretty much rely on authors for business, charging a writer a fee in return for publishing his books. (By the way, subsidy presses are also known as *vanity presses.*)

You will not find subsidy presses in your handy-dandy *Writer's Market.* A better place to look is in the back of publishing magazines, where subsidy presses often advertise. What are these publishing magazines? There's *Publishers Weekly, Writer's Digest, Writers' Journal,* and *Poets & Writers,* for starters.

Some of the better-known subsidy presses include the following:

- AuthorHouse: www.authorhouse.com
- BookSurge: www.booksurge.com
- Dorrance Publishing Company, Inc.: www.dorrancepublishing.com
- Infinity Publishing: www.infinitypublishing.com
- iUniverse: www.iuniverse.com
- Ivy House: www.ivyhousebooks.com

✔ Melrose Press: www.melrosepress.co.uk

✔ Vantage Press: www.vantagepress.com

✔ Watermark Press: www.watermarkpress.com

✔ Xlibris: www.xlibris.com

Subsidy presses can be a great place to begin your copyediting or proofreading career, what with the amount of published material that goes through them. Plus, their quality control is not as stringent as it is at a major press, so they're more likely to forgive your fledgling errors. (I know you never make them, but . . .) However, subsidy-press budgets tend to be pretty tight, so don't expect bells-and-whistles treatment. And I'll whisper this: Some of the books can be downright dreadful. Just a word of warning.

Making a Book

In recent years, some publishing houses have grown so vast that they now house specialized honeycombs of busily buzzing bees. In addition to the dizzying publishing divisions for fiction, nonfiction, music, academic, ad nauseam, the hive of a publishing house also contains distinct editorial, publishing, sales, and marketing departments.

If you become a copyeditor or proofreader for one of these publishers, you will be one bee — albeit a very important one — in a honeycomb of a very large hive. You don't need to be familiar with every stage in the book-publishing process, but it doesn't hurt to know how that industry functions.

The movers, shakers, and machines that move a typewritten manuscript to a beautifully bound book (or a fully accessible Web site) are part of something known as the *production process*. Production can be further broken down into the editorial stages, the production stages, and the manufacturing stages, each with their own actors. In the sections that follow, I walk you through a typical process at one of the big publishing houses. There are always exceptions, however, so don't be surprised if things work differently at some companies.

The editorial stages: Acquiring a book

Think of the editorial stages as everything that takes place before a book can be considered ready for polishing and publication.

Meeting the people

I'll start by introducing who's who on the editorial side of the business:

✔ **Editor-in-chief:** Oversees the editorial direction and related policies of the imprint or publishing house, including content, style, budgets, and the editorial staff.

✔ **Acquisitions editor:** Works with the editor-in-chief to acquire content and make decisions about upcoming title lists. The role varies from publisher to publisher: This person can have the actual title *acquisitions editor* or can be called an *editor, senior editor,* or *executive editor* depending on seniority and on how much staff and list management responsibility the position carries. Some acquisitions editors are heavily involved in editing, and others do the acquiring and then assign the actual editing to a more junior editor.

✔ **Associate editor (or editorial project manager):** Works with the acquisitions editor in preparing manuscripts for production. This person works directly with the author and is the acquisitions editor's right-hand guy or gal. An associate editor will begin to acquire books as well.

✔ **Assistant editor:** Handles some of the more mundane (but absolutely crucial) editorial and administrative tasks, such as researching competing titles, logging and doing reader's reports on submissions, logging contracts and royalty statements, and writing copy for sales sheets.

✔ **Developmental editor:** Sometimes works with the acquisitions editor and author to help the author further develop a manuscript. This person may actually play the role of the author if the author cannot do the recommended or necessary rewrites.

Not every editorial department has each of these editors on staff, and not all positions are needed for each book. A developmental editor, for example, is only called upon for certain situations. Position titles can also vary between publishing houses.

Why isn't the copyeditor on this list? The copyeditor is part of the team of people who polish a manuscript, as I discuss in the upcoming sections on the production process.

Proposing a project

Usually, everything starts with the author — or, more accurately, the author's agent. Sometimes a publishing house contacts an author to write a book, but that's not the norm; it happens most often with people who have name recognition. The majority of manuscripts come to a publisher unsolicited, and these can be divided into ones that are submitted through a literary agent (which gives them a better chance of being noticed) and ones that come in directly from an author *over the transom* (which gives them a slim chance of being noticed).

An agent submits a manuscript on behalf of an author to several publishing houses. A good agent plays matchmaker, pitching a manuscript to editors and publishers that he thinks make the best potential mates. If the author has a strong hook — for example, she's well known and brings a built-in audience with her — the agent may be able to submit only a query letter or book proposal containing a book outline or table of contents; an introduction; and a completed sample chapter, often the opening chapter of the book.

And what about those unagented submissions, and even submissions from agents that the editor doesn't know? If they're kept at all (and often they aren't), they go into what's called a *slush pile* — a reserve of manuscripts and proposals that sit until an assistant editor gets around to looking through them when it's a light week for submissions. Published winners do get pulled from the slush pile, but it doesn't happen very often.

Assessing the proposal

Who are these acquisitions editors? They're the people at a publishing company who help create headline news. Thanks to acquisitions editors, Anderson Cooper sold his memoir to HarperCollins for $1 million, and Oprah raised eyebrows with her cool $12 million book deal.

Because publishing a book is an expensive endeavor, the acquisitions editor holds a book proposal closely to the light, assessing the entire package of information to determine whether the subject matter is appropriate for the publishing house or imprint. If the proposal passes muster, the acquisitions editor works with the author to fine-tune and better complete it for easier acceptance by the publishing house. Sometimes a developmental editor is called in to help the author at this stage.

Going through committee review

Next, an internal editorial committee or board usually receives the proposal. The acquisitions editor meets with the committee and makes the case for acceptance of the manuscript by the publishing house. If the committee agrees and decides to take on the manuscript, the acquisitions editor pushes the proposal along to another internal — and sometimes external — group of people who further scrutinize the subject matter and outline for any holes in the research that need to be fixed before a book deal can be penned. For academic works, it's not uncommon for additional peer-review panels of experts in the field of the book's topic to be brought together for suggestions and comments. All these hands, and we've just scratched the surface!

The acquisitions editor then takes the manhandled proposal back to the author, who addresses and incorporates the suggestions and changes and submits a final book proposal.

Generating a contract, at last!

Finally, the publisher creates a contract with the author to acquire and publish the book. The contract includes a summary of the book and a delivery date of the manuscript from the author to the publishing house. At this point, the author can officially consider the book acquired and start blocking off his calendar for all-night writing or revising sessions.

Revising the manuscript

After a book is acquired, an acquisitions editor may assist the writer in reworking the flow of the book, the table of contents, the characters' voices, and so on. Then, the author does her job, creating a manuscript that meets the publisher's expectations.

But let's be clear: The author is never set free to work completely on her own. The creation of a manuscript is a collaborative process. The editor (usually the one who acquired the project) edits the manuscript line by line and discusses queries and suggestions with the author, who works on the text and sends it back. The two of them may tackle the entire manuscript at once or work on it piece by piece. Together, they create a manuscript that is ready for production.

The production stages: Polishing a manuscript

After the manuscript is received from the author — either in pieces or complete — things rapidly begin moving through the production process.

Meeting the people

Let's run through the key players in the production process:

- ✔ **Production manager or director:** Deals with printers and manufacturing costs, liaising with the acquisitions editor and the managing editor

- ✔ **Managing editor:** Assigns projects to the production editors and oversees the schedule for the movement of all elements of all books through the production process

- ✔ **Production editor:** Guides a manuscript through all stages from word-processed file to bound books by hiring a copyeditor (and perhaps a fact-checker), working with the design team, communicating queries to the acquisitions editor or author, and doing whatever else is necessary to get a book into print

- ✔ **Copyeditor:** Works magic on the manuscript to ensure consistency, clarity, accuracy, and adherence with house style

✔ **Designer:** Works with the acquisitions editor to plan the format of the book, decide how to lay out the text and graphics on each page, and choose the fonts for the various page elements

Assigning a production editor

The first step of the production stage is the transmittal of the manuscript from the acquisitions editor to the managing editor, who assesses the individual strengths and availabilities of his production editors to choose an editor for the book. Oftentimes, production editors work on a handful of books simultaneously.

The production editor is responsible for guiding the word-processed manuscript through each stage of the production process. The manuscript jumps to and from the production editor's desk as it moves through the various stages, always returning after changes have been made. Some production editors are little more than glorified traffic cops, while others serve as midwives who support all stages of labor and delivery.

The production editor first puts her arm around the manuscript's shoulders to get more familiar with the book's content and tone. She may just leaf through the pages, or she may hunker down to read the entire work and begin to formulate a game plan: Who will copyedit the book? What level of edit is needed? What timeframe do we need to get this done in?

The production editor is at the center of everything that happens on the production side. She works with every member of the book team (designer, acquisitions editor, compositor, managing editor, and even the author) to get the manuscript into print.

This person also identifies elements of the manuscript that will need to be designed and prepares a list of codes for typecoding. This list is given to the copyeditor and design team; while a copyeditor is coding the manuscript (see Chapter 16), the design team is deciding what each coded element will look like.

Getting a copyeditor (and perhaps a fact-checker) involved

The editorial analysis begins when the production editor hands off the manuscript to a copyeditor — someone like you! Depending on the size of the publishing house, the copyeditor may be a staff member or a freelancer brought in to address all content, grammatical, and stylistic issues in the manuscript.

The copyeditor may query the author for more information, suggest changes to make the content more understandable by the intended audience, and smooth awkward sentences or transitions. Although the copyeditor keeps his keen eyes cocked for libelous or slanderous language, an additional fact-checker may be brought in to confirm or correct any factual details in the work and to ensure that permissions have been collected for any quotes, photos, or artwork within the book.

As I note in the previous section, the copyeditor also typecodes the manuscript for typesetting by inserting codes to identify where each designed element occurs (see Chapter 16).

Designing the book

While the manuscript is being copyedited, the production editor contacts a designer (or design team). With the input of the acquisitions editor and keeping in mind the original book proposal, the production editor and designer make decisions about what the book will look like. The designer plans the format of the book, decides how to lay out the text and graphics on each page, chooses the fonts for the various page elements, and finalizes the cover designs.

Revising the manuscript (again)

After the copyeditor finishes her work with the manuscript, the production editor sends it back to the acquisitions editor and author for approval and any necessary rewriting. The manuscript is also checked against the book proposal to determine that it reflects everything the author said it would be way back when he first submitted it.

The manufacturing stages: Creating a final product

Finally, we're ready to turn the manuscript into a book!

Meeting the people

As I've done for the editorial and production stages, I want to introduce the key players in the manufacturing stage:

- **Compositor or typesetter:** Converts electronic manuscript files into page proofs that conform to the design specs

- **Production editor:** Remains integral to the process by sending typeset pages to the author and one or more proofreaders, compiling revisions, and forwarding them to the typesetter; sending camera- or print-ready copy to the printer; and reviewing page proofs and a sample copy of the bound book

✔ **Proofreader:** Reviews the typeset pages in search of errors made by the compositor or missed by the copyeditor

✔ **Printer:** Turns camera- or print-ready copy into bound books

Typesetting pages

After the revised manuscript gets the big "okay" from the author, it goes into what is called *prepress*. Prepress involves sending the manuscript to a type-setter, also known as a *compositor,* who is almost always out of house. The book's International Standard Book Number (ISBN) is also obtained at this stage.

The typesetter transforms the manuscript into typeset pages, or *galleys,* and often a limited number of these galleys are bound and sent as samples to book reviewers. This first version of the book is called the *first pass.* The first pass is also sent to the production editor, who sends copies of the galleys to a proofreader — someone like you!

Proofreading and revising galleys

The proofreader reads the galleys against the author-approved manuscript, looking for errors either made by the typesetter or not caught by the copyeditor — anything from minor spelling snafus and improper word breaks to *widows* and *orphans* (words hanging out by themselves at the top or bottom of a page or column). The proofreader also makes certain that typeface and fonts are consistent, illustrations and their corresponding descriptions are correct, and the table of contents is accurate. This whole process is called *slugging,* and while the proofreader does his thing, the author does the same.

All proofread copies are returned to the production editor, who collates all changes and corrections into a master copy of galleys. The master copy is then sent back to the typesetter, who generates a second version called the *second pass.* This second pass is returned to the production editor who — gasp! — brings in two proofreaders: one to proofread the slug against the second pass and one to cold-read the second pass.

Any pages with additional final corrections are sent to the typesetter, until a complete set of error-free, camera- or print-ready pages is created. A *camera-ready copy* is the copy the printer uses to photograph and print the final book. These days, you more commonly hear the term *print-ready* because the final pages are actually electronic files that are sent to the printer along with clean printouts.

Sending the book to the printer

The production editor, yet again, gets his grubbies on the work. He sends the camera-ready copy to the printer, along with directions as to the design and other aspects of the book. Before completing the entire print run, the printer sends a set of page proofs — sometimes called *bluelines* — back to the production editor for final approval. These proofs are either loosely bound or in separate sheets.

When the book is fully printed, but before it's bound, the printer may send a set of *F&Gs* (a term that stands for *folded and gathered* pages) to the production editor to be sure that no major errors have crept their way in.

After this, the book is finally bound, the cover or jacket is attached, and a sample copy is sent to the production editor for final approval. Ta-dah! The only thing left to do is complete the entire print run and send it to the publisher's warehouse for distribution. Oh, and promote the heck out of the thing.

Talking the Talk

In this section, I list some book-publishing terms to keep in mind so you can communicate like a pro. For even more lingo, check out the glossary in Appendix B:

- **Author's alteration (AA):** An author's change or other alteration to laid-out text that is not a printer's error.

- **Bad break (BB):** An incorrectly hyphenated word at the end of a typeset line.

- **Bluelines:** Also referred to as *blues,* these are proofs of the final book that can be supplied as loose pages or can be bound. Bluelines represent the editor's last chance to catch any errors before the presses start rolling.

- **Bound book:** The finished product, ready to be sold.

- **Cold read:** The process of reading a piece of copy straight through, with nothing to compare it against.

- **Copy:** The actual words of a manuscript.

- **F&Gs:** A set of galleys that may be sent to the production editor after a book is fully printed and before it is bound, to make sure no major errors have crept in.

- **First pass:** The first set of page proofs that are proofread against the dead copy. These are nearly always in separate sheets, often blown up for easier markup.

- ✔ **Foul manuscript:** The proof pages of a previous pass that are no longer used because an updated, corrected set of proofs has been produced.

- ✔ **Four-color process:** The process used to produce the full range of CMYK (that's cyan, magenta, yellow, and a *key* color — black) for a full-color image.

- ✔ **Galleys:** Another term for a set of page proofs, often reserved for the first set of proofs that is oversized for easier editing.

- ✔ **Imprint:** A set (or *line*) of books that usually share a common look and feel (or *brand*) and are marketed to the same segments of the population.

- ✔ **Manuscript:** A book in loose pages or an electronic file submitted to a publishing house for evaluation and/or publication.

- ✔ **Page proofs:** A set of pages that are composed according to the design specifications for review to ensure that the type is correctly set and that art and other display elements are correctly placed. Also called *galleys* or *typeset pages*.

- ✔ **Perfect binding:** A binding method for paperback books in which the folded and gathered signatures are cut and then glued to a cover.

- ✔ **Printer's error (PE):** An error made by the typesetter or printer in production.

- ✔ **Print-ready:** Used to describe electronic files that have final approval for printing.

- ✔ **Print run:** The number of copies of a publication that are to be printed.

- ✔ **Proof:** A sample of typeset and/or laid-out material that is checked against an original or earlier version.

- ✔ **Second pass:** The second version of page proofs from a manuscript, with implemented corrections from the first pass.

- ✔ **Typeset pages:** A set of page proofs, usually loose-leaf, that are composed according to the design specs for review to ensure that the type is correctly set.

Chapter 3

Other Publishing Opportunities

*B*ook publishers aren't the only companies in need of people passionate about the written word. There is a whole slew of written material out there, and it all needs copyeditors and proofreaders. Think about the different things you get in the mail, like magazines and journals; and what about those stacks of form letters and freebie samples? They come from somewhere, and that somewhere — more often than not — has a marketing and communications department. Plus, consider all the Web sites you visit in a given week. Someone writes the stuff you read online, which means that someone (we hope) edits and proofreads it.

In this chapter, we'll consider what your roadmap may look like if you're destined to be a copyeditor or proofreader but books aren't your first love. It's impossible to detail all the opportunities available to you — the world is full of writing, and it all needs the type of TLC you can provide — but I cover some of the biggies here.

Majoring in Magazines

Think about the last time you ran out to your mom 'n' pop grocery store and found yourself in the magazine aisle — there were more magazine types and titles than you could digest in one sitting, right?

There are as many different magazines as there are people, tastes, and trends. The magazine industry refers to genres such as general interest (*Consumer Reports*, *Reader's Digest*), fashion and beauty (*W*, *Cosmopolitan*), health and fitness (*Self*, *Men's Health*), business (*Fortune*, *Business Week*), news (*Time*, *Newsweek*), and celebrity and entertainment (*Us Weekly*, *Star*).

But guess what? These are just the *consumer* magazines — the ones marketed to people buying magazines at a mom 'n' pop grocery store. In addition, there are *trade* publications — those marketed to people who work within certain industries. In the sections that follow, I offer some insights into the two camps of the magazine world.

Meeting the major consumer magazine players

As in the book publishing world (see Chapter 2), mergers and acquisitions have reduced the number of consumer magazine publishers in recent years. Following are some of the conglomerates you should get to know:

- **Advance Publications, Inc.:** Most importantly, Advance owns Condé Nast, publisher of such magazines as *Glamour, GQ, The New Yorker, Vogue,* and *Wired.* It also owns Fairchild Publications (*Jane, W,* and *Modern Bride*), the Golf Digest Companies (*Golf Digest* and *Golf for Women,* naturally), and Parade Publications (publisher of the news-magazine insert *Parade*), among others.

- **Hearst Magazines:** You've definitely heard of the magazines under Hearst's belt — titles like *Good Housekeeping, Redbook, Marie Claire,* and *Seventeen,* as well as *Town & Country, SmartMoney,* and *Popular Mechanics.*

- **PRIMEDIA:** Calling itself "the leading targeted media company in the United States," PRIMEDIA publishes nearly 100 branded magazines, like *Motor Trend, Snowboarder, Surfer, Soap Opera Weekly,* and — no kidding — *Truckin'.*

- **Time Inc.:** Yes, Time Warner gets around. Its hands are in books, cable, movies, online ventures — and lots of magazines: *Time, Life, People, In Style, Real Simple, Field & Stream, Popular Science,* and enough others to read until you're blind.

A positive side to these conglomerates? If you freelance, you may be able to do a little copyediting or proofreading shape-shifting by covering editing tasks for two or three different titles, after you get your pencil in the door. (See Chapter 18 for suggestions on how to find work in consumer magazines.)

Riding the trade winds: Industry publications

Trade publications or journals — also known as *business to business* (or *B2B,* if you want to impress your friends) publications — are geared toward people working in specific industries. Trade publications exist to provide expert coverage in news, case studies, trends, new products, and governmental issues pertaining to an industry.

Work in manufacturing? There's a manufacturing-trade publication just for you. Marketing? Choose from direct marketing, promotional marketing, and more. Just name an industry, and you can bet there's a trade magazine that addresses it — hospitality, aluminum siding, snack food, fertilizer . . . trust me, you can't conceive of the number of publications out there.

Understanding the editorial structure

Like consumer magazines, trade publications keep their heads above water through advertising (see the sidebar "Church and state: Editing and advertising"). But their editors can take much of the credit, too. Some trade publications are large, but many are quite small, with one or two editors doing just about everything:

- ✔ Overseeing and directing the focus of the publication
- ✔ Conducting research for writing
- ✔ Editing articles to maintain house style (if one exists)
- ✔ Acting as a liaison between the publication and writers
- ✔ Dealing with clients' marketing or advertising departments

Trade journalism is a fast-growing writing field, so finding writers for these types of magazines is also a pretty big part of the editor's life.

Meeting some of the trade publication players

While book and consumer magazine publishers tend to be concentrated in big cities like New York, Chicago, Los Angeles, Boston, Philadelphia, and San Francisco, trade journal publishers are more widely distributed around the United States — maybe even in your own backyard.

Most trade journal publishers have Web sites advertising the many industries in which they publish their many titles. Oftentimes, these Web sites include the all-important staff lists, mailing addresses, and e-mail contacts you need when searching for work opportunities. Or you can go to www. publishingcentral.com and get the deets on every trade publisher you can handle.

Take a look at the smattering of publishers I list here, and note how many different industries they cover:

- ✔ **Advanstar Communications (www.advanstar.com):** Ah, life sciences, fashion, and power sports. A lovely cocktail, yes, but these industries are also the focus of Advanstar, which has offices in such cities as Cleveland, Santa Ana, Ft. Lauderdale, and London.

✔ **Kalmbach Publishing Co. (www.kalmbach.com):** From birds to beads, Kalmbach publishes hobby and special-interest magazines, all from its offices in Waukesha, Wisconsin. Be sure to take a look at its online job listings.

✔ **Meredith Corporation (www.meredith.com):** These guys publish *Better Homes and Gardens,* sure, but there's also *Successful Farming, WOOD,* and *Garden Shed* to contend with. Plus *American Baby* (aw, idn't dat cute). They have offices in the usual publishing cities, but there's also one in Des Moines, Iowa.

✔ **National Business Media (www.nbm.com):** Focusing on awards and custom gifts, promotional apparel, sign making, and automotive magazines, NBM is located in Broomfield, Colorado. The Web site includes everything you need to contact editors.

✔ **Target Media Partners (www.targetmediapartners.com):** You know those flimsy classified-ad weeklies you pick up from wire bins at the grocery store? Target Media has its paws all over them. Head to the Web site and check it out.

Another starting point for finding work in this business is to make a short list of industries that interest you (or you know something about). Call a business within each industry, and ask someone in its public relations department which trade publications the company receives.

Making a magazine

To get a magazine from desk to aisle (or mailbox) requires a well-oiled team of writers, editors, and proofreaders who, as deadlines draw near, may hardly have the time to high-five each other in the hallway before another draft makes its way through the rounds. In this world, deadlines are referred to as *closing dates,* and they are the drop-dead dates for the final submission of advertising materials, copy, and editorials for a specific issue.

Every magazine is different, but as I do with books in Chapter 2, I want to help you get familiar with the people, processes, and parlance you may encounter in magazine land.

The people

I'll start by introducing the editors — and there are *lots* of editors:

✔ **Editor-in-chief:** This person oversees the editorial direction and related policies of the magazine, including content, style, budgets, and the editorial staff. This guy or gal is also the one who writes the monthly "ed letter," usually found in the beginning pages of the magazine.

✔ **Managing editor:** The managing editor works with the editor-in-chief to manage staff, inspire content and the layout of an issue, and make decisions as to which pieces will run when. Some writing, editing, and budget work also fall onto this person's plate.

✔ **Copy supervisor:** Also known as the *copy chief,* this is the person who oversees the copyeditors and proofreaders. Often, this position reports directly to the managing editor.

✔ **Associate editor:** The associate editor edits and reads feature articles, sometimes writing content as well. This person also gives the okay to the look and feel of the cover and may be the one blessed with representing the magazine at events.

✔ **Staff editor:** The staff editor helps the associate editor, sometimes acting as a go-between with writers and the publication.

✔ **Assistant editor:** The assistant editor is the member of the senior editorial staff who handles routine work and "front-of-the-book" and "back-of-the-book" departments. This editor may also be required to write and edit features of the publication.

✔ **Executive editor:** The executive editor is mostly concerned with daily work — think deadlines, deadlines, deadlines — and also ensures copy and style quality and compliance.

✔ **Contributing editor:** This is an editing or writing contributor who is not part of the in-house staff. Contributing eds write the articles and later read them in the magazine, sometimes not even resembling their original versions.

Not every editorial department has each of these editors on staff, and not every position carries these exact titles. But I hope this list gives you some idea as to the many eyes, hands, and brains that go over magazine copy before it's published.

The process

For simplicity, I'm going to explain the process one measly article goes through before it's considered ready to launch. To get a true feel for the craziness of magazine publishing, you need to multiply this process by however many articles and pieces are within a particular issue. Oh yeah, and remember this happens every week, month, or quarter.

A person with a title like *senior writer* first receives a draft of a story from the main writer or contributing editor. The senior writer reads it and suggests changes, working with the associate editor to lift the level of the story. At the same time, the editors at the top of the chain read the story with a slightly different eye, making sure the content is in line with the vision of the magazine and suggesting their own changes where needed.

Church and state: Editing and advertising

In the magazine world, money doesn't only talk, it squawks — loudly. Along with subscriptions, advertising money keeps magazines afloat. Run an article unflattering to an advertiser, and you run the risk of losing lots of money.

To give you a sense of how this situation affects a magazine, a metaphor is used in the industry: church and state. The *church* represents the creative editorial staff, and the *state* represents commercial advertising. Just as we strive in government to separate the sides, so, too, does the magazine industry try to prevent advertising from influencing editorial decisions.

Like in real life, the lines between church and state often get blurred, especially in trade publications and local consumer magazines. In these types of publications, advertisers are often guaranteed editorial column inches as part of their purchase. How does this complicate things? Well, not only are writers not going to write anything offensive about advertisers, they're going to write unnaturally glowing features about them. How's that for an editorial/advertising overlap?

The article is then forwarded to the copy supervisor, who reads and forwards it to the copyeditor, if the editorial staff has one. These fresh eyes read it for sense and logic, checking that the context is correct, the spelling and grammar accurate, and the house style adhered to. Other facts, like names, titles, and Web addresses, are researched by a fact-checker for accuracy. After these steps are complete, the article is sent to the executive editor for another sweep.

With issues resolved and answered, the article flies back to the copy supervisor, who gets a proofreader involved to correct any niggling errors and problems with readability. The article then zooms back to the executive editor's team to read it, make fixes, and push it back up to the managing editor and the editor-in-chief for a final okay.

The magazine manufacturing process can involve prepress services, such as advertising and ad layout; printing; fulfillment; and distribution. As with most things, the Internet and PDFs have greatly changed magazine manufacturing, although magazines oftentimes outsource pieces of the manufacturing process. Typically, an approved article is sent to the printer, who shoots the file onto photo paper (in the biz, referred to as *Kodaks*) and returns it, where it's reviewed one final time by editing staff before final printing.

The parlance

In this industry, the word *book* is slang for the magazine. To help you avoid confusion if you enter this world, I offer a list of terms you may smack into while ferrying proofs back and forth. To be fair, some of this jargon does overlap with book production (see Chapter 2), so be aware.

- **Alley:** The two margins in the middle of a page spread.

- **Back of the book:** The back pages of a magazine that contain indexes, endnotes, and other such boilerplate information.

- **Backbone:** The bound edge of a magazine.

- **Blow-in cards:** Those annoying subscribe-now or smell-me cards blown between the pages of a magazine. (If they're stuck within the binding, they're called — ta-dah! — *bind-in* cards.)

- **Bluelines:** Also referred to as *blues,* a mock-up of the final magazine that is folded and bound — and printed in a shade of blue. Any changes made after the bluelines are pricey.

- **Callout:** A few sentences pulled from an article, blown up, and placed prominently on the page to break up copy. It's intended to attract attention and entice further reading.

- **Center spread:** Just like it sounds, an article or ad that covers the two center pages of a magazine.

- **Column inch:** A measurement of space for copy that is one column wide and one inch deep.

- **Content:** Anything within a magazine that is not advertising.

- **Coverlines:** Short lines of copy (sometimes referred to as *cutlines*) placed on the cover of a publication to tempt newsstand browsers to purchase it.

- **CQ:** Scribbled next to a word, it's magazine talk for *This word is spelled correctly, capiche?*

- **Editorial inventory:** A slush pile of sorts containing unpublished articles for future use.

- **Filler:** A short article or editorial used to fill blank space.

- **Fixed elements:** Elements within a magazine whose positions remain constant from issue to issue, including the magazine title and editorial page.

- **Front of the book:** Beginning pages of a magazine, usually including editorials, the masthead, and departments.

- **Four-color process:** A process used to produce the full range of CMYK (cyan, magenta, yellow, and a *key* color — black) for a full-color image appearance.

- **Gatefold:** A fold-out advertisement or article printed on a larger piece of paper and folded to the size of the magazine.

- ✔ **Graf:** A paragraph.

- ✔ **Head:** A headline.

- ✔ **Lead time:** The time it takes from planning to the newsstand (or mailroom).

- ✔ **Masthead:** A section detailing the publication's ownership and staff members, as well as contact information.

- ✔ **Perfect binding:** A method of folding and cutting magazine pages to create a flat spine on which copy can be printed. It's convenient for inserts but doesn't allow the magazine to lie open flat and is more expensive than side stitching.

- ✔ **Side stitching:** Also called *saddle stitching,* the stitching where pages are bound together by stapling the bound ends of the sheets.

- ✔ **TK:** Editorial shorthand for *information to come.*

- ✔ **Well:** The main section of a magazine where feature articles are published.

Trying on the Corporate Style

Maybe you thought that, by now, the paperless office would be a reality. Well, think again. Information is an important product for companies, and anybody who works in an office can attest to the flood of letters, memos, marketing materials, reports, surveys, brochures, and invitations filling the hallways and hands of the staff. Then there is the growing field of *custom publishing* — the production of customer-oriented magazines and newsletters by corporations, nonprofit organizations, and trade associations. Unfortunately, downsizing has resulted in smaller and smaller marketing and communications departments. Make that *fortunately* — for you, anyway.

Considering your possible role

If you've ever read Dilbert, you are aware that the corporate world has a reputation for endless approval processes, board approvals, and review, review, review. As a corporate copyeditor, you could be responsible for as much as *content editing* (maintaining accuracy of the information presented, making the material easily understandable and effective, and questioning the logic of a document's layout) or as little as quickly correcting blatant grammatical errors before a document or publication blows out the door.

If you want to work for the suits, keep a few things in mind:

- ✔ **The author reigns.** Unlike in the publishing world, final say of how a document looks and feels sits firmly with the person who wrote or created it. Whether good or bad, there's a mentality here of "leave it with the professionals." And sometimes that *is* good, if money is the bottom line. Imagine having to be the person to tell that big corporate donor that his sappy writing style isn't up to company par. Yikes!

- ✔ **The deadline reigns, too.** It's terrible to admit, but if you have to choose between creating quality and meeting a deadline, the deadline will win almost every time. That's sometimes true in the publishing world as well, but here's a key difference: In the publishing world, deadlines are months in the making; in the corporate world, deadlines may be days, or even hours, in the making.

  If an invitation is due to hit the post office by 5 p.m. on Friday, it's going to be done by 5 p.m. on Friday — and neither you nor your mighty red pencil will stop it. Soothe yourself with my assurance that corporations take accuracy as seriously as the next guy; no one wants to see mistakes in print. But the priorities of money, message, and professional ego win every time.

- ✔ **You may be alone.** Depending on how large the company is, there may be only one person to review and finalize a piece of information. Being the only proofreader or copyeditor on staff has its advantages, but disadvantages tag along, too. You may be able to help hone the company's message, develop (or improve) a house style, and generally be a champion for clarity and consistency. But being the keeper of style can leave you open to challenges from the non-editorial types as well.

  If you're editing solo, you may need to determine how to most effectively communicate editorial issues with non-editorial staff members. That may mean setting aside the proofreading symbols I show you in Chapter 9. Consider your in-house audience, and decide how house style can best be conveyed to people who aren't as in love with words as you are.

  Does it ever make sense to use proofreaders' marks in the corporate setting? I'd say yes. You may find that teaching other staffers the tools of your trade generates enthusiasm for your cause and for the English language. But the call is yours, and it depends greatly on your specific work environment.

To be successful in this setting, you have to be an all-rounder. You'll work on projects that vary greatly — annual reports, press releases, internal memos, customer magazines, the corporate Intranet, and any other piece of marketing communication that the suits can dream up. You need to be disciplined, setting up a system for prioritizing deadlines, communicating the system effectively to the people who dump things on your desk to deal with, and enforcing it with grace.

✔ **You may get more benefits than expected.** If you land a full-time corporate job, you may be blessed with myriad benefits you never imagined. Sure, there's the paycheck, health insurance, retirement package, and stability. But there's also something to that steady drone of nine-to-five. Depending on the amount of in-house production of print and Web communications a corporation does, the number of deadlines to juggle in a corporate environment can be fewer than those in the publishing world proper, but the system of daily deadlines can still help you develop working habits that benefit you in any environment. The fixed flow of related work can help you get into a rhythm, cut your teeth, and develop your own style. Plus, being part of a corporate network means you have the potential to make connections for other work; if you invite somebody out to lunch, it may be a valuable steppingstone to something else.

Cracking the company exterior

Looking for copyediting or proofreading gigs in the corporate world isn't much different from looking for any other type of work (see Chapter 18). You've got to pick up the paper, call your friends, and vroom out onto the information superhighway.

I'd also encourage you to make a list of companies you'd love to work for. It may be a short list if you're focusing only on companies in your local area, or it may be considerably longer if you're willing to relocate. If you need inspiration, check out *Fortune* magazine's listing of the "100 Best Companies to Work For" (go to www.fortune.com and click on <u>Best Companies to Work For</u>). When you have a list in hand, go to each company's Web site and take a look around. You may find an employment page, but even if you don't, take down the contact information to make some calls and inquire about positions. Larger companies usually have human resources departments that can give you the type of information you need, including a contact name for submitting a résumé. Also check out job boards that focus on opportunities in corporate communications (the code term you'll be searching for), such as the one at www.pubmgmt.com.

Searching for Even More Opportunities

I've touched on books (in Chapter 2), magazines, and corporate bodies. Is there anyplace else you can hang your editorial hat? You betcha.

Becoming a news junkie

Newspapers are furiously busy with fast-paced reporters, deadly daily deadlines, and gruff-voiced editors barking from every doorway. At least that's how they are depicted in the movies, and there's a modicum of truth to that portrayal.

The role of the copyeditor takes on a whole new meaning in the high-stressed headquarters of the dailies. Newspaper and wire-service copyeditors tend to have more responsibilities than copyeditors in the book or magazine worlds. To get a job in this field, you're usually expected to be well-versed in journalism, and a degree in that subject may be prerequisite. A newspaper copyeditor may have a hand in deciding which story goes where on the page and is the person who writes all those clever headlines you read each day.

If your preference is to proofread for a newspaper, keep this in mind: By the time you get your grips on a newspaper article, it has already been set in its final layout stage, and changes are not happily received. As with corporate copyediting and proofreading, the deadline is the devil wreaking wrath on the joint — regardless of what errors will keep the article at just good enough.

Bottom line: Although the goal of polished copy is the same for copyeditors and proofreaders of newspapers and those working in other fields, the job descriptions are very different. For information about copyediting newspapers, be sure to check out the American Copy Editors Society Web site: www.copydesk.org.

Taking your skills online

Anybody who has moseyed about the Internet can attest that it's a potential goldmine for copyeditors and proofreaders. You've probably seen hundreds of errors between visiting Web sites, ordering goods, and filling out surveys online. Some of these are memorable typos, like the online catalog that boasts "Our goat is total customer satisfaction." Baaaah . . .

When you encounter an error, send an e-mail to the Webmaster of the site. (This person's contact information is usually at the bottom of the homepage or nestled within an "About Us" page.) Your e-mail should contain the error and a note about yourself, and be sure to attach your résumé. See Chapter 18 for suggestions on how to phrase this type of e-mail.

Do you ever peruse e-zines like *Inc.* or *Slate*? These Web-based publications tend to update and post articles every few days or so. So? These publications need editors and proofreaders just like the tree-based kind. And e-zines are more opportunity-friendly than print magazines, which require in-house eye-ballers due to quick deadlines and layout issues. E-zines are cool for other reasons as well: They have a reputation for being more cutting-edge than the traditional 'zines, and they're Internet-based, which means you can edit them from just about anywhere.

When taking on a copyediting or proofreading job with an e-zine, you'll sometimes be handed access to the *back-end,* administrative tools of the Web sites themselves. Many Web sites are constructed and maintained using *modules,* or tools that allow Web site administrators to update specific content within a site. Need to update the news page? Use the news module. Have a new calendar event to add? Use the calendar module.

Using a module, you can simply log in to the e-zine's administrative site and make edits and corrections to the copy itself. Most times, you use a module that works much like Microsoft Word. Webby types refer to it as *WYSIWYG* (that's "wizzy-wig," or "what you see is what you get"). You don't need a crash course on HTML to do this stuff. Other e-zines request that you cut and paste corrections into a Microsoft Word document and e-mail everything to the editor. With e-zines, all these tools and all this flexibility make it even easier for you to work while sipping coffee in your flip-flops.

Working with printers and typesetters

Though not an abundant source of work, the commercial printing industry is a different marketplace to explore. Here, business demand is determined by the needs — printing, advertising, and the like — of the general business community. Who do you think prints all those glossy magazines? Commercial printers, of course. Telephone books, advertising collateral, direct mail? They print those, too.

Good printing and typesetting firms have proofreaders, sometimes part-time, to review typeset copy before it is returned to the customer. The goal is to keep more of the profits by minimizing any printer's errors (or PEs) returned by the customer's in-house proofreader.

Check your Yellow Pages (also printed by commercial printing firms) under "Printing" or "Typesetting" for local commercial printing opportunities.

Part II

Conquering Copyediting

The 5th Wave   By Rich Tennant

"Oh, he's brilliant all right. But have you ever noticed the grammar in his memos? 'Org need helicon antenna...Org need ion cyclotron...Org need neutron analyzer...'"

In this part . . .

If you've set your sights on becoming a copyeditor, this part is for you. (If you've set your sights on becoming a proofreader, I still think you should cozy up with these chapters; knowing what a copyeditor does places your own job in context and gives you a professional edge.)

First, I help you peek inside the daily life of a copyeditor and different kinds of copyediting styles. Next, I delve into the details of what makes a superior copyeditor and cover some niche markets. Finally, I encourage you to pump some mental iron by watching the editing process in action.

Chapter 4

So, What Does a Copyeditor Do?

*H*ave you ever read a story in which, suddenly, your blonde-headed protagonist became a redhead? Or her beloved poodle turned into a collie? How about that document you read that referenced Smith University in Massachusetts? (It's Smith College.) Or maybe you stopped and scratched your head when a character described the majestic view of the Atlantic Ocean from his San Diego apartment.

Flub-ups like these are not only confusing; they could shatter a reader's confidence in a novel, a brand, or a product. One minute, you are relying on a work for information or mind-numbing enjoyment, and the next, you are aware of the language itself, stumbling over words like a strawberry blonde over a crouching border poodle.

Here's where a copyeditor could have changed things. Think of the copyeditor as the behind-the-scenes magician whose role is to make the letters and words, the punctuation and paragraphs . . . disappear! And right before your trusting, unsuspecting eyes! Poof!

The copyediting process, although methodical, is straightforward enough: It's a thorough, careful reading (or multiple readings) with an eye on the language and a brain on the intent. The copyeditor's mind questions both the commas (*What's that doing here?* or *Shouldn't there be a pair here?*) and the content (*Harry? I thought his name was Henry?*) of a story, brochure, annual report, magazine article, poster, e-mail, or anything else that contains words. Like a magician, the copyeditor is armed with the skills and tools to tweak and manipulate the tangible, black-lettered reality of words until they dissolve into an intangible understanding. If a copyeditor does her job correctly, the mechanics are invisible to the reader, so that nothing interferes with the reader's experience of the story or with the message.

So, what does a copyeditor *do*, exactly? Who does a copyeditor work with? And where in the stage of writing does the copyeditor come in? I tackle all these subjects in this chapter.

A Day in the Life of a Copyeditor

Where does the term "copy" come from? As an English word, it's related to "copious"; both are from the same Latin root that means *plenty* or *abundance*. But you can think of it as the "10-4! Y'copy?" bandied about by the *Reno 911!* crowd. Copy is the message that comes across.

What's the difference between copyediting and proofreading? To phrase it the way it would be on the SATs, proofreading is to high school what copyediting is to college. In high school, you are fed — sometimes forcefully — information that you are then expected to spit back out in some form; but in college, you are granted the right to build upon that information, offering your opinions and suggestions for improvement.

Clearly, there is overlap in the types of work expected of copyeditors and proofreaders. I discuss this subject later in the chapter. But copyeditors step deeper into the intricacies of voice and language, plot and argument, and they maintain grammatical and tonal consistency. I discuss this subject later in the chapter, as well! Before we tackle those topics, I want to clarify where the copyeditor fits into the publishing process.

The big picture: Perfecting a product

Depending on the setting — a newsroom, a magazine, a publishing house, a nonprofit organization, a corporation — copyeditors may work with house editors, writers, designers, and a whole slew of other creative types. You create, maintain, and fine-tune style sheets; meet tight deadlines; and often work late hours, occasionally waiting at a desk for the next round of documents. Sometimes the name of the game is Hurry Up and Wait; other times, your desk is a picture of disarray, overrun with brochures, reference guides, dictionaries, usage manuals . . . and all the hair you've pulled out in frustration.

The copyeditor is part of a team that wants the same thing: a near-perfect assembly of language that best conveys an idea. Each part of this team relies on you: The author or managing editor hopes you smooth out kinks in the words and meaning of the information presented; the publisher or company or organization expects the edited piece to nicely fit into its general family of produced information; and the reader or intended audience wants to glide through the information without tripping over grammar, punctuation, syntax, and spelling.

A keyboard and a quiet space

Back in the day of the typewriter, a copyeditor's toolbox brimmed with pencils, erasers, sharpeners, and sticky notes. Sometimes those are still the tools of a particular job, but more and more often, electronic editing is the norm. I discuss this topic in depth in Chapter 17, but here are just some of the key advantages of editing on-screen:

✔ Efficiency: You can nudge most software programs into doing some of the work for you by customizing toolbars, assigning keyboard shortcuts, and creating macros for your oft-performed tasks.

✔ Accuracy: You can catch many typos through spell-check without batting an already beleaguered eye.

✔ Clarity: For clearer edits and queries, you can track all changes made to the original document, insert color-coded comments, and save separate versions to delineate between drafts and final edits.

✔ Design consistency: Templates within a program help speed and simplify design, as well as maintain the branding of a company or organization.

For smaller jobs, you may want to print the document and conduct a line-by-line reading. But you'll likely be expected to insert your corrections into the electronic file and send the completed job back to the editor or author via e-mail, instead of packing hard copy pages into an envelope and shipping them.

As for where you should work, find a quiet place to sit and read — aloud, if necessary. But understand that a private space of your own is a luxury that may not be available in the corporate world of work cubbies. If your workspace is flanked by compulsive sneezers, chatty-Kathys, and the ubiquitous speakerphone voice-mail listeners, invest in a pair of noise-canceling headphones.

After other folks have discussed the piece to be created, and after it's been written, you're called upon to wave a wand (or a cursor, or even a fine-tipped marker) over it and work some magic. Depending yet again on the circumstances, you may deal directly with the author, with whom you can discuss expectations, deadlines, and how heavy your hand should be; or you may work with an in-house intermediary — a managing editor or a project manager — who provides all the essentials to get the job done.

The little picture: Reaching for resources

Is it *10 percent* or *10%,* or even *ten percent*? *Data is* or *Data are*? And did that country call for a *cease fire* or a *cease-fire*? Technically, each of these examples may be correct, depending on the house style of the organization you're working for. *House style* is the set of editorial conventions followed by the publishing house or other organization that hires you.

House style is separate from the style followed by a specific industry. For instance, a medical journal may follow AMA style, but it will also have its own house style that specifies anything not covered by the AMA manual or any place in which its practice departs from AMA style.

I give the whole subject of house style a thorough treatment in Chapter 14, but know this: This key issue here is consistency. Consistency helps to make the mechanics of language invisible, and house style makes consistency possible.

If an official house style does not exist, you have the option of perusing previous publications to see if you can get a handle on a particular issue, whether it's the treatment of industry-specific language or hyphenation and number conventions. As the copyeditor, you can also create a set of acceptable conventions yourself, best compiled by keeping a list of things you pick up while going about your business. I discuss how to compile a thorough style sheet in Chapter 15.

Here's a quick rundown of the sources and resources you want to have on hand while you're editing (see Chapter 14 for lots more detail):

- ✔ **A house style manual or style sheet.** Before starting a job, ask whether an established house style exists.

- ✔ **A general manual of style.** As I explain in Chapter 14, there are many style manuals out there — *The Chicago Manual of Style, The New York Times Manual of Style and Usage, The Associated Press Stylebook and Libel Manual* . . . Before getting started, ask which manual the organization or publisher follows.

- ✔ **A house dictionary.** In the editing world, the granddaddy of all dictionaries is *Merriam-Webster's Collegiate Dictionary*, now in its 11th edition. You'll get to know it better as *Web 11*.

There are several "Webster's" out there: *Random House Webster's* (RHW) and *Webster's New World* (WNW) are the biggest, and *American Heritage* (AH) is another well-known choice. Be sure you use whichever one your employer or client prefers.

- ✔ **A thesaurus.** A favorite of copyeditors is *The Synonym Finder* by J. I. Rodale (Warner Books). The Internet is also a popular place to head for suggested replacements for words, although Web-based thesauri have their limitations.

- ✔ **A usage guide.** You want to get familiar with *Garner's Modern American Usage by* Bryan A. Garner (Oxford University Press).

- ✔ **A handbook of English usage.** College handbooks, such as *The Little, Brown Handbook* by H. Ramsey Fowler and Jane E. Aaron and *The Penguin Handbook* by Lester Faigley (both published by Pearson Longman) are big sellers that offer overviews of writing style, grammar basics, industry styles (such as APA, CMA, and MLA — see Chapter 14), and more.

- ✔ **Subject-specific reference materials.** The cardinal copyediting rule is this: Look Up Everything. Is the copy peppered with foreign words? Are you expected to verify city streets and highways? Is the job for a fashion magazine? Or the sports page? Go 'head — fill your shelves with medical and foreign-language dictionaries; quotation books and trademark checklists; atlases and street maps; even the Bible, Koran, and Talmud, if you think you'll need them. Or at least become familiar with where you can locate these types of references when you need them.

- ✔ **Industry-specific publications.** Previously published materials are great for checking the consistency of usage and language — even accepted jargon — within a particular industry.

- ✔ **Trusty online resources.** As you delve deeper into the world of editing, you will come to trust certain Web sites and user groups to help you make the best decisions in particular circumstances. (Plus, you can commiserate with others who do what you do for a living!)

Everything is game for looking up. *Everything.* Place names, foreign words, company titles, religious holidays, archaic spellings, industry jargon, compound adjectives, book titles, song lyrics — the list continues *ad nauseam.* If you don't find an individual entry in your style guide, consult a dictionary or other appropriate resource, and confirm, confirm, confirm. I discuss this aspect of copyediting in detail in Chapter 5.

The itty-bitty picture: Sweating the small stuff

Okay, there's a manuscript in your inbox and a style manual on your desk — now what? Your job is to thoroughly read a document, which usually means going over it again . . . and again . . . and again.

Line by line, word by word, you conduct a careful, concentrated, whole-brain reading of the work. From the header to the endnotes, you answer these questions: Does this (word, phrase, sentence, paragraph, section, chapter, book) work? Will the intended audience understand this? If not, what can I do to help make it clearer? And yes, you also cover spelling, usage, and every scrap of punctuation (including apostrophes that face the wrong way).

Ideally, a copyedit is done in two rounds. On the first read, you want to deal with structural and language-use issues. Your goal with the second read is to spot and correct mechanical errors that you may not have caught on the first read. Depending on the time available to you and the difficulty of the piece, you may need more than two rounds to do the job right.

While there is no one way to skin a copyedit, a good place to start is by cursorily scrolling or flipping through the pages for the things your eyes more easily pick up. Give your document a quick scan. Then go back for more.

The proofreader who reads your manuscript will study usage, spelling, punctuation, layout, and all the other details of the piece just as excruciatingly. In fact, many of your efforts will be duplicated when you pass a project off to a proofreader (assuming that's part of whatever editorial process you're in). And why not? In the publishing world, errors are like moldy strawberries — they make you not even want to open the fridge.

In the next section, I spell out some issues that both the copyeditor and proofreader keep their eyes peeled for. Then I return to the subject of how to skin a manuscript, offering lots of ideas on how you may end up doing your job.

The Marriage of Proofreading and Copyediting: Identifying the Overlap

Both proofreaders and copyeditors need to follow house style, and they need to be able to spot inconsistencies, spelling errors, typos, and grammar wrongdoings.

Here are some things both of you look for:

- **Mechanical errors:** These tend to be errors of convention or house style, such as

  - Hyphens and dashes

  - Capitalization

  - The treatment of numbers

  - Quoted information

  - Abbreviations, acronyms, and initialisms

  - Italicization, underscores, and boldfaced type

  - Charts, tables, and graphs

  Remember: If there is no established house style or hierarchy of style for you to consult, let consistency reign.

- **A consistency of parts:** Here are the types of questions you're going to ask: Do page numbers correlate with those in the table of contents? Does data in a chart match the facts in the copy? Does information in the endnotes match the footnotes in the document?

Parts to check for consistency include

- Footnotes and endnotes
- Photographs and illustrations and their respective captions
- Tables of content and page numbers
- Charts, graphs, and maps and their respective keys
- Placement of page numbers, headers, and footers

✔ **Grammar and usage errors.** This is where you use what we in the industry call your *editorial judgment.* Your role is not to impose your own preferences of syntax and diction upon a piece; rather, you are to make sure the writing is clear, the thoughts well presented, and the tone appropriate for the intended audience.

Here's a sampling of items you're looking for:

- **Sentence fragments and run-ons:** Make sure each sentence is grammatically complete and can acceptably stand on its own. Keep in mind that exceptions exist. Some house styles allow for fragments because they help create a conversational tone. (You find fragments in books *For Dummies,* for example.) And if you're working on a literary piece, even run-ons may be allowable depending on the author's style and intent.

- **Subject and verb agreement:** The subject(s) and verb(s) of a sentence must agree in number and tense.

- **Inconsistent parallelism:** Be sure that sentences containing a series or other matching elements are grammatically equal.

- **Confusing pronoun references, incorrect pronoun cases, and uncouth pronoun use:** A pronoun becomes confusing when a reader is forced to guess what *it* or *they* refers to. Your job is to ensure the reader never has to guess.

- **Essential and nonessential clauses:** Essential clauses and nonessential clauses both convey additional information about a word or phrase in a sentence. The principal difference is that a nonessential clause can be eliminated without changing the overall meaning of a sentence, while removing an essential clause alters the meaning of a sentence.

- **Apostrophes run amok — or missing completely:** It's shocking, the examples of this transgression you can find just on the way to work in the morning: *Bagel's and Cream Cheese, Its Going to Be a Hot One!, Baker and Son's,* and on and on.

  The only time you ever use *it's* (with the apostrophe) is for the contraction of *it is.* Period. Everywhere else, you use *its.*

- **Errant or missing capital letters:** Capitalization varies by house style, so be sure to check the reigning guide before you get started.

• **And, of course, spelling and punctuation:** Some copyeditors keep a list of commonly misused or misspelled words to keep these recurring mistakes in the forefront of their discerning brains. Other copyeditors keep the list to impress their friends at parties. I share just such a list in Appendix A.

A Copyeditor Apart: Editing Content

Okay, now we're ready for the juicy stuff: what sets the copyeditor apart from the proofreader. The distinction is content editing: A copyeditor does it; a proofreader doesn't.

Content editing requires close collaboration with the author or managing editor of a project. Here are just some of the questions you ask yourself as you read:

✔ Is the author's diction and tone suitable for the intended audience?

✔ Is the presentation (such as the argument or plot) organized rationally or appropriately?

✔ Is the layout logical?

✔ Are quotes or other borrowed material properly attributed?

If the answer to any of these questions is *no,* you carefully rework and smooth these spots as discreetly as possible, without disrupting the author's purpose or voice. Think of yourself as a gardener; you prune and cut this leaf and that one with the goal of leaving the garden looking and feeling as organic and true to the original as possible.

What, exactly, does this pruning entail? Here are some of the things you do:

✔ Clarify ambiguous statements or assertions

✔ Correct structural, organizational, or conceptual problems

✔ Point out inconsistencies and discrepancies

✔ Streamline or revise figures of speech, redundancies, hyperbole, and euphemisms

✔ Fix (or suggest how to fix) anything else that may muck up communication with the audience

You may also be asked to smooth awkward transitions, keep an eye out for biased language or stereotyping, and point out libelous or otherwise salacious statements that could expose the author or publisher to lawsuits. (For the stickier, hairier issues, you are expected only to point out potential problems and possibly suggest changes to resolve them. You do this through a process you will come to love: the query. I discuss querying later in the chapter.)

All the while, you maintain the appropriate tone and the author's own language. This is key, and I discuss it in detail in the upcoming section "Maintaining authorial voice: The most important section in this book."

 Depending on the type of manuscript or document you edit, you may be given a note (also called a *style sheet*) from the author with information on slang, jargon, figures of speech, or acronyms unique to the particular genre or audience. If you're working on a fiction book, you may get a list of characters and their characteristics, as well as details of the world in which the characters interact. If you don't get such resources and believe they'd be helpful, ask whether this information exists.

Pruning the text

Does all this work sound overwhelming? If a project arrives to you in rough shape, it may feel that way. But if you stick with this profession, you'll also get to work on good pieces of writing that make you want to weep with relief and joy. And, of course, the rough projects help you get better and better at your job.

Here, I offer some ideas for trimming and shaping even the most unwieldy language. Following are some offenses that you'll encounter frequently:

- **Clichés and other figures of speech:** Your goal is not to eliminate every cliché or convoluted metaphor you encounter. Rather, you should try to rework areas in which these issues of speech cloud the message, create confusion, or are not suited to what the author is attempting to say.

  Take this example: *It goes without saying that, in this day and age and at this point in time, Joe should seriously consider what makes him tick or he's going to go nowhere fast.* Ooh, gripping.

  Aren't you pretty much saying the same thing with *Joe needs to figure out what makes him tick*? One idiom is enough. If the language sounds trite, hackneyed, or just plain tired, blow fresh air into it.

- **Euphemisms, business-ese, and jargon:** Writers sometimes use one type of word or phrase to represent another type of word or phrase to make the former sound more agreeable, more important, or (ahem) more complicated than it really is.

  The world of politics all but owns the catalog of euphemisms; consider *collateral damage* for unintended civilian casualties, or, worse, *friendly fire*. But none of us is immune. We say that someone has *passed on* when he's died, a woman is *expecting* when she's pregnant, and we're eating *sweetbread* when munching on the organs of an animal. Ew.

Business-ese and jargon work the same way. For example, in most cases, *utilize* and *effectuate* can be replaced with good ol' *use* and *cause*. BTW, those undecipherable chat-room abbreviations? They're undecipherable because they're understood only by a specific audience. Say CUL8R to such jargon, unless you have confirmed that the audience will pick it up as a wink-wink, nudge-nudge.

✔ **Redundancies:** Many writers pick up phrases that sound just fine when spoken but are unnecessarily verbose. You may want to stalk and tag such things as *past history* (what history isn't in the past?), *plan in advance* (one doesn't plan in hindsight), *major breakthrough* (aren't all breakthroughs major?), and *he thought to himself* (that's usually who hears the thinking).

Redundancies have a fan base, it seems. Amy Einsohn's *The Copyeditor's Handbook* (University of California Press) has a good list of redundancies, and funwithwords.com lists a fair few (`www.fun-with-words.com/redundant_acronyms.html`). Richard Kallan's *Armed Gunmen, True Facts, and Other Ridiculous Nonsense: A Compiled Compendium of Repetitive Redundancies* (Pantheon) is a fun resource as well.

✔ **Inconsistency:** This is a biggie, and this is where a thorough style sheet (see Chapter 15) makes your life bearable. When working with book manuscripts, great copyeditors also keep running lists of facts to reference as the book progresses.

For example, a fiction editor keeps notes on characters (*page 12: Zoey Jacobs, brown hair*), places (*page 32: Tulsa, Oklahoma; childhood home*), and other information (*page 102: Mother broke leg in Christmas-light accident*). If *Zoey* becomes *Zoe* on page 51, you want to query the change.

Inconsistencies occur just as easily in corporate documents, especially when older names or conventions creep into new communications. Maybe the *Mid-Atlantic Division* recently became the *Eastern Coastal Region*. Your job is to make sure it stays that way.

✔ **Passive voice:** Surely you've had the grammar-check function on your word processing program suggest that you rephrase a sentence in the active voice. But what is that robot trying to tell you? In the active voice, something or someone does the acting; in the passive voice, there is action being done to that same something or someone.

Here's some passive voice for ya: *It was discovered that Laura did not do her homework*. The author isn't saying who discovered it; she's just pointing out that Laura is a slacker. The active voice rewrite may be *The principal discovered that Laura did not do her homework*. Here, we reveal who did the discovering.

Does every sentence require active voice? Well, that's where your editorial judgment comes in. Despite what you may have been taught, the passive voice can be perfectly fine. Sometimes it doesn't matter who discovered what, and sometimes we just don't know. In mystery novels, it may be exciting to let the audience wonder who outed the slacker — it's more important that Laura got caught.

Bottom line: Read everything in context (including in the context of the house style for a particular project), and use your well-stocked head.

As a copyeditor, you hold the keys to more than errors in spelling and grammar. You are the pin-striped (or pajama-wearing, if you work from home) gatekeeper charged with protecting copy against awkward, convoluted, or otherwise bad writing. You check for language and usage consistency and compliance with house or industry style. You make sure the information presented is free of anything factually incorrect or, worse, libelous. In a nutshell, you make the copy as clean as possible before it's handed to the proofreader (assuming that's who sees it next).

You've been a great crowd: Knowing your audience

I admit it: I would be somewhat embarrassed to show up at a nightclub in my sensible shoes and frumpy work pants. Likewise, if I wore my way-too-drapey "girls' night out" halter top to a business meeting, I may be accused of, um, questionable negotiating tactics.

Audience matters, and language that's completely appropriate for one audience may raise the eyebrows of another. For example, a guide to Web-content management ought to provide a definition of *HTML* the first time it is used. (By the way, that's *hypertext markup language.*) That same definition in a newsletter for computer hackers would be construed as unnecessary, if not insulting.

As copyeditor, you've got to make judgment calls, and the audience should always be a key factor in your decisions. Here are some other examples to get you thinking:

- ✔ Depending on the audience, you may or may not need to spell out abbreviations like *PC, CPA,* or *mph.*

- ✔ Common open compounds are not hyphenated unless ambiguity could result. Your judgment call comes with determining whether something is ambiguous to a certain audience. For example, using hyphens in *real-estate salesperson* and *small-business owner* may be overkill for folks in the know.

- ✔ When editing books that are part of a recurring series, you can assume the readers know something about the characters and storyline from past installments. For example, they probably don't want to be reminded every time that the main character's cloak of invisibility was bestowed upon him by the slain king.

> The last people you want to offend are repeat customers; they're the ones who have the stamina to stand up all night waiting at the bookstore for the latest edition to go on sale.
>
> ✔ Despite what you were taught in grade school, contractions and informal language deserve their day on stage, although they're more likely to be used in books like this one than in a *Forbes*-100 annual report. Darn tootin'!
>
> On the flip side, readers of academic journals or textbooks are less apt to be frustrated by the brambles of highfalutin scholarly language. For a scholarly audience, the tone of the writing can be, well, less entertaining without much repercussion. The readers will do the work to get to the heart of the message or the results of the study. So if you're editing a less-than-inspiring article or chapter, use a lighter hand with the words and pay more attention to consistency in the details.

When you're in doubt about whether something is appropriate for your audience, the query is your friend. Stay tuned: A complete discussion of queries is coming up at the end of the chapter.

Maintaining authorial voice: The most important section in this book

Okay, so a good copyeditor makes style and usage corrections and considers how information will be interpreted and understood by the audience. A great copyeditor has another trick up her sleeve — one that blurs any traces of her hand in the work.

Channeling the author

Say it's necessary for you to rewrite or add one or two sentences for clarity. You want to be sure that your language flawlessly maintains the integrity of tone and consistency of the author's voice found within the rest of the document. It's that gardener thing again: Weed and prune, but keep it close to the original.

If you're not sure about the exact language an author would be comfortable with, you have every right to leave a note along the lines of "Consider changing this sentence to . . ." Most authors appreciate help in strengthening their language, especially when the help is presented politely.

Here's where I should talk about what a copyeditor doesn't do. A copyeditor doesn't arbitrarily change things because that's how he would do it if the document were his. A copyeditor doesn't rewrite or add whole chunks of text, nor does he reorganize the logic or fix faulty development in plot; these are things the author should handle. The copyeditor's job is to ask questions and make suggestions using queries.

So, how do you best maintain the author's voice? If the author's sentences are clear, factual, and adequately woven together, let them stand as is.

Asking what's expected of you

Before you start a job, talk to the author or managing editor. You may want to get an idea of the types of projects this person has worked on before. More importantly, you want to find out what he or she expects of you. Specifically, you need to ask how light or heavy an edit is required on the document.

Going heavy when an author expects you to go light could turn a great working relationship into something . . . well, not. Gauging the difference is part intuitive and part knowing who you are working with. The following guidelines may help.

Here's what you do during a light (or *baseline*) edit:

- ✔ Correct inconsistencies in the mechanics of the body text — spelling, capitalization, punctuation, abbreviations, use of hyphenation and dashes, font and font sizes, and everything else your eyes take in.

- ✔ Correct inconsistencies in the other parts of the document — footnotes and endnotes; tables of content and page numbers; placement of page numbers, headers, and footers; and charts, graphs, and maps.

- ✔ Correct grammar and usage errors, but do not change anything that is not an outright error.

- ✔ Flag awkward or confusing language, but do not revise it.

- ✔ Bypass benign areas of wordiness and jargon, but query unusual words that may not be accessible to the audience.

- ✔ Flag information that seems incorrect or is not factual.

- ✔ Flag information that may require permission for use, as well as statements or language that may expose the author or publisher to lawsuits.

During a heavy edit — the kind that may require a backhoe — you do the following:

- ✔ Correct all errors and inconsistencies in grammar, syntax, and usage.

- ✔ Rewrite areas of wordiness or confusing or awkward construction.

- ✔ Flag and query inappropriate or overused figures of speech, jargon, or sentiment.

- ✔ Check and revise information that seems incorrect or is not factual.

- ✔ Query and suggest changes or fix discrepancies and conflicts in content (or, if fiction, in plot, setting, and character details).

✔ Flag and suggest changes in language that promotes bias or stereotyping or is otherwise insensitive to a particular section of the readership. For fiction, query the intent of bias-heavy language if it is difficult to discern a reason for the language in the context of the piece.

✔ Suggest changes to the layout or order of information for clarity or a more logical progression of an argument.

Perfecting the fine art of the query

Being a copyeditor is not synonymous with being a mind reader, and nobody expects you to know everything. When you encounter a reference you don't understand, or when you come across a factual inconsistency, or when pictures or tables referenced in a work are nowhere to be found, what are you to do? Let out a great sigh — this is where the query comes in to save the day.

If you speak with the writer or managing editor before going about your task, here's some information to get that can serve you well: what kind of writing or editing this person has done in the past, and how comments or queries should be addressed. Some writers and editors are happy to see notes written directly in their files, on their proofs, or on their manuscripts. Others may not be so thrilled.

Querying on hard copy or in electronic files

Normally, a copyedited manuscript is returned to the assigning editor, who resolves what queries she can and accepts whatever changes she thinks are uncontroversial before sending a cleaner document to the author. Here's what you need to know: the assigning editor's preference for how you present your queries.

If you work on hard copy, knowing the editor's preference is crucial:

✔ Some editors don't mind if you write notes on the document itself because it will not be the same document that goes to the author. Plus, sometimes self-adhesive stickies can get lost, and that may be a source of frustration.

✔ Other editors prefer stickies because they can remove anything they've resolved and don't have to distract the author with those queries. These are the harried editors who hope they don't have to create a cleaner document to send to the author.

✔ Still other editors prefer that you create a separate notes document with the queries numbered sequentially. You write a number or letter on the manuscript page that requires a query, and the separate document contains the actual queries. This method is particularly helpful if the document you're working on requires lots of queries.

If you write queries on the pages themselves, circle them or draw boxes around them. Doing so alerts everyone who follows you in the production process that those marks are queries, not corrections. If the assigning editor asks you to write queries on sticky notes, you still mark corrections and changes directly on the hard copy. Attach the sticky note near the queried item, and write the page number on the lower right-hand corner of the note (just in case it falls off somewhere down the line).

If you copyedit electronic documents, you probably won't have to ask about an assigning editor's preferred working method because it's easy for the editor to just resolve or remove whatever you question or change in the document.

Minding your manners

Queries should be as clearly written and straightforward as possible, and the tone of your notes should never be sarcastic or demeaning. Write *Will the audience understand this reference?* instead of *What does this mean?* Doing so could mean the difference between a thoughtful rewrite by the author and the ripping of your note for the trash.

And if there's a word more beautiful than any other for queries, it's this: *consider* — as in *Consider recasting sentence as . . .* , or *Consider replacing* utilize *with* use, or *Consider moving paragraph to end of document.* This word exudes respect and concern without offending, and it may be your only way of nudging a change in language for the better.

It's important to tread lightly, as even a seemingly obvious error may be a bit of technical jargon or insider speak. But if you're not sure, or if it's not clear, query away — you'll be doing the writer and the readers a favor. And remember, after the publication is in print, it's too late to do anything more than shake your head.

Here's some helpful language for addressing inconsistencies and errors in queries:

What you want to say	A better query
This makes no sense!	Confusing. Clarify by indicating who is talking.
Awkward	Consider revising as edited to improve [insert problem here].
Fix these numbers or this total.	Numbers do not add up to total. Please reconcile.
This is completely offensive!	May be construed as biased. Consider striking.

(continued)

What you want to say	A better query
What does "this" mean?	"this" = refers to [possible reference] or [possible reference]?
Why are you using two words for the same thing?	If "mainframe" and "server" are equivalent here, consider using one term for both references.
Huh?	Will the audience understand what this word means? If not, consider changing.

Sometimes the easiest thing to do is to revise the sentence yourself and then say "OK as edited?" followed by an explanation for why the change was made. For instance, I once edited a document in which the author wrote "he was depraved from a father." I suspected the author meant "deprived of," so I made the change and wrote: *OK as edited? "Deprave" means "to malign or corrupt."* That way the author saw the problem but didn't feel obligated to accept my change.

Chapter 5

What Makes a Good Copyeditor *Great*

In This Chapter

▶ Ensuring accuracy

▶ Keeping an eye out for legal and ethical issues

▶ Editing notes, bibliographies, and more

You've mastered spelling and punctuation. Grammar and diction have warmed up to you; in fact, you're best buds. And editorial judgment just called your cell phone. You're all good.

But, wait. What if you don't want to settle for *good*? What more can you master before swimming deeper into the wordy waters? There are the mechanics of copyediting, then there's the mind-set — the psyche, if you will — of a copyeditor. If you do the job well, you're part detective, part lawyer, and just slightly obsessive (in the best way, of course).

Let's get psyched!

Checking (and Checking and Checking) Facts

Fact-checking is simply the verification of factual accuracy. A copyeditor is not always asked to perform this task, but all copyeditors should know how to fact-check.

Getting the details right doesn't matter to everyone. But for some people, everything they read is like a game of "gotcha." Copyeditors should be among those people. Let me illustrate:

At www.dummies.com, you can find out all about the *For Dummies* series, part of the John Wiley & Sons family of educational and reference books.

While Ms. Reader will absorb that information no problem, accepting that it is correct, Mr. CE may find his brain stopping and starting: Is `www.dummies.com` the official *For Dummies* Web site? Is the series published by John Wiley & Sons? Is John Wiley & Sons the official name of the company, or does the company prefer different names for marketing, corporate, and legal purposes? (If Mr. CE has said these things aloud, Ms. Reader at this point may glare in his general direction and take her book to a quieter place.)

To prevent a proliferation of the *look-at-me-my-life-was-tough-wait-no-it-wasn't-I'm-so-sorry-Oprah* type of fictions, larger magazine and publishing houses have on-staff fact-checkers who wade through the mucky details of fact before the piece of writing lands in your hands. That said, your job of making the copy as clean and error-free as possible may include making certain all information is accurately presented. Ensuring accuracy never hurts in this resource-heavy society. It's not enough to knit your eyebrows at an article's assertion that the sun is 100 billion miles away from Earth; you must yank at and unravel that knit to either confirm or correct it. (By the way, the estimate of the sun's distance from Earth is actually between 91 and 93 *million* miles.) Weights and lyrics, company names and animal classifications, car models and supermodels — it's all game to be researched and checked for accuracy.

You may be thinking, *With everything else on my plate, I have to do this, too? Why, why, why?!* Get up off your knees, and let me explain. Checking factual declarations is about more than helping to cover the heinies of others. Copyeditors can be the unsung averters of costly problems (can you imagine having to reprint a textbook because of the astronomical assertion in the previous paragraph?), awkward slights (you don't want to thank Sally Butts for her generous donation to your cause, only to find out later that her name is Betts), and even lawsuits.

There are different levels of fact-checking depending on the kind of text:

- ✔ **Fiction:** Here, you're dealing with internal consistency (does a character's hair color change between one chapter and the next?) and with references to real-world things (is that constellation really visible in the northern hemisphere in winter?).

- ✔ **Nonfiction:** You're not expected to redo an author's research or to verify statistics, but if you spot things that seem illogical, do query them. No matter how tight your deadline, you must make sure you've at least checked anything capitalized (names of people, places, and products); any dates, times, or references to real events; and any assertion that could potentially be libelous.

Eyeballing brand names

Though the Internet is not always a copyeditor's ally, it's a great research tool to confirm correct spellings of brand names, the producers of said brands, and the conglomerates that inevitably rock the brands' cradle. First, use your favorite search engine to pick out your particular proper noun. Most times, your friendly search engine will suggest a corrected brand name, should it suspect that *Macrosoft,* for example, is faulty.

If you are unable to find an official maker's Web site, or if you are unable to attain clear consensus through the search engine, you may need to flag the name. So do the initial check yourself, but if your answers turn up conflicted, ask the author to verify.

With business names, pay close attention to unusual typographical features. Is it MicroSoft or Microsoft, 7-Eleven or 7-11, NBC or N.B.C.? Check each name for capitals, midcaps, internal wordspacing, numerical characters, non-alphabetical characters (Yahoo!), and internal periods. Every business name you check should appear on the style sheet you create (see Chapter 15).

If you're editing fiction, keep in mind that it's fine to use brand names of products to add a sense of reality. For other types of writing, writers should consider using generic terms: *cotton swabs* instead of *Q-Tips, bandages* instead of *Band-Aids,* and *cheese puffs* instead of *Cheetos.*

If you're not sure whether a product name is truly a brand name (and therefore in need of capitalization), here are two options:

- ✔ Check your handy-dandy dictionary, such as *Merriam-Webster's Collegiate Dictionary,* 11th edition. Look up *Band-Aid,* for example, and you find out that there is, indeed, a trademarked *Band-Aid* for a small adhesive strip with a gauze pad. (However, there's also *band-aid,* used as an adjective.)

- ✔ Mosey on over to the International Trademark Association's Web site at www.inta.org. It has a searchable database that Pop Rocks this world. Look for the "Trademark Glossary" in its "Publishing" pull-down menu.

And please, to keep a reader's eyes from crossing, do not muck up nice words with those © or ® signs unless you absolutely have to. They're startling to the eye, silly to the feel, and completely unnecessary in magazine articles and running book copy. Trademark lawyers may try to insist that these symbols be included in running text, but they're not legally required except when the writer mentions a product (such as a competitor's product) in an advertisement.

Verifying people and place names

As if misspelling or misrepresenting a brand name isn't bad enough, you also have to worry about the names of people and places. Is that actor's name Nicholas Cage, or Nicolas Cage? (No *h* for this Cage.) What about Quatar? Is it Qatar? (The latter.)

Here are a few resources you want to have handy to check people and place names:

- ✔ The Internet Movie Database (to friends, *IMDb*) bills itself as "the biggest, best, most award-winning movie site on the planet." And it's the closest thing to a definitive resource on name spellings for actors, directors, producers, and other stars (even the B-movie variety). Check it out at www.imdb.com, but be aware that you may occasionally run across an error. If you work frequently on copy that deals with films and celebrities, keep a printed guide on hand as well, like *Leonard Maltin's Movie Guide* (Signet), which is updated annually.

- ✔ What IMDb is to pop culture, the *Cambridge Biographical Encyclopedia* (Cambridge University Press) is to historical figures. Unfortunately, it's not (yet) available online. In this tome, you get a brief synopsis of world leaders and cultural personalities, living and dead. A "How to Use" section explains the format and cross-references and includes a pronunciation guide — great for dinner-party talk about Marcel Proust (pronounced *Proost*) and Johann Wolfgang Goethe (that's *Gur*-tah). Don't have the *CBE*? No problem — there's a "Biographical Names" section in the endpages of the *Merriam-Webster's Collegiate Dictionary*.

- ✔ For geographical names, may I suggest the latest edition of *Merriam-Webster's Geographical Dictionary*? If you'd rather use the Internet, run the spelling through a search engine and find a generally accepted consensus.

- ✔ For a whole collection of authoritative sources, you may want to try www.bartleby.com, your one-stop shop for unlimited and free access to *Columbia Encyclopedia* (Columbia University Press), *The American Heritage Book of English Usage* (Houghton Mifflin), Bartlett's *Familiar Quotations* (Little, Brown), Gray's *Anatomy of the Human Body* (Lea & Febiger), and Strunk's *The Elements of Style* (W. P. Humphrey), among others.

As good as many online resources are, a copyeditor ought to have printed resources as well. Errors can creep in with scanning and transcription, so Web versions of printed books are always second-best. Any quotation from an online source should be checked against the print version if there is one.

With that caveat in mind, here's a go-to guide of fact-filled Web sites to keep on hand while editing:

- ✔ Movie stars, directors, and other film-related ephemera: The Internet Movie Database at www.imdb.com

- ✔ Domain names: Go Daddy at www.godaddy.com

- ✔ Famous, and not so famous, quotations: Bartlett's *Familiar Quotations* at www.bartleby.com

✔ Sneaky spellings: My favorite online word source — Merriam-Webster OnLine at `www.m-w.com`

✔ Elements of editing: Strunk's *The Elements of Style* at `www.bartleby.com`

✔ The official database for trademarks: The International Trademark Association at `www.inta.org`

✔ Cooking hints, kitchen tips, and measurements galore: The Food Reference Web site at `www.foodreference.com`

✔ Biographies, businesses, and the ways of the world — anything you need: Infoplease at `www.infoplease.com`

✔ Links to just about every resource you could ever possibly need: *The New York Times* Newsroom Navigator, which lists recommended Web sites organized by research category, at `www.nytimes.com/navigator`

Spying Potential Offenses: Three Ways to Save an Author's Backside

Imagine that you're reading a document written by a pro: someone who knows how to use the English language (including how to spell) and how to present an argument, sales pitch, or plot line with clarity and style. Here's my warning: Don't ever assume that a near-perfect presentation means you can coast through a job. Sometimes evils lurk beneath the surface of such a document.

A great copyeditor must be on high alert for the following three-alarm issues.

Recognizing the need for permissions

The responsibility of obtaining permissions to reprint copyrighted material — be it song lyrics, a snippet of poetry, or even a dictionary entry — falls on the author of the work. And who do you think is responsible for alerting the author to copyright wrongdoing? That's right, it's you — the copyeditor. You are not responsible for knowing whether a quotation, passage, or artwork requires permission. You are simply responsible for flagging it and asking the question.

Amid the jumble of legal language contained in section 107 of the copyright law (officially called the *U.S. Code*), you find something called "fair use." Teachers, students, and most nonprofit organizations may use some excerpted materials without infringing on copyright laws. The rest of us, however, must get permission to use somebody else's work.

Here's the nitty-gritty: Up to 250 words total of a text (continuous or from different parts of the work) can be used, if the text is a standard prose work. When it comes to poems, lyrics, and the like that themselves may be much shorter than 250 words, then using even a line or two can cause trouble.

But a legal issue wouldn't be a legal issue without confusing addendums, and you need to know about one called *public domain.* This term is used for works that are either ineligible for copyright protection or whose term of copyright protection has expired and may not be renewed. What makes a work ineligible or why the copyright runs out is too boring to mention here. The important thing to remember is this: For works in the public domain, no permission is necessary for use; they can be quoted to the author's content, whether in books, on Web sites, or on the biggest billboards you've got.

Where can you confirm whether a work is considered public domain? Check these Web sites, or enter "public domain works" into your favorite search engine:

✔ **Project Gutenberg (www.gutenberg.com):** This site doesn't claim to include every free-use work known to humankind, but it contains electronic versions of more than 19,000 public domain books and other documents, and its nifty author and title searches greatly simplify your work.

✔ **Bartleby.com (www.bartleby.com):** Worthy of another mention, this site is a great source for public domain works, with separate search menus for reference, verse, fiction, and nonfiction.

Sniffing out plagiarism

In the world of words, there is no greater intellectual offense than plagiarizing somebody else's work or ideas — and it's not always committed by some malicious malcontent. You know that plagiarism includes copying large sections of text from another source without including a citation, but what about actions that are more difficult to sort out and put your finger on?

We're all bombarded with so much information every day that it's easy to understand why an author may not know exactly where she has picked up certain facts or ideas. An author may not even know that an offense has been committed.

To avoid having a big red *P* affixed to your — or your author's — chest, be mindful of the following when reading a work:

> ✔ Exact words from books, magazines, television shows, Web sites, songs, or other media must be cradled in quotation marks and credited with the source and the author, if available. Ideas from the same must be restated by the author in words that greatly differ from the original, and they, too, must be credited with the original source and author.
>
> ✔ Visual material, such as pictures, illustrations, and charts, must be credited with the source and an author or originator. The author must track down the copyright owner; otherwise, you can't use the image.
>
> ✔ Information received through an interview or conversation with another person — however informal and whether by telephone, by e-mail, or in person — must include a citation and may include the date of the interview.

Keep in mind that facts that are common knowledge do not need to be supported with citations. For example, if an author writes that World War I took place between the years 1914 and 1918, you do not need to pull down a dusty tome from the shelf to get another author's name for a citation.

If, while you are copyediting, a storyline rings fantastically familiar or you suspect that an article covers a topic you've already read, either flag it for the author or do some research to locate the other source. If you do the research and confirm overlap with another source, flag that the plagiarized portion be corrected. Experienced copyeditors will call or e-mail the editor as soon as plagiarism is suspected, because it can take time to correct the problem and may have an impact on the production schedule.

You can check for plagiarism by using many of the same methods and resources I present in the "Checking (and Checking and Checking) Facts" section earlier in the chapter. The Internet can be your best friend in this task.

Here's the bottom line: When in doubt, flag or query anything that looks like it is not properly attributed. The assigning editor will normally go through the queries, passing along only those that he cannot resolve without the author's input, so it's better to query than to ignore.

Walking the line with political correctness

What do _Tron_, Rubik's Cubes, parachute pants, and political correctness have in common? They all got their start in the '80s. And while _Tron_ is now a cult classic, Rubik's Cubes are tradeshow freebies, and my husband (thank heavens) no longer wears those awful swishing things, political correctness is here to stay.

The copyeditor's job is to point out when an author strays too far over the fine line between being wisely cautious and being a little silly.

Writing shouldn't offend people, nor should it coddle them. It should be sensitive to language or sentiment that unnecessarily excludes or alienates whole groups of people — especially your readers. Moreover, copyeditors are *expected* to flag or change language that promotes bias or stereotyping of others (based on gender, religion, race, sexual orientation, age, or a mental or physical disability). That said, you must find a precarious balance between eliminating language you personally find unacceptable or offensive and allowing the author to fully express himself. Your goal should be to keep an ear to the ground for those transgressions the author may not be aware he is committing.

When people rail against political correctness, they're usually stating that it has run amok. The label "PC" is, more often than not, applied disparagingly. However, you do need to watch out for things that could genuinely offend readers. Following are some things you may ask your author about:

✔ Gender:

- Is it necessary to refer to an object or country as *he* or *she* when *it* would suffice?

- Is there a reason to use such terms as *male nurse* or *female doctor*?

- Is the generic use of *he* appropriate? (For example, *Every director must report to his office by 9:00 a.m.*)

- Can *chairman* and *fireman* be changed to the more gender-neutral *chair* and *firefighter*?

✔ Race:

- Is it necessary to point out racial differences? (For example, *The board comprises six men and three African-American women.*)

- Is there reason to use such archaic terms as *oriental* (instead of *Asian*)?

✔ Disabilities:

- Is it appropriate in context to mention a disability? (*Despite his prosthesis, he was a profitable stockbroker.*)

- Should you consider changing such negative references as *confined to a wheelchair*? Perhaps *wheelchair-supported* would be equally clear.

Don't let the whole PC thing get out of hand. A term like *differently abled*, while well intentioned, reads strangely euphemistic and maybe should be struck for a more acceptable term, like *developmentally delayed*.

For some PC mirth, check out Henry Beard and Christopher Cerf's book *The Official Politically Correct Dictionary and Handbook* (Villard), offering an entertaining lexicon of politically correct terms.

A note of caution: While it is necessary in journalism and most corporate communications to maintain an impartial tone, fiction is a whole different game demanding much different rules. Don't immediately fire on descriptions of people as "yokels" or change dialogue that contains controversial language and subject matter. Bias-heavy language may be part of the characterization of a person, or part of the story, and shouldn't be touched by the hands of anyone other than the author. If you can't discern the intent of the offending language in context, querying the author is always an option.

Becoming a Sourcing Expert: Footnotes, Endnotes, and Bibliographies

You know how it is when you're talking to a coworker about his weekend and he starts telling you about how nice the weather was, and then he goes on to say that he was quarreling with his significant other and they've decided they're really not all that happy with their relationship and maybe they need a break from each other and now there is this barista he keeps running into at the coffee shop around the corner who gives him a grande latte but only charges for a tall . . . and you're thinking, "Whoa, T.M.I."

You've been there. You know what I mean. Sometimes you just don't need all that data.

Footnotes and endnotes are tools to use in instances where an author wants you to know that he's got more info if you want it, but he realizes that you probably don't. This note system lets authors get on with their narratives and not bore everyone with what particular issue of the *Farmer's Almanac* they got their prediction from and on which page it was found. The system is also vital for providing citational support for assertions, and for giving the source of quotes.

Especially if you're interested in copyediting academic texts, whether books or journal articles, knowing how to handle footnotes, endnotes, and bibliographies can make you a hot commodity.

Marking the notes: When the foots justify the ends

Let's recap what your high-school English teacher was getting at when you were struggling with that report on the hole in the ozone layer: Anything in the main body of your text that needs further explanation should be referenced using the note system. Notes can be in the form of footnotes or endnotes. Both work the same way:

- ✔ A reference mark is placed in the running text.
- ✔ An explanation is listed with that same reference mark at the foot of the page (for footnotes) or at the end of the manuscript (for — hazard a guess? — endnotes).

"Marco?": The reference mark

The term *reference mark* refers to the number or symbol placed in running text (or a table) that alerts the reader that there is more information to be found elsewhere about some piece of information he just read. You create a reference mark by placing a small symbol, letter, or number immediately after the sentence or clause containing the information to be referenced. The mark should be formatted as *supertext* (smaller and set slightly higher than the rest of the line of text):

> "We didn't need to look far to witness the socioeconomic toll such a dictatorship had on its people," Bob said upon his return. "It was written on the wearied faces of each and every Minsk citizen."[3]

If a document contains many notes, they should be numbered, starting over at the beginning of each chapter. If the footnotes are few, their numbering can run consecutively throughout the work. If there are very few notes, use symbols such as these:

- ✔ Asterisk (*)
- ✔ Dagger (†)
- ✔ Double dagger (‡)

Also use symbols if the author is using superscript numbers for other things, such as mathematical equations.

While you won't see this situation often, when both footnotes and endnotes are used, suggest that the endnotes be referenced with numbers and the footnotes with asterisks, daggers, and so on.

If the manuscript has way too many footnotes or endnotes, suggest that the author consolidate them. For instance, sometimes one reference mark is enough to cover multiple notes within one long paragraph.

Now, where to place those marks . . .

Always place reference marks after the material they explain. Put them at the end of a sentence or clause, after the punctuation. One exception: They should be placed before a dash, never after.

Not great:

> Atlanta's efforts to curb downtown traffic during the 1996 Summer Olympics dramatically improved the health of children with asthma[2] and people of all ages with chronic obstructive pulmonary disease.

Better:

> Atlanta's efforts to curb downtown traffic during the 1996 Summer Olympics dramatically improved the health of children with asthma and people of all ages with chronic obstructive pulmonary disease.[2]

In some instances, reference marks are placed before a closing parenthesis, if they refer to the information inside the parentheses.

> After two years of shared residency, they applied for her green card (although he previously stated he had misgivings about the strength of the marriage[3]).

"Polo!": The reference note

Footnotes and endnotes can be used to reference just about anything that the author doesn't want included in the main text. There are four typical uses:

- ✔ Alerting readers that material was borrowed
- ✔ Identifying the source of statements or quotations
- ✔ Presenting background or supplementary material that is way too much information for most people
- ✔ Referencing other parts of the work

Why use footnotes instead of endnotes, or vice versa? Well, most people use footnotes because they are easier to read: You don't have to keep flipping to the back of the book. But many publishers prefer endnotes, purely for the aesthetics. With endnotes, the main pages remain clean and "untechnified." The publishers' great fear is that when you pick up the book in a bookstore and see tons of footnotes at the bottom, you'll think, "Whoa. This is gonna be a drag to read."

Here's a brief rundown of how to use each type of note:

- ✔ **Footnotes:** Generally, footnotes are placed at the bottom of the page on which a statement to be cited or otherwise noted appears, typically in a font smaller than that of the running text. They should always begin on the page on which their reference marks appear.

  Don't let your note get lost in transition. If a footnote carries over to the next page, the break should fall midsentence so the reader knows the note continues beyond that page.

- ✔ **Endnotes:** Endnotes are grouped in their own section and placed after the main text and appendixes and before the bibliography. Endnotes are oftentimes in a smaller text than the running copy. A simple heading of *Notes* is sufficient to differentiate this section from the others.

  If an endnote is added to or deleted from the slew of notes, the entire lot of them has to be renumbered from that point on.

Now, just to complicate matters, there are two terms that publishing types sometimes bandy about to describe types of footnotes and endnotes:

- ✔ **Content notes:** These are additional things an author or editor wants you to know about that statement or fact or whatever else the reference mark is attached to.

- ✔ **Source notes:** These indicate where the statement or fact came from, with no peanut-gallery commentary.

Content notes and source notes are not treated differently within the same text; these are just good terms to know so you can communicate effectively with authors and editors.

Want more confusion? Well, there are also *parenthetical notes,* which — as the name implies — are tucked within parentheses and inserted within the copy itself.

Nailing down note styles

There are as many different manuals of style that dictate how to reference things as there are industries and audiences. Most of us caught wind of this in high school, where we probably followed the Modern Language Association's style for our carefully referenced research papers (um, yeah).

In your copyediting adventures, you may encounter any number of manuals of style. You need to be sure to have the latest edition of a given style guide at all times, and to be sure when accepting a job that the publisher is using the same edition. A lot of stuff changes between editions, believe it or not. Here are some of the most frequently used manuals of style:

- ✔ **American Medical Association (AMA) style:** The *American Medical Association Manual of Style* contains definitive guidelines for medical writing.

- ✔ **American Psychological Association (APA) style:** The *Publication Manual of the American Psychological Association* is used by many academic disciplines, including the social sciences and humanities.

- ✔ **Chicago style:** *The Chicago Manual of Style* seems to be the most widely used within the book publishing world. Have a copy within arm's reach while editing. And, for the record, its official title is appended with the following: *The Essential Guide for Writers, Editors, and Publishers.*

- ✔ **Council of Science Editors (CSE) style:** *Scientific Style and Format: The CSE Manual for Authors, Editors, and Publishers* covers all areas of science and related fields, including the responsibilities of authors, editors, and peer reviewers in scientific publications.

- ✔ **Modern Language Association (MLA) style:** The *MLA Handbook for Writers of Research Papers* claims to be the official guide for nonfiction writing. Academics who don't use APA style often use MLA.

In Chapter 14, I discuss these and other style guides in detail.

How a footnote or endnote is reflected in a work depends on the guiding style for the document or manuscript. Next, I show you a few different ways to reference a book, sorted by APA, MLA, and Chicago style.

American Psychological Association (APA) style

APA uses parenthetical citations for sources, so footnotes and endnotes are used for explanatory notes and copyright permissions only.

Parenthetical source citation:

> A recent book chronicles Abraham Lincoln's bouts with depression (Shenk, 2005).

Content footnote or endnote:

> [2] See Shenk (2005), especially chapters four and seven, for examples of Lincoln's bouts with depression.

Modern Language Association (MLA) style

MLA recommends using footnotes and endnotes for source citations only.

Source footnote or endnote:

> [2] Joshua Wolf Shenk, <u>Lincoln's Melancholy: How Depression Challenged a President and Fueled His Greatness</u> (New York: Houghton Mifflin, 2005), 135.

Chicago style

Chicago style encourages the use of footnotes and endnotes for content, and it doesn't establish word or sentence limits.

Content footnote or endnote:

> [2] While this theory that Lincoln suffered from depression has been bandied about in academic circles, a recent book is an easier read to get an idea of the extensive research available to support this idea. See Joshua Wolf Shenk's *Lincoln's Melancholy: How Depression Challenged a President and Fueled His Greatness* (New York: Houghton Mifflin, 2005), especially chapters four and seven.

Footnote or endnote source citation:

> [2] Joshua Wolf Shenk, *Lincoln's Melancholy: How Depression Challenged a President and Fueled His Greatness* (New York: Houghton Mifflin, 2005), 135.

Dizzy? Don't worry — your managing editor (or whoever else is elbowing you for editing) will likely provide you with examples of that particular publishing house's style on footnotes and endnotes.

Copyediting this stuff: The bitter dessert

Save the footnotes and endnotes for after you've read everything else. Get a sense of what the story or information within the running copy is trying to tell you, then go back and read all the notes from start to finish. And keep your feelers out for the following:

- Are the notes in proper order?
- Are the reference marks placed properly within the text?
- Does the note that the reference mark corresponds to seem appropriate and correct?
- Do the notes have any obvious errors (misspellings, incorrect italics, and so forth)?
- Is the format for each consistent and identical?

When reviewing footnotes and endnotes, the three most important things to check for are

- Consistency
- Typographical errors
- Consistency

Do the first and third items seem similar? I stress consistency because such little details can mean the difference between a book that rings of professionalism and a book that clangs of shoddiness. While many readers don't notice inconsistencies in reference notes, some do. Sloppy notating can bring the accuracy of the entire piece into question. And authors want people to know how accurate they are, right? Otherwise, why have all those little notes?

Bibliographies: Reeling in the resources

Reference notes can also refer a reader to a *bibliography:* the list of works an author has used in putting together her own work. The bibliography is alphabetized and usually placed just before the index.

While bibliographies can be formatted in many ways, a typical entry looks like this:

> [2] Simpson, C., State of the Nation's Air Quality, *Lung Health Association,* 2004: 49–51.

From this entry, you can tell that the author of the source material is C. Simpson, the article is called "State of the Nation's Air Quality," the publication is *Lung Health Association,* the date of the publication is 2004, and the information is on pages 49–51. You can trust that if the author went to such pains to write out all that information, it ought to be accurate; you don't have to go to the library and look it up. But you do need to understand how it's laid out so you can compare it with other entries. Let's assume the next entry is as follows:

> [3] M. Josefson, *On Mexican Wifehood,* Staten Island Chronicle; 2006: 18, 16.

After comparing the two, you may query the author about these things:

- Should the article name be in roman and the publication name be in italics?
- Should the "M." be placed after "Josefson," as in the first example?
- Should this entry be alphabetized by "Josefson"?
- One entry has a comma before the year; the other, a semicolon. Which should prevail?
- Should the pages be reordered to "16, 18"?

As with footnotes and endnotes, bibliographic entries can differ by style. Here's an example of American Psychological Association (APA) style:

> Shenk, Joshua Wolf (2005). *Lincoln's Melancholy: How Depression Challenged a President and Fueled His Greatness.* New York: Houghton Mifflin.

And an example of Modern Language Association (MLA) style:

> Shenk, Joshua Wolf. <u>Lincoln's Melancholy: How Depression Challenged a President and Fueled His Greatness.</u> New York: Houghton Mifflin, 2005.

Chicago style suggests different bibliographic entries depending on whether the readership for the manuscript or paper is within the realm of the sciences or the arts, history, and literature. Here's a sciences bibliographic entry:

> Shenk, Joshua Wolf. 2005. *Lincoln's Melancholy: How Depression Challenged a President and Fueled His Greatness.* New York: Houghton Mifflin.

And an arts, history, and literature bibliographic entry:

> Shenk, Joshua Wolf. *Lincoln's Melancholy: How Depression Challenged a President and Fueled His Greatness.* New York: Houghton Mifflin, 2005.

Again, chin up — you should receive examples of acceptable bibliographical entries before you begin a project.

Chapter 6

A Handful of Copyediting Specialties

*R*eady to take your copyediting skills beyond the margins? One way to make yourself more valuable to potential employers is to identify a publishing niche and focus your training, freelancing, and/or job-hunting efforts on it. In this chapter, I offer details on three niches I happen to know a good deal about: editing fiction, converting British text for a U.S. audience, and editing cookbooks.

Maybe none of these three specialties interests you. Maybe you're more inclined to pursue work in the fields of education, medicine, science, finance, sports . . . name your pleasure. If that's the case, my advice is to search the Web and *Writer's Market* (see Chapter 2) to get a sense of the publishers who focus on that specialty; read as many books or articles that relate to that field as possible; and, while you're reading, pay close attention to the conventions used in the writing.

The next logical step is to identify the style guide(s) most often used by editors working in your field of interest. In Chapter 14, I list a variety of style manuals, including the *American Medical Association Manual of Style,* the *Publication Manual of the American Psychological Association,* and *The Gregg Reference Manual* (a favorite of business writers). If you want to edit online content or technical materials, you may want to become familiar with *Read Me First! A Style Guide for the Computer Industry,* Second Edition by Sun Technical Publications (Prentice Hall), or the *Apple Publications Style Guide,* which is available online at `http://developer.apple.com/documentation/UserExperience/Conceptual/APStyleGuide/AppleStyleGuide2006.pdf`.

With lots of reading and style research under your belt, you'll have more confidence — and more to offer — when you start knocking on the doors of the publishers in your field of interest.

Editing Fiction

How would you like to get paid to read a bestseller or peruse the publications of your favorite genre? Fiction editing is one way to use your skills for fun and profit. But there's much more to copyediting a novel than plopping a manuscript on your beach towel and letting your love of literature go wild.

Letting the author's voice reign

The author's voice and poetic license reign in the pages of fiction. Some of the topics I cover in Chapters 4 and 5 may need to be folded up, stuck in a book, and put on a shelf, because they won't necessarily apply here.

When you edit fiction, you perform some of the same tasks as when you edit corporate and other nonfiction materials. For example, you may be charged with formatting the manuscript (see Chapter 16), and you usually correct spelling, grammar, and punctuation issues. (I say *usually* because, depending on the context, the author may actually want misspellings or incorrect grammar left alone.) But that's where the similarities end. Copyediting fiction doesn't require adhering to a publisher's house style manual. Instead, it requires doing everything possible to maintain the integrity and cohesion of a story and to preserve the voices of the author and the characters. The author's voice *is* your house style when you copyedit fiction.

In Chapter 4, I stress that maintaining the author's voice is the most important part of your job. In fiction, voice is even more crucial than in nonfiction. Creating a specific voice is how a fiction writer communicates and engages the audience. It adds an entire layer of meaning — sometimes acting as a character itself — over the surface of the general storyline and details of a novel. Think of the drastic difference between the style and tone of a Stephen King novel and that of a Jackie Collins novel, and you'll see what I mean.

Fiction editors and writers rely on copyeditors to use common sense and a light touch. You need to keep an ear to the ground for the author's voice and style, and you need to keep your paws off the editor's territory. That means no comments on character development, no "improvements" to the plot or suggestions on how you'd change the story, and no scratching at the dialogue to make it more "correct."

But you *are* allowed to finesse language that sounds awkward or may confuse a reader. Say you come across two ancillary characters with the same name; you may want to suggest a change to one of the names to ensure a reader understands that they are two distinct characters. Or maybe the writer uses a word six or seven times in the matter of three lines; you may want to flag it and suggest other words to break up the monotony.

Let me say it again: The author's voice *is* your house style when you copyedit fiction. Listen to that voice to figure out the pace and the preferences of grammar, diction, and expression that hold the consistency of the novel in place. Is the cop eating a *donut* or a *doughnut*? When that alien said "Nanu nanu," were the words in italics or not? Is the author consistently using a dash to introduce interior monologues and the thoughts of characters? Careful readings and a sensitive ear will reveal these kinds of things and much more. You may even want to read a fiction manuscript out loud.

With fiction, one reading is never sufficient for a thorough copyedit. Your first reading gives you a sense of the pacing of the storyline; the complexities of the plot, subplot, and characters; and the consistency and construction of language and voice. You can also catch typos and other obvious errors during the first read. During a second reading, your goal is to catch discrepancies that can ruin a story. If the author writes that Bianca has been ga-ga over Guy for the past five years, never paying attention to other men, how can she later reminisce about dating Gordon?

With each character, fact, and event presented, the author builds a world that is credible in its consistency. Who cares that the centaur has three heads and is pink? We can believe that, except if that same centaur inexplicably turns blue, in which case you need to query. (If said centaur has chameleon tendencies, it's probably best to let the reader in on that ability before she suspects a mistake.) As I explain in Chapter 4, the query is your best bud when you need to respectfully point out things that just don't jibe within the world the author has created.

Ensuring continuity and chronology

Readers of fiction are much different than readers of newspapers or textbooks. Rather than reading for information or to learn a new task, fiction readers want to be entertained. For that to happen, they need to be able to get past the words, forget where they are, and become oblivious to the passage of time. For a reader to have this experience, a novel must have internal coherence.

Nothing is more frustrating to a reader than errors in continuity and chronology. What are these things?

✓ **Continuity:** This word refers to the overall logic and consistency of a story's internal world. It applies to characters and relationships, plots and subplots, places and the things within them, and events and timelines. Your job is to ensure that the reader can depend on the descriptions of these elements to remain the same throughout a work.

✓ **Chronology:** If a story begins on a beautiful summer day, it doesn't make sense if later that evening it starts snowing. If we're told in one chapter that Dusty's parents died when she was very young, she can't later introduce her new boyfriend to her mother.

How can you possibly remember everything when you're editing a lengthy manuscript? During your first read, you start to keep track of all the people, places, and things you encounter in the world of the novel. With each subsequent read, you add to the list. The result is your style sheet for that work. Here's what such a style sheet should include:

✓ **Design elements:** Are there reference notes? If so, are they located at the bottom of each page or at the end of the chapter? Is there artwork, and is it always in the same place on the page or in a chapter?

✓ **Words, language, and usage:** Are certain words always capitalized? Did the author hyphenate *red-headed mistress*? Does the story contain invented or non-English words, *padre*? Do the characters speak in slang? Does the text use the serial comma and spell out numbers?

✓ **Proper names:** List all the characters. If they have pets, list those too. List any place names mentioned, whether cities or bars or grocery stores. Note the types of cars (or rocket ships or whatever) they drive. Whenever you see a proper name, include it.

✓ **Character traits of major players:** What makes each character unique? What do these people (or animals or aliens or whatever) look like? Where did they grow up? Who did they date? Are they married? Do they have accents? How about tattoos?

✓ **Miscellaneous information:** Who is on the cheerleading team? Do Cameron and Cory live on the same street? Are they in the same town? Where was the pivotal ball game, again? If the author has cleverly weaved historical events and names into the mix, make sure Watergate isn't happening in the '90s.

✓ **Your changes:** Did you add a hyphen to *real-estate salesperson*? Correct the spelling of *quicky mart*? If so, write down the change, and note the page number(s) where it appears. That way, if you need to go back and undo a change for any reason, you save a lot of detective work.

Depending on the length and breadth of a novel, your style sheet could be extremely long and detailed, with entries the likes of *Pg. 6: Amanda (Schilling, p. 23; born El Centro, California, p. 103; married Danny, p. 104) — caramel-colored hair, rainbow tattoo on right shoulder.*

I recommend that for each entry, you include the page number of its first occurrence in the story, as well as any information that should be kept in mind about that entry and any places in the story that the information changes or is updated. If you need to query a certain reference, include that in the style sheet, too.

Sometimes you may need to make sketches of the streets, places, and even relationships you come across. If the story establishes in Chapter One that Chris lives in Indianapolis and Joan lives in Houston, you can't have Chris walking to Joan's house in Chapter Five. And when the book opens with Aryn marrying Leah's brother, Teddy, you want to make sure that everybody is in their proper familial places for the remainder of the story — unless somebody dies or gets divorced, which you'd keep track of, too.

You use the style sheet to determine the logic and laws that guide the story, cross-referencing resources to keep the internal world in check. If something seems physically impossible or defies the internal logic of the novel's world, query it to bring the inconsistency or error to the author's attention.

After you finally finish combing, recombing, and letting the piece set under a hair dryer, you type up your list (if you didn't create it electronically), alphabetize the entries, and submit your final product with the finished job. While the author and editor *ooh* and *aah* at your thoroughness, you can flip your hair back, polish your knuckles on your lapel, and toss off, "It was nuthin'."

Handling dialogue

Speaking of *nuthin'*, dialogue within a work of fiction is worth talking about. Do you speak in flawlessly constructed and grammatically perfect sentences? I don't. Unless you're editing a science fiction tale, characters within a story are expected to speak the way the rest of us do: with slang, in dialects, and sometimes using otherwise cringe-worthy words like *ain't* and *uh-huh* and *Wuzzup!*

So, let's go over the rules of grammar and diction in fiction: There are no rules. The words and ways in which characters speak are part of the characters themselves, and to change them would be not to understand the story or the author's intent. When reading dialogue in fiction, you need to believe that most things are there for a reason, and with the poetically licensed blessing of the author.

That said, you could find along the way that the dialogue of a character seems out of place with previous voice, vocabulary, or setting. Your Southern belle may become ruffled and exclaim "Blimey! That was none too brill!" leading you to wonder whether the stress-inducing event in question has inadvertently turned her cockney. And did that Civil War soldier really tell his buddy that he set his wristwatch by the setting sun? If he did, what to do? Query the offense; bring it to the author's attention and explain why you find it inconsistent.

Tapping into genres: Mystery, romance, and fantasy

One dark and stormy night, he peered into her heaving cleavage, kissed her eyeballs, and invited her to slay the 18-headed dragon. Each genre of fiction has its own form, style, and subject matter. While it's not absolutely necessary that you enjoy what you're reading, wouldn't it be more fun if you did? If you have a favorite sort of story, you may be one step ahead in the game of copyediting for publishers of a particular kind.

A fiction editor should know the conventions of various genres to help a writer meet the expectations of the publisher and, most importantly, the audience. For example, what are some typical settings for a mystery novel? How detailed does a fantasy reader expect a plot to be? What kinds of conflict do romance characters come up against? How multifaceted should each sexy siren be?

Read and analyze as many recently published books and stories as you can that are in the genre you hope to work in. Most publishers have pages of requirements for genre copyediting. When you get an editing job, be sure to ask for those requirements. And even before you get an editing job, feel free to contact a publisher to ask for them; they're a great way to improve your understanding of how a certain type of book is created.

Here are just a few fields of fiction and some tidbits about what kinds of mysteries you need to master for each:

✔ **Elementary, my dear Watson.** Mystery fiction is extremely popular these days. It's that nail-biting, edge-of-your-seat stuff that tears us out of our own lives and leads us along by bread crumbs into a puzzle or suspicious whodunit event. As the copyeditor, you keep close tabs on the teaser information peppered along the paragraphs to substantiate the evidence and keep coherence in check.

✔ **Edit your heart out.** Whether you find them silly or sensuous, the satiny soap-opera sagas of romance novels are rife with drama and happy endings, making them among the more fun reads. However complex the plot and subplots, romance novels tend to focus on a romantic relationship between two (or more) people and nearly always wrap up with an emotionally satisfying ending. Of course, some romance authors push the envelope with cattiness and adultery, so know what you're getting into — and ask to see the publisher's guidelines for clarity.

✔ **The plane! The plane!** Fasten your seatbelt, and get ready to venture forth into fantasy. On the outside, this fiction may seem built of fluid, amorphous bricks of changing colors and physical properties. But the custom-built worlds of science fiction and its kin are held to their own laws and practices, which makes for one fascinating read. Fantasy editors must know and thoroughly understand the layers of the unique universe to enforce the particular laws that effectively suspend the disbelief of the readers. This means steering steady words, slang, and syntax; the facts of the futuristic themes; the voice and tone of the drama; and the historical coherence of the place and plot.

To be an effective genre copyeditor, you must care and have respect for the craft. Really. If you don't truly love the work, the novelty of telling your friends that you are a sci-fi editor will wear off more quickly than that author can churn out the latest *Attack of the Killer Mutant Fish* title. If you don't dig the details or aren't at least curious about it, edit something else.

Translating British Materials for a U.S. Audience

Someone (perhaps George Bernard Shaw — we don't know for sure) once described Great Britain and the United States as "two nations divided by a common language." The truth is, people in the United States are not always aware of the many differences between British and American writing, even if they realize that *favourite* isn't quite right or it's not appropriate to refer to a policeman as a *bobby*.

Thanks in part to one Noah Webster — father of the first American dictionary — we Yanks may dream of living in a Monty Python world of boots and bonnets, but we no longer commit such talk to paper.

Considering the market

Isn't it brill that there's literature from across the pond that requires our translation? Think *Bridget Jones's Diary* — some Yank had to modify the language to make sure we got it when Bridget got into her beau's britches.

How often might you encounter this type of translation? U.S. publishers keep an eye out for British novels that burn up the best-seller charts over yonder, and they often want to handle the hotter titles for a U.S. audience. (*Harry Potter*, anyone?) If you work for a publisher with international tendencies, you could very well be asked to do this kind of job.

Oddly enough, I was a proofreader for the *For Dummies* series published in England. I was responsible for proofreading British books to maintain the authentic English voice, spelling, punctuation, and style — which can be much terser than American style and favor things such as commas and colons much more. To do that job, I had to know what British lexical and punctuation differences needed to stay in the book and why.

Sharing a few of my favourite guidelines

Following are a handful of guidelines to help you recognize some Briticisms and convert them to Americanisms:

- ✔ **Singular and plural noun agreement:** Is *team* a singular or plural noun? Would you say *The group are coming to a meeting*? While (I hope) this example doesn't sound right to you, it's perfectly acceptable to the British ear. Pay specific attention to singular and plural noun agreement. Use your American ear and translate collective nouns to the way you know they should be for your audience.

- ✔ **Regular and irregular verbs:** He who *smelt* it . . . er, *smelled* it? This is a tricky one. While the British allow for both regular and irregular verbs (*burnt, dreamt, smelt*), Americans generally lean toward *burned, dreamed,* and *smelled.* This goes for *amid* (as opposed to *amidst*), *while* (as opposed to *whilst*), and *among* (*amongst*) as well.

- ✔ **Hyphenation:** Hugh Grant may be a heartthrob in Houston, but in London he's a heart-throb. The heart palpitations he creates in the United States may be reduced by beta blockers, but in the United Kingdom, they require beta-blockers. Many British compound nouns are written with hyphens while their American counterparts are spelled as open or solid compounds.

- ✔ **Punctuation, period:** It is not unusual to see *Dr, Ms, Mr,* and *Jr* in British publications. Make sure to add the period for an American audience.

- ✔ **Dates:** In U.K. publications, dates (whether spelled out or abbreviated) appear in a day/month/year format. For instance, *4 July 1776* and *4/7/1776* each refer to the day we claimed our independence from Britain (albeit not from British bands and the like). Verify and change such dates to the U.S.-friendly month/day/year format.

- ✔ **Times:** Although it's 4.40 p.m. in England, it's 4:40 p.m. (with a colon) on our turf.

- ✔ **Measurements:** Metric facts and figures must be converted to U.S. standard for an American audience. That includes kilometers, kilograms, and Celsius.

Then there's *analyse* and *minimise,* some strange *ou* combinations, and other tricky spellings to look out for. Take a look at the following word list to taste a sampling of British English:

- ✔ **Living on the edg:** Although *acknowledgement* and *judgement* are preferred in England, spell them *acknowledgment* and *judgment* for a U.S. audience.

- ✔ **The beachwear of linguists:** Brits love the *oe/ae* digraphs in *manoeuvre, encyclopaedia, anaesthetic,* and *foetal.* Us? We prefer the more demure *maneuver, encyclopedia, anesthetic,* and *fetal.*

- ✔ **Mind your o's and u's:** Drop that *u* from *behaviour, colour, honour, neighbour, humour, favourite,* and their ilk. Instead, use the Americanized *behavior, color, honor, neighbor, humor,* and *favorite.*

- ✔ **Be wize and memorise:** Don't go suffix soft with *organise, apologise, standardise, specialise,* and *analyse;* try a *z* on for size and go *organize, apologize, standardize, specialize,* and *analyze.*

- ✔ **Taking the el:** While you'll be *travelling* (two *l*s) in London, you'll be *traveling* (one *l*) in New York. Same goes for *jeweler* and *reveler* (not *jeweller* or *reveller*).

- ✔ ***M* and *M*'s:** Hey, I love BBC *programmes* as much as the next Yank, but in my neck of the words it's *programs.*

- ✔ **Licence to confuse:** Although a lawyer in the United Kingdom must have a *licence* before he can be on the *defence* team, he'd better get a *license* to sit on the U.S. *defense* team. Same spiel for *offence* and others.

- ✔ ***Tre* wrong:** In most cases, *metre, centre,* and *theatre* are British variants and should be changed to *meter, center,* and *theater.* But be careful: Proper nouns — Kodak Theatre, for instance — should be kept intact.

- ✔ **Keep your logue in cheque:** American preferences over *catalogue, dialogue, banque,* and *cheque* are *catalog, dialog, bank,* and *check.*

- ✔ **Other errant English-isms:** *Tyre* and *pyjama* can be changed to *tire* and *pajama.* Skeptical of *sceptic*? You should be — it's *skeptic.* Craving a *draught* after *ploughing* your garden? No? How about a *draft* after *plowing*? Sounds delicious.

This list is by no means exhaustive. And neither is the following list of British words that need replacing for a U.S. publication:

- ✔ The British *flat* is an American *apartment.*

- ✔ British babies are pushed in a *pram* (for *perambulator*), but Yankee youngsters sit pretty in *strollers.*

- ✔ *Trolley* and *chemist* may or may not need to be altered. Check context, and rule out the Briticisms if the author means *shopping cart* and *pharmacist.*

- ✔ Trash *dustbin* and *rubbish bin* for the good ol' *trash can.*

- ✔ Where's the *city centre*? You can find it downtown.

- ✔ What could it mean to pull your *knickers* over your *bum* in the *loo*? Easy: Pull your *underwear* over your *bottom* in the *bathroom* or *toilet.*

- ✔ From A to *zed?* Chiefly a British thing, *zed* is the letter *z.*

When you suspect a Briticism but cannot decipher it on your own, search the Internet for a usage example and translate the word appropriately. Type the word or phrase into your Google search field and then type *location:UK* (no space after the colon, lowercase *l*). Your search will return hits from U.K. Web sites only. Or have a copy of a good British English dictionary on hand, like the *Shorter Oxford English Dictionary* (Oxford University Press). For punctuation differences, pick up a copy of *New Hart's Rules* (the British style bible), which is available here through Oxford University Press.

How do you know that *knock-on effect* is a domino effect or a *Heath Robinson machine* is a Rube Goldberg machine? For extra credit, brush up on your idioms with one of the British dictionaries for advanced learners of English, such as the *Oxford Advanced Learner's Dictionary* (Oxford University Press), the *Longman Dictionary of Contemporary English* (Pearson Longman), or the *Macmillan English Dictionary* (Macmillan), all of which are written with a bias toward British English but show patterns in American English too. (Don't get the American English–only versions of these books.)

Heading into the Kitchen

If cooking is your cup of tea, you can have your cake and edit it, too. The recipe testers who work in labs aren't the only people who have to be technically proficient for a cookbook to work. Recipes can easily get lost in the translation from the cook to the book. Consider the woman who detected something fishy in her Key lime pie, only to find that she used the called-for tartar sauce instead of the truly needed cream of tartar. Ouch.

Cookbooks are similar to handyman how-to books: They present a list of necessary materials and step-by-step instructions on how to bring them together into something tangible. However, many cookbooks also have narratives woven throughout that you edit much as you would a novel.

Getting familiar with the specialty

In a loving household, dinner means more than reaching for the phone and a take-out menu. As the world around us becomes more demanding, the art of cooking is becoming increasingly important as a binder, holding families together like a honey apricot glaze over diced fruit. And well-written cookbooks not only instruct, educate, and entertain — they also become companions, as important to our kitchens as our very hearths.

Do you notice a hint of sappiness in this intro? Cookbooks are all about the feelings behind the food. Cookbook copyeditors pay as much attention to the voice of the writing as they do the technical aspects of the recipes.

If you want cookbook editing to be your thing, how do you begin? At the bookstore (or the library). Go to the cooking section, and try not be overwhelmed. Start pulling titles from the shelves, and notice these things:

- **Audience:** Recipes for bachelors and slouches are far less complicated than those for the Julia Child set.

- **Consistency:** How are the abbreviations for *tablespoon* and *quarter cup* handled? Is it a *Kalamata* or *kalamata* olive? A *rib eye* or *rib-eye* steak? Do we combine the first *4* ingredients, or *four*? Does the serving contain *3g* or *three grams* of protein?

   Review the list of ingredients against the steps of a recipe. Does the recipe suddenly call for chocolate when no chocolate is included in the ingredient list? Are the ingredients listed in the order in which they're called for?

- **Logic and completeness:** Think of the recipes as trials, and picture each part of the experiment as you read along. You don't need to know everything about cooking to catch an error like "add two cups of salt" to a batch of brownies. Do the steps include an oven temperature? An approximate cooking time and numbers of servings per recipe? Are the directions clear and consistent?

A typical cookbook contains at least 100 recipes. With that many to check, you quickly figure out how the recipes are supposed to look and feel. And if you need help figuring it out, a great style guide to have on hand is *Recipes into Type* by Joan Whitman (Collins).

Measuring up

Cookbook copyeditors need to be aware of cooking terms and measurements. You don't have to be an expert on these, but some familiarity may alert you when something is amiss.

Here are some equivalencies to keep in mind:

✔ A cup of liquid equals 8 U.S. fl. oz.

✔ A pint equals 2 cups.

✔ A quart equals 2 pints.

Formally, a *dash* of liquids equals about six drops (where 76 drops make 1 teaspoon). In most recipes, however, a dash just means a small amount.

A *handful* is a term used when the amount selected isn't going to ruin the recipe, like adding nuts to the top of brownies. If you must, think of it as ½ cup — more if you want more, less if you want less. Query the author when the use of "handful" refers to something you wouldn't want to pick up, like olive oil.

A *pinch* is a small amount of a dry ingredient, about ⅛ teaspoon or less.

A *shot* is a unit of alcohol, roughly 1½ fl. oz.

A *level spoonful* has the excess scraped off with an edge (other than your thumb, ideally). A *rounded spoonful* has about as much above the top of the spoon as below it. A *heaping spoonful* is as much as the spoon can hold.

The three basic spoon sizes are as follows:

✔ Tablespoon (Tbs), 15 ml (equal to three teaspoons)

✔ Dessert spoon, 10 ml

✔ Teaspoon (tsp), 5 ml

Formatting recipes

If you're going to teach an old dog a new trick, you need to first record each tool he needs for that trick. Then you need to logically explain the stages of assembling those tools into the trick itself. The same process applies with a recipe. Kinda.

Grab your go-to cookbook, and you'll notice that each recipe follows the same general format. Typically, recipes start with a brief description of the dish, followed by a list of necessary ingredients in the order in which they are mentioned in the recipe directions, then detailed directions — step by every careful step — on how to create the dish. The more elaborate the dish, the longer and more detailed the ingredient list and directions.

More elaborate cookbooks may include wine pairings, cross-references with other recipes for full meals and dinner plans, acceptable ingredient substitutions, and nutrition values for each serving. Each piece needs to be checked for consistency and accuracy.

If the cookbook you're asked to edit is part of a series, the publisher may have strict guidelines for you to follow to keep the series consistent. If the cookbook is intended to be part of a future series, it may be your responsibility as the copyeditor to create the guidelines. Lucky you!

If the publisher hasn't furnished guidelines, keep track of the order in which the first recipes are laid out. Are the ingredients listed first, or are they incorporated within the recipe directions? If the author includes comments or tips, are they interspersed within the recipe, are they noted in a sidebar, or are they at the end of the recipe? All these subtle variations are important to the integrity of the book and should be consistently applied to every recipe within it.

There's one other thing I feel I must note: While you are welcome to actually cook the dishes you come across in this niche, if you find that they are terrible, don't take it upon yourself to make improvements. Even if you know that tweaking that Heirloom Tomato Sauce with balsamic vinegar — just like Grandma's — will save thousands of people from grimacing over pasta, keep it to yourself.

Chapter 7

The Copyediting Process in Action

*T*his is the voyeuristic section of the book. In this chapter, I do the same sorts of things I do when I'm copyediting alone in my office . . . while you watch.

Copyediting is different from some other disciplines — take math, for example. In math, there's usually just one right answer. You either get it right or you get it wrong. And when you get it right, what's the big deal? Most everybody else got the same answer.

While some of copyediting deals with right and wrong answers (how many different ways can you spell *exhibitionism*?), much of it has to do with using judgment. You're editing for structure and clarity, and there's always more than one way to get it right.

This is what I love about copyediting: When I'm faced with something that doesn't quite work, I get to suggest fixes. Fun.

You don't believe that it can be fun? I'll prove it. First, read the examples that follow. Then look through my edited versions to see what changes I've made and queries I've posed. (I've also included a few notes for your eyes only in the examples.) To indicate my edits, I use marks that are similar to those a proofreader uses (see Chapter 9).

We'll start with you reading a short fiction piece . . . while I'm in my, um, naughty copyeditor's outfit.

Example One: Dabbling in Fiction

Rest assured, there's no need for your faithful Carmine red here. I want you to read the following example once, twice, and maybe a third time before moving ahead to the edited version. Some things will be easier to spot than others; some you may not see or understand at all until the end. That's how we figure this stuff out, right?

In this example, we need to edit for consistency, style, and grammar, keeping in mind the following:

- ✔ We need to use a serial comma.
- ✔ We need to spell out numbers one through ninety-nine.

Ready? Here goes:

The original

An excerpt from *White Russian Rail* by Christapher Dunbar

The train stopped at the border just after 1:00 a.m. I missed the midnight dead-line to be out of Belarus and was now in the county without a valid visa. I braced myself for a difficult customs interogation. However, there was another, less-daunting purpose of the stop at the Polish border that I looked forward to witnessing. This was the adjusting of the train's wheelbase to accommodate the differing widths of track used in Belarus and Poland.

Russia and its former states uses a realway gauge of five feet. It was adopted in the 1840s when an American engineer sells the idea to the Russia tsar. There was no standard at that time, but the rest of Europe used, and still uses, a more narrow gauge. Some historians have hinted that this was an important factor in Germany's inability to take over Russia-they couldn't easily get their troops beyond Poland by rail.

The Belarussian customs forms were unreadable to me. There was no English section. Nor did I have a pen. A heavyset woman who resembled a prison guard came to my cabin and helped me. She wrote "nyet," "nyet," "nyet," in three boxes and spoke at length in Russian about the other boxes. I didn't understand a thing she said, but I did the best I could with both forms. Soon, five officials (resembing riot police) boarded the train and came to my door. One said something that seemed to indicate that he was already impatient with me, so I gave him my passport. He exchanged glances with the others, and they took turns inspecting it, no longer interested in the stack of other passports in their hands.

Mean-while the train kept moving slowly in one direction and then the other. When it stopped between direction changes, eerie noises came from below. It was the sound you would expect a large chain to make if it was snapped under load. Then there was an intermittent clanging of what had to be an enormous tool chest, dropped from a great heighth. At other times, it sounded as though the other cars were getting sheared in half by the jaws of a fearsome metal-munching creature. It was dark and the windows were cloudy. I caught glimpses of workers toiling beneath yellows lights. I couldn't make out the surroundings but I noticed that the loud noises echoed as if our train were housed in some structure with concert-hall acoustics.

I heard talking outside my cabin's door—it was Russian punctuated by the words "Washington D.C.," "American" and "Dollars." Finally, a calm, savy-looking riot-police chief came in and sat down next to me. "Where. Are you. From," he asked, in a way that made me feel that I had already lied to him.

"The United States," I said with out any hint of deception.

"Why are you traveling in Belarussia?"

"I am a tourist."

"Tourist, yes," he contemplated. "May I see . . ." he took my declaration papers off the table. "Do you have any other money. Russian rubles, Belarussian rubles." His questions lacked the inflection of inquiry. Rather they fell flat, like statements.

"I do have less than one million Belarussian rubles." This wasn't much money, but more than I wanted to forfeit.

"Where is your first declaration papers." "I don't have any."

"You were given such papers when you came to Belarussia."

"I came to Belarus by trian from St. Petersburg. There was no one to greet me when I passed through the border." This was <u>true</u>.

"I see," he said slowly. "Do you know it is illegal to take Belarussian ruble's out of the country. You cannot do this, you see."

The final shakedown, I thought. I countered with, "I thought I might buy something to eat on the food car."

Our conversation continued like this. He would point out something questionale, I gave some lame excuse that he didn't seem to care about, and then he would let the initial objection drop. When I described the contents of my luggage to him. He became overly concerned that the only gift that was given to me during my visit to Belarous was hand tooled wooden box. He felt Belarussian clothing would make a nice present for a "nice man" such as myself. I agreed wholeheartedly. After a lengthy discussion about nothing much in particular, he decided the rubles I was taking out of the country would not be a problem after all. Then he shook my hand and left. He did not return my passport. This was the adjusting of the train's wheelbase to accommodate the differing widths of track used in Belarus and Poland.

I heard more breaking of large metal pieces and the pounding and whirring of some kind of motor. I closed my eyes and tried to sleep. Ten minutes later, the chief came back in. "Excuse me." he stated, "How did you enjoy the country of Belarussia."

"I . . ." I didn't know what to make of this second visit, but told him, "I thought it was wonderful." We continued our chat where we left off and he spoke passionately about the language of Belarus, which was becoming outlawed by the Belarussian president, Lukashenko, and how it would always be spoken—even if Russia and Belarus joined again. He pointed out differences in the pronounciations of words and told me there were areas in Russia where everyone still spoke Belarussian. I told him more about my visit. He thanked me and we shook hands. Then and he left again. Still no passport.

I watched the workers through the window. I could now see that the train was in a large barracks-style structure. It was wide enough for three sets of tracks, running parallel. 1 by 1, the train cars were separated and elevated. The jacks were ten-to-twelve-feet tall and mounted in concrete. They were operated by a vertical screw, roughly eight feet high. It resembled the hose used by coin-operated vaccum cleaners that you see at car washes. At the bottom of the screw was a motor with a housing the size of a quarter beer keg. I watched as my car rolled into position. Four jacks, one at each corner, began to lift the car. Beneath the car was a section of both the five-foot-wide track and the narrower-with track, running between it. The workspace was a huge pit, like you would see at an automotive lube shop. While the screws turned, railway police paced the yard, perhaps looking for double agents. Heavy men with beefy arms slaved over the manual part of the process and struggled with the jacks. Along the side of the track ran a cable pulley system. It was in constant operation but did not have a purpose I could discern. At the ends of my car, I saw the connecting cars sitting slightly below me, at ground level. I could not see how long the barracks structure was.

The cars were eventually rejoined with all the noise and enthusiasm of their separation. The train lurched forward, then backward, then stopped. Outside, a tone sounded and a tired voice came back on the PA system. It was a woman speaking in either Russian or Polish, but it was too muffled to know for sure

We sat there for almost an hour longer. Then the riot-police chief came back in. "I think you have nothing to declare," he told me. His eyes were red.

"Yes, that is true," I feigned a smile.

"I think you are a happy man," he said sincerely. He reeked of booze.

"Well, my visit has made me happy," I said, trying not to appear alarmed.

"I think the Belarussian people are the best people." He was swaying and had had to prop himself against the doorway to keep his balance. "And I hope to see you again. Not in minsk but outside in the country. Like Brest. It is really wonderful country."

And I was like, "I hope so too."

We shook hands for a third and final time. He left, and the official to whom I initially gave my Passport appeared. Before giving it back to me, she made me stand so she could check beneath the bench—perhaps for stowaways. There were none.

My suggested edits

An excerpt from *White Russian Rail* by Christopher Dunbar

Query: Is this name spelled correctly?

The train stopped at the border just after 1:00 a.m. I missed the midnight deadline to be out of Belarus and was now in the county without a valid visa. I braced myself for a difficult customs interogation. However, there was

If a hyphen can be removed without causing confusion, as in this case, remove it.

another, less daunting purpose of the stop at the Polish border that I looked forward to witnessing. This was the adjusting of the train's wheelbase to accommodate the differing widths of track used in Belarus and Poland.

Russia and its former states uses a realway gauge of five feet. It was adopted in the 1840s when an American engineer sells the idea to the Russian tsar. There was no standard at that time, but the rest of Europe used, and still uses, a more narrow gauge. Some historians have hinted that this was an important factor in Germany's inability to take over

Query: When was this? Specify which war.

Russia—they couldn't easily get their troops beyond Poland by rail.

The Belarussian customs forms were unreadable to me. There was no English section. Nor did I have a pen. A heavyset woman who resembled a prison guard came to my cabin and helped me. She wrote "nyet," "nyet," "nyet," in three boxes and spoke at length in Russian about the other boxes. I didn't understand a thing she said, but I did the best I could with both forms. Soon, five officials (resembing riot police) boarded the train and came to my door. One said something that seemed to indicate that he was already impatient with me, so I gave him my passport. He exchanged glances with the others, and they took turns inspecting it, no longer interested in the stack of other passports in their hands.

Meanwhile the train kept moving slowly in one direction and then the other. When it stopped between direction changes, eerie noises came from below. It was the sound you would expect a large chain to make if it was snapped under load. Then there was an intermittent clanging of what had to be an enormous tool chest, dropped from a great height. At other times, it sounded as though the other cars were getting sheared in half by the jaws of a fearsome metal-munching creature. It was dark and the windows were cloudy. I caught glimpses of workers toiling beneath yellow lights. I couldn't make out the surroundings but I noticed that the loud noises echoed as if our train were housed in some structure with concert-hall acoustics.

Query: The use of an uncountable "load" is unusual; can we change to "a load"?

I heard talking outside my cabin's door—it was Russian punctuated by the words "Washington D.C.," "American," and "Dollars." Finally, a calm, savy-looking riot-police chief came in and sat down next to me. "Where. Are you. From," he asked, in a way that made me feel that I had already lied to him.

These words should be italicized because they represent the words themselves.

"The United States," I said with out any hint of deception.

"Why are you traveling in Belarussia?"

"I am a tourist."

"Tourist, yes," he contemplated. "May I see . . ." he took my declaration papers off the table. "Do you have any other money. Russian rubles, Belarussian rubles." His questions lacked the inflection of inquiry. Rather they fell flat, like statements.

"I do have less than one million Belarussian rubles." This wasn't much money, but more than I wanted to forfeit.

"Where is your first declaration papers." "I don't have any."

I don't mind that this question is mis-worded and ends with a period rather than a question mark. This is the character's voice.

"You were given such papers when you came to Belarussia."

Emphasizing this word doesn't help the story, in my opinion. And if the author still wants it emphasized, that is more effectively achieved with italics.

"I came to Belarus by train from St. Petersburg. There was no one to greet me when I passed through the border." This was true.

"I see," he said slowly. "Do you know it is illegal to take Belarussian ruble's out of the country. You cannot do this, you see."

Especially when you work on hard copy, you have to train your eye to catch an extra space between sentences. You can catch this error easily when editing electronically by running a global search for two spaces and replacing them with one (unless your document requires two spaces in some instances).

The final shakedown, I thought. I countered with, "I thought I might buy something to eat on the food car."

Our conversation continued like this. He would point out something questionable, I gave some lame excuse that he didn't seem to care about, and then he would let the initial objection drop. When I described the contents of my luggage to him, He became overly concerned that the only gift that was given to me during my visit to Belarous was hand tooled wooden box. He felt Belarussian clothing would make a nice present for a "nice man" such as myself. I agreed wholeheartedly. After a lengthy discussion about nothing much in particular, he decided the rubles I was taking out of the country would not be a problem after all. Then he shook my hand and left. He did not return my passport. ~~This was the adjusting of the train's wheelbase to accommodate the differing widths of track used in Belarus and Poland.~~

This errant sentence appears to have come from an earlier paragraph. You shouldn't need to query its removal because the error is obvious.

I heard more breaking of large metal pieces and the pounding and whirring of some kind of motor. I closed my eyes and tried to sleep. Ten minutes later, the chief came back in. "Excuse me," he stated, "How did you enjoy the country of Belarussia."

"I . . ." I didn't know what to make of this second visit, but told him, "I thought it was wonderful." We continued our chat where we left off, and he spoke passionately about the language of Belarus, which was becoming outlawed by the Belarussian president, Lukashenko, and how it would always be spoken—even if Russia and Belarus joined again. He pointed out differences in the pronpunciations of words and told me there were areas in Russia where everyone still spoke Belarussian. I told him more about my visit. He thanked me, and we shook hands. Then and he left again. Still no passport.

I watched the workers through the window. I could now see that the train was in a large barracks-style structure. It was wide enough for three sets of tracks, running parallel. 1 by 1 the train cars were separated and elevated. The jacks were ten to twelve feet tall and mounted in concrete. They were operated by a vertical screw, roughly eight feet high. It resembled the hose used by coin-operated vaccum cleaners that you see at car washes. At the bottom of the screw was a motor with a housing the size of a quarter beer keg. I watched as my car rolled into position. Four jacks, one at each corner, began to lift the car. Beneath the car was a section of both the five-foot-wide track and the narrower-with track, running between it. The workspace was a huge pit, like you would see at an automotive lube shop. While the screws turned, railway police paced the yard, perhaps looking for double agents. Heavy men with beefy arms slaved over the manual part of the process and struggled with the jacks. Along the side of the track ran a cable pulley system. It was in constant operation but did not have a purpose I could discern. At the ends of my car, I saw the connecting cars sitting slightly below me, at ground level. I could not see how long the barracks structure was.

Sidebar notes (margin):

In most cases, numbers less than 10 are spelled out. And numerals never begin a sentence.

You may be tempted to use hyphens here, but they should be removed. If the sentence were worded differently ("ten- to twelve-foot-tall jacks"), hyphens would be necessary. As for the numbers, you need to check house style to know if they can remain spelled out.

You may want to query to suggest shortening this paragraph a bit. The last four sentences could probably be cut without losing essential information. However, if you've been asked to do a light copyedit, you may not want to tread on this ground.

The cars were eventually rejoined with all the noise and enthusiasm of their separation. The train lurched forward, then backward, then stopped. Outside, a tone sounded and a tired voice came ~~back~~ on the P.A. system. It was a woman speaking in either Russian or Polish, but it was too muffled for me to know for sure.

> There was no previous voice on the P.A. so the word *back* has to go.

We sat there for almost an hour longer. Then the riot-police chief came back in. "I think you have nothing to declare," he told me. His eyes were red.

"Yes, that is true," I feigned a smile.

"I think you are a happy man," he said sincerely. He reeked of booze.

"Well, my visit has made me happy," I said, trying not to appear alarmed.

"I think the Belarussian people are the best people." He was swaying and had had to prop himself against the doorway to keep his balance. "And I hope to see you again. Not in minsk but outside in the country. Like Brest. It is really wonderful country."

~~And I was like~~, "I hope so too," I said.

> The tone shifts here, so you want to make a change that brings it in line with the rest of the passage.

We shook hands for a third and final time. He left, and the official to whom I initially gave my passport reappeared. Before giving it back to me, she made me stand so she could check beneath the bench—perhaps for stowaways. There were none.

Wrap-up

Be advised that my edits to the above piece reflect what I feel is required to make this story clear and readable. My personal style, generally, is not to edit heavily. Other copyeditors may have wanted more clarity in what was happening in the train yard. Others may have taken issue with the deliberately mispunctuated quotations. It's really up to the individual reading it to decide what direction a piece should take. And bear in mind that if the author doesn't want to accept the suggested changes, it's the author's right to do so (although the author should be prepared to explain why).

Example Two: Touching on Technical Writing

Read the following technical writing example a few times before venturing on to the edited version. And don't be discouraged if you don't catch everything on the first try.

For this example, our goal is to edit for consistency, style, and grammar, keeping in mind the following:

- ✔ We can't use the serial comma.
- ✔ We need to use numerals when referring to a specific measurement.

The original

The Tape Dispenser

INTRODUCTION

Though shapes and sizes vary widely, the overall size of the standard

office tape dispenser is between 7 and 7.5 inches long, 3 to 4 inches tall

and 3" wide (at its thickest part. The dispenser described in this docu-

ment is 7.5 inches long, 3.5 inches wide (at its tallest part) and 3 inches wide (at its thickest part); it is designed to dispense a roll of .75-inch-wide one-sided sticky tape on a 1-inch core.

A standard tape dispenser consisted of three (3) parts: the dispenser base, the tape spindle and the cerrated metal cutter,

DISCUSSION

Dispenser base. The oval dispenser base is the piece on which all other parts are attached. The plastic base is weighted withs and, and two 1.75- by 1.75-inch non-skid appliqués are attached to the bottom of the plastic base; the sand and appliqués prevent the tape dispenser from moving when tape is pulled from the spindle and dispensed. The top of the dispenser base is hollowed into a 2 inch deep and 1 inch wide recess for the tape spindle and tape roll. Both sides of the hollowed recess contain a .4-millimeter L-shaped, notched cradle in which the arms of the tape spindle rest.

Tape spindle. The plastic tape spindle is 2.5 millimeters at its thickest point and is 3.5 millimeters wide (including two .7-millimeter arms on both sides) and is designed to fit within the one-inch core of a roll of .75-inch one-sided stickie tape, while the tape spindle is pushed into the core of the tape roll until the spindle is snug within the core and the spindle arms are seen on both sides of the tape roll, such that with the sticky side of the tape roll facing down, the arms of the tape spindle are placed into the l-shaped notches in the tape-dispenser base. If placed within the notches correctly, the spindle will whip around allowing the tape to be pulled from the tape roll and placed upon the serrated metal blade.

Serrated metal blade. The serrated metal blade are attached to the tape dispenser base with raised serrations facing the tap spindle. It is 1 inch long with a .25-inch flat surface on which tape sticks after dispensing, preventing the end of the tape from having to be freed from the roll each time tape is needed.

Conclusion

To dispose a tape roll, the dispenser is placed upon a level surface. A tape roll is placed on the tape spindle and the arms of the tape spindle are placed into the L-shaped notches in the dispenser base. The tape is pulled from the roll toward and beyond the serrated metal blade until the desired length is reached. The tape is pulled down until it sticks to the flat surface of the serrated metal blade and is then cut and freed; and the end of the tape roll will remain stuck to the fat surface of the serrated metal blade for ease of dispensing further pieces.

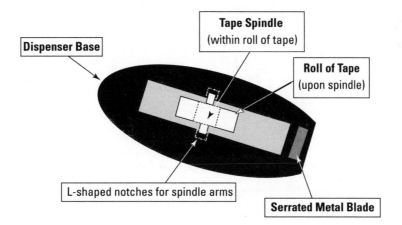

Tape Spindle (within roll of tape)

Dispenser Base

Roll of Tape (upon spindle)

L-shaped notches for spindle arms

Serrated Metal Blade

My suggested edits

The Tape Dispenser

INTRODUCTION

> Query: This piece would benefit from a better introduction. I suggest "The tabletop tape dispenser is an effective tool for storing and dispensing one-sided sticky tape."

Though shapes and sizes vary widely, the overall size of the standard office tape dispenser is ~~between~~ 7 to ~~and~~ 7.5 inches long, 3 to 4 inches tall and 3 wide (at its thickest part) The dispenser described in this document is 7.5 inches long, 3.5 inches tall ~~wide~~ (at its tallest part) and 3 inches wide (at its thickest part); it is designed to dispense a roll of 0.75-inch-wide one-sided sticky tape on a 1-inch core.

A standard tape dispenser consists of three (3) parts: the dispenser base, the tape spindle and the serrated metal cutter.

DISCUSSION

Dispenser base. The oval dispenser base is the piece on which all other parts are attached. The plastic base is weighted with sand, and two 1.75- by 1.75-inch nonskid appliqués are attached to the bottom ~~of the plastic base~~; the sand and appliqués prevent the tape dispenser from moving when tape is pulled from the spindle and dispensed. The top of the dispenser base is hollowed into a 2-inch deep and 1-inch wide recess for the tape spindle and tape roll. Both sides of the hollowed recess contain a 4-millimeter L-shaped, notched cradle in which the arms of the tape spindle rest.

Tape spindle. The plastic tape spindle is 2.5 millimeters at its thickest point ~~and is~~ 3.5 millimeters wide (including two 0.7-millimeter arms on both sides) and is designed to fit within the one-inch core of a roll of 0.75-inch one-sided sticky tape, while the tape spindle is pushed into the core of the tape roll until the spindle is snug within the core and the spindle arms are seen on both sides of the tape roll. ~~such that~~ with the sticky side of the tape roll facing down, the arms of the tape spindle are placed into the L-shaped notches in the tape-dispenser base. If placed within the

> *L* is used to describe the shape of the notch. The notch is the shape of the capital *L*, not the lowercase *l*.

notches correctly, the spindle will ~~whip around~~ freely spin allowing the tape to be

pulled from the tape roll and placed upon the serrated metal blade.

> Query: Change to "freely spin" okay?

Serrated metal blade. The serrated metal blade ~~are~~ is attached to the

tape dispenser base with raised serrations facing the tape spindle. It

is 1 inch long with a .25-inch flat surface on which tape sticks after

dispensing, preventing the end of the tape from having to be freed

from the roll each time tape is needed.

Conclusion

To dispense a tape roll, the dispenser is placed upon a level surface. A

> Query: Use of the passive voice creates a dangling modifier here. Can we shift to active voice in this paragraph (because we shift from description to instruction)? If not, please rewrite this sentence.

tape roll is placed on the tape spindle and the arms of the tape spindle

are placed into the L-shaped notches in the dispenser base. The tape is

pulled from the roll toward and beyond the serrated metal blade until the

desired length is reached. The tape is pulled down until it sticks to the

flat surface of the serrated metal blade and is then cut and freed; ~~and~~ the

end of the tape roll will remain stuck to the flat surface of the serrated

metal blade for ease of dispensing further pieces.

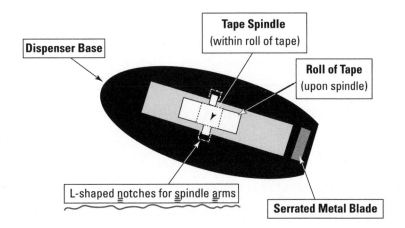

Dispenser Base

Tape Spindle
(within roll of tape)

Roll of Tape
(upon spindle)

L-shaped notches for spindle arms

Serrated Metal Blade

Wrap-up

As in the first example, many of the corrections I made here were no-brainers: a comma that should have been a period or a misspelled word. But other corrections required a decision to be made; something wasn't working, and there were a few ways to fix it. Copyeditors are faced with these decisions every day. And they become easier to make over time.

So now that you know how I work, I have one request to make: Get that image of me with the sharpened pencil to my lip out of your head. You'll be disappointed to know that my naughty copyeditor's outfit is more like sweat pants, a ratty T-shirt, and a pair of hideous footies with rubber soles my mom gave me a few birthdays ago.

Part III

Picking Up a Proofreading Career

The 5th Wave   By Rich Tennant

In this part . . .

Proofreaders find and fix for a living (errors, that is). In this part, I first walk you through what the job entails so you can determine whether the proofreading life is the life for you. I also cover various reading techniques so that errors can just vault out at you.

Next, you can master the cool proofreading symbols (our very own da Vinci code) and spend two chapters watching them in action.

Chapter 8

So, What Does a Proofreader Do?

*I*t's a familiar scene: You're ordering lunch with a few coworkers, the waiter is hovering above you, and you find yourself trying to decide between the Human chicken and the Mandarin lamp.

"Did they even glance at this menu before printing it?" you ask yourself.

When you stop and look around, you have to wonder how so many professionally printed items can be laden with so many errors — especially when you consider that the people printing them should know that their sloppiness brings into question how much care they're putting into other details of their business, like meat refrigeration.

The good news: By spotting the occasional misspelling, you already know you don't have to be a word nerd to be able to correct the mistakes littering the printed world around us. You just have to pay attention. And there are rewards to noticing mistakes. Catching an embarrassing typo in a theater program gives you something to chuckle about during intermission. Spotting that same error when you're the publicist's proofreader can mean job security.

Proofreading is not gene-splicing. Attentive people can perform it adeptly after some stimulating lessons and several practice tests. Proofreaders are normal people like you and me. Cast aside the image of the serious, bifocaled loner surrounded by heavy tomes, blue pencils, and fine wines. (Well, you can keep the wines if you want.) You don't have to fit any certain mold to be a proofreader. You just need to enjoy reading (and you've made it this far, so you can't hate it, right?), tuck a few guidelines under your belt, and be able to focus on what you're doing. This chapter gets you headed in the right direction.

Separating the Proofreader from the Copyeditor

As I show in Part II of this book, copyeditors analyze, process, and transform copy into intelligible, easy-to-understand prose. They look at the big picture. They ask questions like "What's the author trying to say?" and "How will the reader best understand him?" Proofreaders, on the other hand, pore over every last letter and shred of punctuation to hammer the copy into error-free perfection.

To look at it another way, if publishing were like getting dressed in the morning, the copyeditor would review the chosen outfit, bearing in mind the weather and what the day's agenda entails. She may decide on different shoes or a wider belt. She may pick out a different jacket. She may even suggest an entire wardrobe change. She examines the overall appearance and makes suggestions to create the nicest-looking ensemble that ever stood in front of the bedroom mirror. The proofreader then waltzes in and points out the deodorant marks on the shirt.

What Does a Proofreader Look For?

Proofreaders don't see things the way other people do. We scrutinize. When something is awry, our warning buzzer goes off, and we swoop down for a better look. We are charged with catching the errors that everyone, including the copyeditor, has missed.

What separates good proofreaders from bad is practice. The more you do it, the better (and faster) you become at catching errors.

Recognizing common errors

Proofreaders check for many of the same things copyeditors do; see the discussion of mechanical errors in Chapter 4. But proofreaders put an extra emphasis on catching the kinds of errors others are likely to miss:

- ✔ **Alignment:** Proofreaders scan margins, bulleted lists, and everything else that is supposed to align with something else.

- ✔ **Alphabetized lists and sequences:** Proofreaders have a field day correcting lists that are improperly alphabetized. For them, alphabetizing lists is like shooting fish in a barrel.

- ✔ **Captions:** Proofreaders know that captions on photos and illustrations are often not reviewed carefully by others. Copyeditors may intend to go back and read captions after completing the editing of the main copy, but they often forget to.

- ✔ **Columns:** Proofreaders always make certain that columns are formatted correctly.

- ✔ **Dates:** Dates are notorious for being incorrect. When a day of the week is mentioned with a date, proofreaders always check the calendar to make sure that the day of the week and the date correspond.

- ✔ **Headlines:** Proofreaders double-check headlines. When a headline has an error, you don't want to be the person who missed it.

- ✔ **Numbers:** It's easy for writers to mistype a number. Proofreaders review them carefully — especially if they are connected to dollar signs.

- ✔ **Spelling of names:** Proofreaders check the spelling of personal and organizational names against other sources (such as Web sites) when possible.

If copyeditors are the gatekeepers charged with protecting copy against bad writing, proofreaders stamp the admission tickets.

Proofreaders try to keep the above elements consistent with the style of the particular publisher for whom they are working. As I explain in detail in Chapter 15, the *house style,* or style sheet, is a printed document that shows how particular parts of language should be written (such as using one space after a period, not two). When an element isn't addressed by the style sheet, the publisher has a particular style guide to follow, such as *The New York Times Manual of Style and Usage.* The style guide explains things like when to use "each other" and when to use "one another." Lastly, the publisher has a preferred dictionary to give the final word on spelling.

When a proofreader is in doubt about anything, he should look it up, making sure to obey the hierarchy of resources:

1. House style sheet

2. Style guide

3. Dictionary

Pointing out not-so-great writing

Like copyeditors, proofreaders should recognize when a sentence lacks that *je ne sais quoi* (French for "was this translated from an extraterrestrial language?") and be able to politely suggest improvements.

Here's just one example of the kind of improvement a proofreader may make:

> Original: *There were some awards I won at camp, such as "largest fish caught" and "best kisser."*
>
> Revised: *At camp, I won such awards as "largest fish caught" and "best kisser."*

These sentences say the same thing, but the second one is more active, a little tighter, and more confident. A proofreader notices when a sentence can be worded more effectively and may suggest how to fix it.

However, keep in mind that this level of work isn't always expected of — or encouraged from — proofreaders. In some work situations, proofreaders are asked to stick to correcting errors. If you get the message from your employer or client that suggestions for rewording are beyond the scope of your position, take that message to heart.

Reviewing stuff the copyeditor never sees

Not only is the proofreader's job different in scope than the copyeditor's, but it also occurs at a different stage of the production process. Where, exactly, the proofreader comes into play depends on whether you're working with books or magazines.

In book production, the proofreader appears on the scene later than the copyeditor does, after a copyedited book manuscript has been set into *galleys* (typeset pages). For an overview of the book production process, see Chapter 2.

The privileged book proofreaders get to read through an almost-finished product in a recognizable format. They get all the extra goodies that a copyeditor usually doesn't see: aligned margins, running heads and feet, the front matter already laid out . . . (If you don't know what running heads, feet, and front matter are, take a quick read through Chapter 13 where I discuss the anatomy of books and magazines.)

Because book proofreaders see laid-out proofs, they can catch things like problems with alignment or inconsistent running heads and feet. They review tables of contents complete with page numbers, indexes, graphs, and other in-text elements created by the compositor based on the copyeditor's coding (see Chapter 16) . . . all elements that are finalized when a publication is typeset. The proofreader bears primary responsibility for catching errors introduced after copy is transformed into galleys, so don't ever doubt the value of the proofreader's role.

In magazine production, the proofreader may get to see laid-out pages and play a similar role as a book proofreader, checking heads and subheads, callouts and captions. But that's not always the case; some magazine proofreaders do their work before the layout is done. For an overview of the magazine production process, be sure to check out Chapter 3.

Testing Various Ways to Read

When you're trying to find your keys in the morning, and they're not materializing, there are different ways to search for them. You can scan all the places you left them in the past. You can check all your purses (or messenger bags). You can rifle through your laundry, checking the pockets of everything you've worn in the past week. You can even ask your pacing husband if he has seen them. And as a last resort, you can frantically overturn every manuscript, open book, and loose scrap of paper covering your desk, office floor, and window sill and shout to no one in particular, "This doesn't make sense, I just had them last night!" (Okay, maybe that last one's just me.)

There are also different ways to proofread a document. You should try all the techniques I mention here as you home in on the method that works for you:

- ✔ **Scan it first:** To familiarize yourself with a new document, start by skimming the first page in its entirety, taking into account such things as whether the paragraph spacing is consistent, whether the copy is justified or aligned left, and whether the quotes and apostrophes are straight or curly. After you do so, you can then go back for a more detailed read.

- ✔ **Slow it down:** Start out by reading your document slowly — much more slowly than you read for pleasure. Consider the spelling of each word. When you get to punctuation, ask yourself if that (comma, semicolon, hyphen, whatever) belongs there. Make sure there is subject–verb agreement. Look at the small words (*a, of, the*). Notice capitalization. Stop at every number and question whether it should be spelled out or in numeral form. Think hard about each sentence you are reading. When you get to something that is confusing, write a query to the author or editor. Then try some other reading methods.

- ✔ **Pump it up:** Read the document aloud. Your ear may catch mistakes that your eyes miss. Speak each word, pause at each comma, and emphasize each number. If people are around, move one arm dramatically and pretend to be rehearsing a scene for a play.

- ✔ **Stretch it out:** Read the document at arm's length. (This method works best with hard copy; your arms may get tired holding your PC this way.) Pay attention to the overall look of each page. Notice the spaces between chapters and paragraphs. Notice the margins and white space around photographs. Look for errant typefaces or font sizes. See if any captions, labels, or legends are missing. This perspective lets you visualize the shapes of the components of the document.

✔ **Turn it upside down:** Flip the page; that's a great way to catch bad breaks, weird fonts, and the like.

✔ **Inch your way:** Place a ruler beneath the text you are reading. (Again, hard copy is best here; we don't want you to scratch your computer monitor.) Move it down, line by line, as you read. Doing so ensures that you don't skip ahead before you have considered each line.

✔ **Don't look back:** As an alternative to "inch your way," place a ruler above each line of copy to prevent yourself from rereading any lines. Move the ruler down the page in a steady sweep and force your eyes to stay a step ahead.

✔ **Pace yourself:** Hold your finger under the word you are looking at. As you read, sweep your finger across the page in a slow and rhythmic pace. Force your eyes to keep pace with your finger.

✔ **Race yourself:** When you feel ready to speed things up, place a finger at the top left corner of the page, and move it down the left margin in a steady sweep. Try to keep your eyes scanning fast enough to keep up.

✔ **Reverse yourself:** A great way to sleuth for spelling errors is to read a document backwards. This method forces you to analyze each word individually and not in the context of the words around it. This technique is excellent for résumés. (It may be a bit unrealistic for a novel.)

The last thing you want to do when proofreading is sacrifice accuracy for speed. Focus on each page, each paragraph, each word as long as you need to, until you are comfortable it is correct. With time, your proofreading speed will naturally increase.

The best thing you can do to improve your proofreading skills is to keep reading. Whether your medium of choice is Web sites, newspapers, or books of varying genres, cranking up the amount of material you read will train your eyes to quickly spot the difference between *right* and *rite*. Newspapers and magazines, in particular, provide excellent proofreading practice. They get you used to reading copy in bite-size chunks, and they familiarize you with current expressions and common terminology.

Honing Your Skills

In this section, I offer suggestions for how to pump up your proofing skills in anticipation of your first jobs. For lots of job-hunting tips, including ideas for getting proofreading practice to tout on your résumé, be sure to check out Chapter 18.

Taking training courses

Of course, I'd like to believe that the wisdom contained in this book is all you need to fulfill your dream of becoming the world's best and most profitable proofreader. But even I admit that sometimes other training resources can be invaluable.

Training courses are a great investment of your time (and sometimes your money) for two reasons: One, they help you improve your proofreading skills; two, they provide you with tests similar to those that potential employers use to determine whether to hire you.

One-day or several-day training courses are often available for free through temp agencies. This is particularly true in larger cities because law firms and big corporations always need freelance proofreaders. You can also take private proofreading courses that connect you with temp agencies after you're done. If you live in a bigger city, this is a great opportunity. While you may not be reading the most thrilling material, this sort of intense training quickly gives you skills and experience that you can easily translate into freelance employment. You can find local proofreading courses through Internet search engines using keywords like "proofreading course" or "[name of your city]," "class," and "proofreader."

Proofreading for fun (and experience)

If you can't get proofreading work because you've got no experience, and you can't get experience because you've got no proofreading work, you've got a conundrum. Here's a secret to get the ball rolling: Your first jobs will be on the house. That's right, *gratis*. You bite the bullet, proofread some jobs for free, and keep track of every title you work on. These projects will become the "experience" section of your résumé.

And where do the jobs come from? You guessed it: your peeps. And your peeps' peeps. The art of networking through friends and family is a time-honored tradition, and there isn't any crowd who will be more forgiving when you blow a deadline. Start by making contact with everyone whose name appears in your cell phone, your e-mail address book, and your Palm Pilot. Don't leave anyone out; if an old friend isn't interested, he may know someone who is.

Your message can simply be something like this:

Friends, I am beginning my proofreading career. Right now, to gain different kinds of experience, I'm looking for any sort of project that needs a second eye.

A start-up business owner may want you to proofread a new brochure. A restaurant manager may ask you to review a menu. A student may tap you to review a thesis or dissertation. You may even come across a friend of a friend in the publishing industry who is willing to let you shadow her for a day. Whatever happens, understand that people you know are writing things every day, and much of what they write could use your help.

Most people you know, whether they care about their writing or not, want their résumés to be flawless. Knowing this fact makes it easy to pick up side jobs. When someone tells you he is looking for a new job, reply (as nonchalantly as you can muster), "Hmm, I proofread résumés on the side. If you're interested, I could take a look at yours." Then act bored.

Chapter 9

Mastering the Proofreading Symbols

*J*ust as carpentry has its tools to assemble sturdy buildings, so, too, does the blissful world of editing have tools for assembling solid communications. Proofreading marks are shorthand symbols and notes to get your point across as clearly and consistently as possible. Though the symbols may vary slightly among companies or style books, the ones I present in this chapter are standard enough to be recognizable to people in the know (and even some who aren't).

But just as you wouldn't pick up a hammer and immediately begin pounding away (or would you?), you need to study how to use a proofreader's tools. In this chapter, I divide the proofreading symbols into four categories:

✔ Core symbols that change the actual words

✔ Symbols that change or insert punctuation into the text

✔ Symbols that change the look or format of the text

✔ Symbols that affect or change the page layout

Here, I introduce you to each symbol's purpose and how it's drawn. In Chapters 10 and 11, I offer lots of examples of the symbols in use.

Covering Some Basics

Let me be clear: The information in this chapter applies specifically to proofreading jobs done on paper (or *hard copy*). If you're asked to proofread a document electronically, you won't be using these symbols; you'll be making (or at least suggesting) changes to the typewritten words. For the scoop on working with electronic documents, please see Chapter 17.

Before I jump into the proofreading symbols themselves, here are a few notes to tuck away in that memory bank for future reference:

- ✔ If your penmanship isn't anything to write home about (cough, cough), you want to be especially careful in drawing your marks and printing your notes. Directions are worthless if they're not understood.

    Be aware of your handwriting: If you tend to use a mixture of capital and lowercase letters, you have to train yourself to be very precise in the use of only what you want to see set by the compositor. A compositor will set an uppercase letter in the middle of a lowercase word if that's what you write.

- ✔ In especially messy documents, you may find yourself needing to insert *and* delete letters, and possibly make other changes, all within the small space of one word. Rather than muck up an already muddy manuscript, use the simplest mark you can muster to clean it up. For example, rather than attempt to fix every mistake in *conshienshus,* cross out the whole enchilada and rewrite *conscientious* above it.

- ✔ You use the symbols shown in this chapter to draw attention to text that needs correcting. But your actual corrections — the letters or words to be inserted, for example, or your notes to boldface or underline the text — are written in the margin.

    For lines that contain more than one error, you write the corrections in the order in which they occur, separating each with a slash (/). If the same error occurs twice in one line, with no other errors in between, you can use a double slash (//) after your margin note to alert the compositor to repeat the correction (or a triple slash if the error appears three times in a row). I also use a final slash after that last margin note on each line, just to assure the compositor that there is only one instance of that error — that I haven't simply forgotten to include the slash. Don't worry: I show you examples of what I mean later in this chapter, as well as in Chapters 10 and 11.

Keep in mind that some proofreaders use different methods of alerting the compositor to multiple corrections of the same type of error. Instead of using multiple slashes after the margin note, a proofreader may write "x2" or "x3" next to the margin note, for example. And some proofreaders may not add a slash after the final margin note on each line. There is no single correct way to communicate with a compositor; in this book, I show you what I do, but you may need to adjust your notation style to follow the protocol of your employer or client.

The Core Symbols

The core symbols are those that any proofreader (or copyeditor) worth her salt knows and uses on an every-reading basis. Toss that salt over your shoulder, and let's get started.

Insert

In general, the caret symbol (^) is used as a big "Insert something here!" sign to add missing letters, words, whole sentences, or punctuation.

To insert a missing letter, you plant a caret just under the space in a word where the letter is missing, and then you write the inserted letter(s) in the margin. (If it won't make things too messy, I often write the inserted letter above the word as well.) What about when an entire word is missing? In that case, simply plant your caret between two words.

Yup, I see it. This sentence is definitely missing letters. There seems be a   i/s/to/

word missing, too. Good thing we can fil them in using carets.   l/i/

On occasion, an entire sentence or paragraph may be missing, in which case you won't have enough room in the margin to insert the missing text. Write *Insert text from back of page* in the margin, and circle it; then write the missing text on the back of the page where there's plenty of room. If the text needs to be cut and pasted from a different place in the material, write in the margin *Insert text from page X,* and circle it. If you need even more space for the material to be inserted, use separate sheets of paper, numbered consecutively and inserted after the page in question. If a lot of new material is to be inserted between pages 101 and 102, for example, number the pages of new material 101a, 101b, and so on.

If you are making a comment in the margin, you must circle it so the compositor does not set what you write.

Delete

Show your artsy side with the easiest of all marks. A squiggly scribble or hash mark through a letter, a word, a sentence, or punctuation in copy indicates that the information needs to be scrapped.

To delete letters, words, sentences, or punctuation, draw a horizontal line through the text to be removed. After you've struck through the offending text, continue drawing the line up and around in a curlicue. Then draw the curlicue again in the margin next to that line. Make sure to precisely mark the letter(s) or word(s) to be deleted so additional copy is not inadvertently removed.

Are there too many ~~many~~ words here? How about here? This ~~is~~ example   *r*||

is tricky, especially if one doesn't read it carefully.   *r*|

If an entire block of text (such as a paragraph or a page) needs to be deleted, simply circle the entire block of text and draw a curlicue on the top right side of the circle. Then repeat your trusty curlicue sign in the margin.

Close up

To close up or delete a space within a word or sentence, nestle the space between the two parts of this symbol.

Draw the close-up symbol above and below the two parts of the word or sentence to be connected, closing them up like a clam. Then draw the close-up symbol again in the margin.

Regard less of your skill level, you will be able to find the errors a long   ⊃|||

this line by sheer in stinct.   ⊃|

Some common errors dealing with closing up involve words that are used slightly differently depending on whether they are spelled as one word or two: *every day* and *everyday*; *any one* and *anyone*; *some time* and *sometime*; *fare well* and *farewell*; *on line* and *online*; *melt down* and *meltdown*. Spell-checking programs won't pick up these errors, so it's up to you to catch them.

Delete and close up

Ah, a marriage of convenience . . . close up is most often used after you have indicated a deletion.

To delete and close up text, use the delete symbol to delete the undesired text, and draw the close-up clam shape to connect the two undeleted parts. In the margin, draw the curlicue and surround it with the close-up marks.

I am crosssing my fingers that you'll find thee three errors within this ℱ|||

sentence.

Space

Within the proofreading realm, the pound sign (#) is used to indicate that a space must be added to the text.

To add a space, draw a vertical line between the letters to be spaced. Then in the margin, draw the pound sign, which looks like a miniature tic-tac-toe board. (I often draw the pound sign at the top of the vertical line in the text as well.)

Everyone of the students took the courseon writing. This helped them #||

farewell on the test. #|

When two letters or two words are just a bit too crowded, you can insert a *hairline* space, which is a fraction of the full space. Simply draw a vertical line between the letters or words to be separated, write *hair* # in the margin, and circle it.

Transpose

Lord of the Files? A large chunk of the errors you find will involve the inadvertent switching of letters or words. Use this symbol to smooth out transposition errors in one fell swoosh.

To transpose letters, entire words, or sentences, draw what looks like an *S* on its side around the text to be flipped, then write *tr* in the margin and circle it.

He will being to learn the basics, form the start of the course to the bed.

 Transposition errors are so common that you'll quickly get familiar with the more infamous pairs: *form* and *from, bear* and *bare, best* and *bets, causal* and *casual, discrete* and *discreet, tries* and *tires,* and so on. Keep your eyes peeled for them.

Spell out

Is it *10* or *ten*? *TV* or *television*? Well, that all depends on the house style or style guide (see Chapter 14). But if the text says *TV* and the style guide says *television,* you need to indicate that the text must be spelled out. As a general rule, abbreviations are shunned in running copy, acting a bit like pebbles in a somewhat smooth road. In most cases, you want to spell them out.

To indicate that text should be spelled out, circle the text to be spelled out. Write *sp* in the margin and circle it.

13 of the people in the room were shorter than five ft and weighed less

than 25 lbs. There must be 1,000,000 more like them.

 In running copy and dialogue, words and numbers are spelled out unless it's cumbersome to do so (such as with years, phone numbers, and addresses) or unless something is conventionally represented numerically (such as a hotel room or highway number). Many house styles spell out the following: whole numbers from one to nine; round numbers, like one thousand or a million; and numbers that begin sentences. Consult your house style, and — most importantly — be consistent.

Cases: Upper, lower, and small (oh my!)

Incorrect letter casing happens, but there's a symbol to fix every situation.

Creating capital letters

To indicate capital letters, place three lines underneath the text to be capitalized. Then write *cap* in the margin and circle it.

Last I heard, jason lived in New york city, but he's always wanted to move (cap)///

to budapest.   (cap)/

See Chapter 12 for some guidelines on when capitalization is required.

Changing caps to lower case

To indicate lowercase letters, draw a diagonal line through the letter to be lowercased, from the top right to the bottom left. If more than one consecutive letter needs to be lowercased, draw your diagonal line through the first letter and extend the line across the top of the remaining letters. Then in the margin, write *lc* and circle it.

In College, Kendra majored in Mathematics. Now she teaches at a school (lc)//

in town.

Marking small caps

To indicate small caps, draw two lines under the text to be small-capped, and write and circle *sc* in the margin.

Small caps are often used for AM and PM; for slogans, such as VIRGINIA IS FOR LOVERS; for logos, emblems, and signs, such as CLOSED FOR RENOVATION; and for newspaper headlines — KENNEDY WINS!

Though she didn't put it on until well after 3 a.m., Sue's ironic tee made   (sc)/

everybody laugh. It read I'm With Stupid.   (sc)/

Equal space

Every relationship needs space, but unequal space between letters and words throws the coherent relationship of a sentence and paragraph out of whack.

To indicate that space should be equalized, place a caret under the problematic space. Also, place carets under the spaces between the words on either side of the problematic space, and write *eq* in the margin. This type of correction is much easier shown than said.

Melinda wandered through the halls of the museum, looking for history.

She couldn't find him anywhere.

Stet (let it stand)

Everybody makes mistakes, even (gulp!) proofreaders. Here's your chance to override any editorial or other changes you have indicated, using this mark to reinstate original text and say "Ignore any changes made."

To stet a change, draw dots in a horizontal line underneath the text to be reinstated, and write *stet* in the margin and circle it.

The singer k.d. lang prefers to see her name without capitalization.

After the first edit of a manuscript, the manuscript is returned to the author or editor. If the author or editor wishes to override any of your changes, he or she will request that you *stet the original,* meaning that you must return the text to what it was or check to make sure the original text is reinserted.

Punctuation Symbols

What are punctuation symbols? The symbols you use to insert punctuation into running copy. Easiest explanation all day. For some handy reminders about when and how to use punctuation marks, check out Chapter 12.

Comma

Pause and take a breather, why don't you. Commas are the most frequently used punctuation marks, and they're our cue to take a breath or pause in thought. Though comma use is often preferential, the current wisdom is to use commas sparingly. Check your house style for a comma entry before you get going.

To place a comma, put a caret where the comma is needed, then draw a comma beneath the caret. Repeat this action in the margin.

After a two-hour drive‸we finally reached the beach‸where we   ‸||

enjoyed the best tacos I've ever tasted.

There's some controversy over that little thing called a *serial* comma: a comma used before the last entry in a series. (It actually appears before the word *and* or *or.*) While some style guides call for the serial comma (*The Chicago Manual of Style,* for example), others prefer not to use the serial comma, unless — confusingly enough — doing so avoids confusion. (*The New York Times Manual of Style and Usage* owns this explanation.) Lucky for you, your house style should include an entry on serial commas — be sure to check it.

Period

You can't escape this punctuation mark — period. Periods are everywhere within a document: at the end of every sentence; within many abbreviations, such as *Jr., Sr., P.M., B.C., Inc., Mrs., D.D.S.,* and *Ph.D.*; and in lists, including footnotes and endnotes. And, in triplicate, they comprise an ellipsis.

To place a period, put a period in the text where it is needed and circle it — like a bullseye. Repeat this symbol in the margin.

Every sentence takes a period, Mrs‸Smith.   ⊙|

Most acronyms and initialisms — USA, SAT, and LSD, for example — do not require periods. Always check your house style or style guide for preferred usage.

If a sentence ends with an abbreviation, no additional period is needed.

Semicolons and colons

Don't let semicolons and colons frighten you — they're pretty easy to figure out. See Chapter 12 if you need more details about when to use them.

Placing semicolons

A semicolon is used to mark a more distinct break in thought than conveyed by a comma. It is often used with compound lists or series, as in the sentence *Jennifer Lopez has been spotted in San Juan, Puerto Rico; New York, New York; Los Angeles, California; and Rome, Italy.* The semicolon is also used to connect closely related independent sentences: *I am planning to visit China; my plans, however, are preliminary.*

To place a semicolon, draw a semicolon and surround it with carets above and below. Repeat this action in the margin. (Note that some proofreaders circle the semicolon in the margin rather than using carets.)

As a child, I hated to go to bed early; I thought all the fun stuff happened

after I fell asleep.

The mere mention of *comma splices* makes some of us shudder. They occur when a comma is used to join two complete sentences, as in the sentence *I can do anything I want, I'm a freethinking human being.* This is an error. (Well, not the freethinking human being part.) Here, a semicolon should be used: *I can do anything I want; I'm a freethinking human being.*

Marking colons

A colon is used after a sentence to introduce material or a clause that illustrates or adds details to the sentence, such as an explanation, example, or list. It is used when expressing time (*12:00 noon*), biblical references (*Genesis 1: 2–4*), and some ratios (*2:4*). It is also used to introduce subtitles, as in *Finding Memo: My Life of Corporate Communications.*

To place a colon, draw a colon and surround it with carets above and beneath. Repeat this action in the margin. (Note that some proofreaders circle the colon in the margin rather than using carets.)

The following are benefits of colon cleansing: purifying vital inner organs,

eliminating toxic waste, and alleviating skin problems.

One of the most common errors you will see is the use of a semicolon rather than a colon to introduce a list. Be on the lookout.

Depending on house style or your preferred style guide, the first word after a colon may be capitalized when what follows the colon is a complete sentence.

Ellipses

Where were we again . . . oh, that's right: ellipses. Ellipses are used to indicate an omission of words or letters or a trailing off of thought.

To indicate ellipses, draw three dots — like three periods — in the text, and circle them, placing vertical lines between them to indicate spaces in the ellipses. Repeat these marks in the margin. You may also use a caret to indicate where to place the ellipsis.

She opened the door and was at a loss for words. "You've‸," she began,　⊙|⊙|⊙|

"you've got to be kidding! It's so‸um‸amazing!"　⊙|⊙|⊙‖

Publishing and word-processing software often convert ellipses to a condensed format (...). More often than adding ellipses, you will need to replace these condensed ellipses with properly spaced ones. To correct ellipses, draw vertical lines between the dots of the ellipses; in the margin, write *eq #* to indicate that space in the ellipses should be equalized.

Occasionally, four dots will appear when ellipses are used at the end of a sentence or when completing a thought; see Chapter 12 for an explanation. And when in doubt, check the reigning style guide for preferred usage.

Dashes: Long, longer, and longest

Hyphens, en dashes, em dashes . . . do people really care how long a dash is? Well, yes, some people do. And the people who issue your paychecks are probably among that group. Let's talk about which length of dash you use in which situation, so everyone can find you dashing.

Handling hyphens

The shortest of the dashes, the hyphen is used in — duh — hyphenated words (think *self-confident, ex-wife*) and compound modifiers (*red-faced, chocolate-covered*).

To indicate a hyphen, draw what looks like an equal sign (=) in the text, and repeat this symbol in the margin. And, class, it's good practice to put a caret underneath to draw attention to the hyphen.

There was a break-in through the basement-level window of my great-   =|||

aunt's house. The barking of her next door neighbor's jet black dogs

prompted the screaming of their 14-month-old baby.   =||

Inserting the en dash

The en dash got its name because the dash is roughly the same width as the letter *n* in that typeface. An en dash is most commonly used to show ranges, such as ranges of pages, dates, and periods of time. It is also used in place of the hyphen in compound modifiers in which one of the elements is an open compound (think *New York* in *New York–Paris flight* and *Cold War* in *post–Cold War*).

To indicate an en dash, draw the number *1* over a letter *n* in the text, almost like a fraction. Repeat this symbol in the margin. A caret can be necessary at times for clarity. Use your judgment.

Between the years 1945–1963, my grandfather practically lived on the $\frac{1}{N}$ |

London–Paris train, trying to hock his pre–Civil War musket. $\frac{1}{N}$ ||

TIP

Feeling overwhelmed by dashes and hyphens? Train your brain to remember the en dash by associating it with the letter *n* for number: numbers of pages, numbers in dates, and numbers in time ranges.

Indicating the em dash

The em dash is roughly the same width as the letter *m* in that typeface. An em dash is used to separate subordinate clauses in sentences in which commas are also used or in which there is an abrupt change in continuity.

To indicate an em dash, draw the number *1* over a letter *m* in the text, kind of like a fraction. If necessary point a caret from below for clarity. Repeat this symbol in the margin. If house style forbids spaces around an em dash, surround the margin note with the close-up symbol.

The guy on the subway this morning—the one in the Viking helmet and $\frac{1}{M}$ |

bright red roller skates—couldn't figure out why we pointed and stared at $\frac{1}{M}$ |

him.

Some publishing and word-processing software automatically correct double hyphens (--) with an em dash. These programs are not infallible, however, so keep a lookout for double hyphens where em dashes belong.

Apostrophe

What possesses people to abuse the apostrophe so (*Fresh Donut's,* anyone?), I'll never understand. Here's how apostrophes *should* be used: in contracted words or in abbreviated years to replace missing letters or numbers, and to indicate the possessive of nouns and some pronouns.

To place an apostrophe, draw a downward-pointing caret directly next to the text where you want the apostrophe to appear. Then insert the apostrophe in the caret, and repeat the symbol in the margin.

By the time I am in my 60s, I hope I will not care so much about other

people's opinions, but whether that will happen is anybody's guess.   ℣‖

Be mindful of the direction your apostrophes are pointing: Apostrophes always make a backward *c.*

Though generally shunned in the world of academia, some style guides call for an apostrophe to form plurals of letters, figures, and symbols: for example, *Mind your p's and q's,* and *My brother earned three Ph.D.'s.*

Quotation marks

"Frankly," I want to scream at those grammar naysayers, "you should give a damn about how to use quotation marks!" You use them in these ways: to enclose direct quotations or bites from media; to indicate such titles as those of poems, short stories, songs, and book chapters; and to offset technical jargon or language that may not immediately be familiar to your audience.

To indicate quotation marks, draw a downward-pointing caret directly next to the text where you want the quotation marks to appear. Then insert the quotation marks in the caret, pointing in the appropriate direction, and repeat in the margin.

"For the love of it all," exclaimed the editor while reading the lyrics to

"Muskrats on Holiday," why do I have to be the one to read such drivel?"

Quotations within dialogue use single quotation marks, and if the nestled quote ends the sentence, most styles call for a space between the single and double quotation marks. For example, *"And another thing," she continued, "you know how much she loves to say, 'Word nerds think they know everything!' "*

Most word-processing programs automatically correct straight quotes (") with the proper open (") and closed (") quotation marks. These programs are not infallible, however, so check that the smart-quotes feature worked and put the quotation marks in the right directions.

Question marks and exclamation points

Why am I putting these two punctuation marks in the same entry? Why!? Because the proofreading symbols for each are remarkably similar.

To place a question mark or exclamation point, draw the question mark or exclamation point over a caret in the text where it is needed. Repeat the symbol in the margin.

Am I risking clarity by not ending my question with a question mark

thought the writer. You bet your bippy you are

Parentheses

Parentheses are used to enclose incidental material within a sentence (examples, explanations, and other supplementary facts). Whereas dashes are used to maximize such information, parentheses minimize the importance. And — no-brainer — the information in the parentheses is often called a *parenthetical reference*.

To indicate a parenthesis, draw a parenthesis bisected by two horizontal lines in the text where it is needed, making sure the parenthesis faces the appropriate direction. Repeat this symbol in the margin.

Merriam-Webster's Collegiate Dictionary (Web 11, for short) is a regular fix-   〈∕〉

ture on my work desk.

Parentheses do not change the punctuation of a sentence. If a parenthetical reference is at the end of a sentence, the period, question mark, or exclamation point still appears after the final parenthesis. On the other hand, if the material within the parentheses is an independent, complete sentence, it gets its own punctuation. For example, *He likes to lick chocolate pudding from his fingers. (I have to admit, so do I.)*

Parentheses can also be used with numbers or letters in a list, as in *We will need the following before you can board the bus: (a) a permission slip, (b) your lunch bag, and (c) bribe money.*

Brackets

I outline the many uses of brackets in Chapter 12, including using them to enclose the expression [sic], which means that an error in quoted material was present in the original.

To indicate a bracket, draw a bracket bisected by one horizontal line in the text where it is needed, making sure the bracket faces the appropriate direction. Repeat this symbol in the margin.

After the meeting, Syd gave me a copy of his play, "The Mispelled[sic]   [⌐∕¬]

Modifier," in which he writes, "I am *loco*[crazy, in Spanish]for cocoa."   [⌐∕¬]

Formatting Symbols

This family of symbols corrects formatting mistakes and inconsistencies in running copy and in such elements as tables, charts, graphs, and reference pages.

Boldfaced type

Boldface is used to emphasize particular words or phrases within a text. Chapter numbers, chapter titles, headings for lists, and page numbers for references to tables or images are often boldfaced.

To indicate boldfaced type, draw a wavy horizontal line under the text to be set in boldface, then write *bf* in the margin and circle it.

HOW TO EAT A BANANA

Step 1: Pick banana from tree.

Step 2: Peel banana from top to bottom.

Step 3: Dispose of banana peel.

Step 4: Bite into soft fruit, and enjoy.

Italic type

Italics are used to indicate the titles of plays, books, magazines, and newspapers; foreign words or phrases; and words as words or letters as letters, as in "This program is brought to you by the letter *m*." Within creative writing, first-person thoughts can be italicized: *My goodness, Chris is a great writer*, thought Kelly.

To indicate italicized type, underline the text to be italicized, then write *ital* in the margin and circle it.

Did you read The Unbearable Lightness of Being? I read the review in The

New Yorker, and I ran right out and bought it. I recommend it, especially

the chapter on the Czech word litost. Amazing!

Underlines or underscores

Back when I learned to type on a — gasp! — typewriter, underscoring, or underlining, text was one of the only ways to make words stand out. These days, the underscore has been downgraded to occasional usage for Web site addresses and e-mail addresses.

To indicate underscored text, underline the text to be underscored, then write *underscore* or *us* in the margin and circle it.

To see more titles in the *For Dummies* series, visit www.dummies.com and browse our title list.

Roman type

Roman type means no boldface, no italics, and no underscores — just good ol' regular type. The roman-type symbol is usually applied to correct mistakenly formatted copy — kinda like an "Undo this!" sign.

To indicate roman type, circle the mistakenly underlined, boldfaced, or italicized text or punctuation, then write *rom* in the margin and circle it.

She doesn't know **a lot** about typesetting, so it makes sense *that* she got a (rom)||
few things wrong in the layout. (rom)|

Wrong font

These days, when a book is designed, the text is usually "flowed in" from a word-processed document to an electronic publishing program. Sometimes the fonts don't convert properly, leading to obvious — and not so obvious — font inconsistencies.

To correct a wrong or inconsistent font, circle the text that is set in the wrong font, then write *wf* in the margin and circle it.

Sometimes an inconsistent font is very, very obvious. Other times, not so (wf)||
much. (wf)|

Layout Symbols

Use these symbols to indicate a change in the look or layout of the text.

Move left, right, up, or down

Move it, move it! I'm trying to explain these actions over here! Though it's a bit difficult to explain in words, trust me when I say that, as you progress through a document, you'll instinctively know when these actions are needed. An example? Well, say you are reading a series of paragraphs and only one is indented. You would use the move-left symbol at the start of the paragraph to indicate that the text needs to be shifted left.

To move text, use a bracket ([ ) to pull the text in the direction you want it to be moved, as if the bracket were a magnet. Try to align the bracket in the position you ultimately want the text to be. In the margin, write *move left/right/up/down* (whichever is the appropriate direction for this text) and circle it.

Pitfalls in Bulleted Lists

[Information that doesn't line up with respective bullet.   (move left)

• [Inconsistent spacing after bullets.   (move left)

• Wait, this bullet is perfect.

Center

There are times when text should take center stage: chapter numbers and titles, titles of articles or excerpts, headers and subheaders, and the like.

To center text, surround the text to be centered with outfacing brackets ( ][ ). In the margin, write *cntr* or *ctr* and circle it.

] Does this look centered to you? [(ctr)

Run in text

You may not run into this situation often, but sometimes it is necessary to delete the start of a new paragraph and run the copy continuously with the previous paragraph.

To indicate that copy should be run continuously, or to delete the start of a new paragraph, run a backward-*S*-shape line from the end of the top line to the beginning of the next line. Write *run in* in the margin and circle it.

Because this is the start of an idea,

and this is a continuation of that idea, there is no reason this (run in)/

sentence shouldn't be a continuous line. (run in)/

Begin paragraph

When proofreading, you generally do not need to indicate new paragraphs. (That's a copyeditor's territory.) However, you may need to do so in dialogue, if creating a new paragraph for a change in speaker has been overlooked.

To begin a paragraph, draw two vertical lines with a loop like the letter *c* at the top, making what looks like a backward *P* — as in *paragraph*. Place the symbol in the text where you want the paragraph to begin, and repeat the symbol in the margin.

Waggoner asked, "Where would I start a new paragraph?" "Over here," ¶/

Simpson replied, "and make it snappy."

Break or rebreak

You, words in the margins! Break it up, and get back in line with the others! Wait, you need to be told what to do? Okay, here goes . . .

To break or rebreak a line, draw what looks like one step of a staircase before the word to be moved to the next line. Write *break* in the margin and circle it.

Each of these lines should look exactly the

same.

Each of these lines should look exactly the

same.

Each of these lines should look exactly the|same.

Bad break

While not backbreaking work, identifying bad breaks is not something that comes easily to the everyday reader. What's a bad break? In published matter, text is usually justified, causing hyphens to occur in words that fall at the ends of lines. Sometimes, this creates what is called a *double break,* a compound word — a word already hyphenated — broken off in an unsightly matter. (And we can't be having that, now, can we?)

For example, *self-inflicted misery* breaking as *self-in-flicted misery* may leave a reader to wonder whether this is even the same word.

To correct a bad break, delete the hyphen in the word to be fixed, and close up the space. Write *bb* — or, for particularly messy documents, spell out *break* — in the margin and circle it.

I am not usually hot-temp

pered, but when I see bad

breaks, I get all fired up!

When in doubt about a word break, check the word entry in your house dictionary for acceptable breaks. These breaks are often indicated by dots in the initial entry word. For instance, tiramisu is listed as tir·a·mi·su. It's a piece of cake!

Chapter 10

Dipping Your Pencil in the Proofreading Waters

....

....

*R*eady to put your snappy proofreader skills to use? In this chapter, I present a number of short examples of text in need of a proofreader's TLC. I've arranged the examples to mirror the categories of symbols I outline in Chapter 9. At the end of each category of examples, I show you how I would mark the corrections, and I explain some of the trickier aspects of each.

Ready . . . set . . . wait! Don't blow through all these examples in one sitting. Go through the first few in a category, and then take a break. When you think you're ready, move on to the next couple, and the next, and the next. And then, when you've made your way through the whole chapter, take a nap before heading on to Chapter 11. The error-laden passages I present there will take even more concentration.

The Core Symbols in Action

The errors in these examples are among the most common ones writers make. I'm sure you know how easy it is to leave a letter out of a word while typing, or to add an extra one where it doesn't belong. (Who among us hasn't sent an e-mail that we later realized needed another proofread?) The same is true for capitalizing a word that shouldn't be, adding an extra space between words . . . the mistakes are easy. And spotting them shouldn't be too tough either.

Core symbol examples

Insert

This movie is intended for a mature audence. All others will be required to provide a signed leter from a parent authorizing consent. Those who do not have a letter will be asked to leve.

Delete

Suddenly, Larry didn't know whether he was in his own bed or somebody else's. He looked around as stealthily as possibley and wasp startled when Drew whispered in his his ear, "Do you even know who I am?"

Close up

All a round the neighborhood, there were children dressed in costume. Some were cow boys, and others were dressed as princesses. And some of the mothers were seen in cat suits.

Delete and close up

When traveling across different time zones, to prevent jet lag, get plenty off rest, keep yourself hyderated, and set your watch to the destination thime zone to better acclimate your body's clock.

Space

This Web site offers readers information onthe market's latest gadgets, gizmos, and trinkets. Noone can offer you lower prices — we guarantee it. Let us know if you have any questions, and we'll reply assoon as possible.

Transpose

Fans at Yankee Stadium were amazed by the atcion that took place there this afternoon. A seemingly unstopapble team suffered a minor setback when the pitcher injured his ram, but they went on to defeat the home team.

Spell out

3 days ago, I grew another inch. I am just waiting for the day when I am 4 inches taller. That'll be in a year or 2, but I'll finally be able to ride the Tornado!

Cases: Upper, lower, and small

This Summer, ivy bought a sign on EBay that read Parking for Accountants Only. Boy, is that lady calculating.

Equal space

I know a lot of people who love dogs, but Troy is one of those little dogs that doesn't seem to offer much in the way of personality or smarts . Yet everybody stops in the street to pet him. Go figure!

Stet, or let it stand

Iím interested in reading what bell hooks thinks about the relationship ⒸⒶⓅ//
between gender, race, and class.

Core symbol corrected examples

Insert

This movie is intended for a mature auḍence. All others will be required   ⅰ/
to provide a signed leṭer from a parent authorizing consent. Those who   t/
do not have a letter will be asked to leᵃve.   a/

Did you notice all the errors? If not, go back to the example and have another read, taking it more slowly and enunciating every syllable of every word. If you need to, read aloud. Train your brain to strain each letter through your head and out your mouth.

Delete

Suddenly, Larry didn't know whether he was in his own bed or somebody

else's. He looked around as stealthily as possible and was startled

when Drew whispered in ~~his~~ his ear, "Do you even know who I am?"

While *possibley* is not a word and may have been the easiest of the errors to spot, *wasp* is tricky because it is a real word. Reading slowly and aloud helps your brain ring the error bells at words that do not read right in context. Same goes for *his his*.

Close up

All a round the neighborhood, there were children dressed in costume.

Some were cow boys, and others were dressed as princesses. And some

of the mothers were seen in cat suits.

More trickiness! Both *a round* and *around* could be correct depending on the context, meaning that spell-check won't catch this error. You have to do the job that a spell-check function can't: determine what's correct in this context. Turtle says, "Slow and steady wins the race. And will save you face."

Delete and close up

When traveling across different time zones, to prevent jet lag, get plenty

off rest, keep yourself hydrated, and set your watch to the destination

thime zone to better acclimate your body's clock.

In this situation, you use the delete symbol to remove the undesired text, and you clamp the clam shape above and/or below the delete symbol to connect the pieces that remain.

Space

This Web site offers readers information on the market's latest gadgets,

gizmos, and trinkets. No one can offer you lower prices — we guarantee it.

Let us know if you have any questions, and we'll reply as soon as possible.

Even if you're spaced out, conjoined words like these tend to be jarring enough to the eyeball that you'll see them pretty easily.

Transpose

Fans at Yankee Stadium were amazed by the atcion that took place there this (tr)/

afternoon. A seemingly unstoppable team suffered a minor setback when the (tr)/

pitcher injured his tram, but they went on to defeat the home team. (tr)/

Keep in mind that transposition errors are super common, due to fumbling fingers or a touch of dyslexia that we all seem to have at times.

Spell out

3 days ago, I grew another inch. I am just waiting for the day when I am 4 (sp)//

inches taller. That'll be in a year or 2, but I'll finally be able to ride the (sp)/

Tornado!

Don't forget to consult your house style to nose out number nuances like whether to spell out *ten* or use a numeral. If a publisher, editor, or company has any house style preferences, they will include the treatment of numbers. Note that no matter what the style, you normally spell out a number that begins a sentence.

Cases: Upper, lower, and small

This Summer, ivy bought a sign on EBay that read <u>Parking for Accountants</u> (lc)/(uc)/(lc)/(sc)/

<u>Only.</u> Boy, is that lady calculating. (sc)/

To be fair, I am the calculating one. I stepped up the difficulty here to mess you up a little in the hope that the sting will help you to remember this stuff later. The names of the seasons are never capitalized, despite what you see out there in the public realm. And eBay? Don't capitalize that either (unless it begins a sentence). As for small caps, remember that they are often used to represent slogans, logos, emblems, and signs in running copy, hence PARKING FOR ACCOUNTANTS ONLY.

Equal space

I know a lot of people who love dogs, but Troy is one of those little dogs that ⓔⓠ/

doesn't seem to offer much in the way of personality or smarts . Yet

everybody stops in the street to pet him. Go figure! ⓔⓠ/

Honestly, you may not find the need to use the equal space mark all that often, but it's good to know it exists. (Note that when there's an extra space between a word and punctuation mark, you can simply use the close up symbol to remove it, as I show here.)

Stet, or let it stand

I'm interested in reading what bell hooks thinks about the relationship ⓒⓐⓟ // ⓢⓣⓔⓣ

between gender, race, and class.

Because the pen name bell hooks isn't capitalized, we need to stet our correction.

While *stet* is your way to undo a change, think it through before committing it to paper. Steting a stet is not a very clean way to say "I'm sorry, I made a mistake . . . twice."

Practical Punctuation

Here's your big chance to put into practice all that punctuation knowledge you've been accumulating since the fifth grade. And if you need any reminders about how and when to use these punctuation marks, be sure to check out Chapter 12.

Punctuation examples

Comma

The street fair in San Diego California which was sponsored by local

businesses, had booths for restaurants bars, and clothing stores and every

attendee got free samples. Slurp!

Period

Under the cloak of darkness, Mikey Jr ripped off his pajamas, ran to the window, and jumped Instead of falling, he swooped up past the trees, gliding above the wires. His father, a PhD, couldn't even explain it!

Semicolons and colons

There is not a lot of research on this elusive reptile, it is nocturnal and very difficult to see in the daytime. Further funding would enable us to fulfill our mission statement We strive to make the mysteries of the world less mysterious.

Ellipses

After reading Veronica's story, he didn't know what to say.

"Well it's, uh ," Joe began, "It's all right, I guess."

"Hm ," Veronica replied, her voice trailing off.

Dashes: Long, longer, and longest

My sister in law hand selected a book for me to read on my New York Los Angeles flight a post Cold War spy novel. It turned out to be only so so.

Apostrophe

Since the 80s, the Smiths have been one of my favorite bands. Its not that theyre more talented than any other band; its just that Morrisseys voice and big hair make me happy.

Quotation marks

Do you know what the local paper said about my poem The Overeater? It takes the cake . . . and the burger, and even the french fries.

The other paper wrote only the following: It's not all that.

Question marks and exclamation points

"Huh " she bellowed, "What did you say "

"Thanks a whole lot " I screamed, "Now the whole auditorium is listening "

Parentheses

The covert operation nicknamed "Project Meatbeard" required us to gather the following: 1 WD-40, 2 chewed gum, and 3 rotten eggs. Fortunately, each was already under my bed.

Brackets

Alternative titles for the external profit report include *earnings statement* and *operating statement.* (Note that profit reports distributed to managers inside a business are often called *P&L* profit and loss statements.)

Punctuation corrected examples

Comma

The street fair in San Diego California which was sponsored by local businesses, had booths for restaurants bars, and clothing stores and every attendee got free samples. Slurp!

I used the serial comma in this example — the comma that appears after *bars* and before *and.* In the real world, you want to check the almighty house style guide to determine whether to add or delete the serial in the particular copy you're working on.

Period

Under the cloak of darkness, Mikey Jr ripped off his pajamas, ran to the window, and jumped Instead of falling, he swooped up past the trees, gliding above the wires. His father, a PhD couldn't even explain it!

Periods are everywhere, but these days, there seems to be a tendency to streamline punctuation in copy. You may come across a house style manual that dictates the removal of periods from *Ph.D., D.D.S.,* and *M.B.A.* That's just some publishers' way of smoothing things out. And that's their right.

Semicolons and colons

There is not a lot of research on this elusive reptile, it is nocturnal and very

difficult to see in the daytime. Further funding would enable us to fulfill our

mission statement:We strive to make the mysteries of the world less

mysterious.

Did you spot the comma splice here? The comma in the first sentence valiantly tried to hold two independent clauses together, but sorry, comma — that's a job for the semicolon. Good job for figuring out that there needs to be an introductory colon before the mission statement.

Ellipses

After reading Veronica's story, he didn't know what to say.

"Well it's, uh," Joe began, "It's all right, I guess."

"Hm," Veronica replied, her voice trailing off.

Her voice trailing off was your freebie hint: Ellipses are used to indicate an omission of words or letters or a trailing off of thought.

The rules about ellipses are complex and involve knowing whether the house style follows the three-dot or four-dot rule (see Chapter 12). Be sure to defer to house style for any given project.

Dashes: Long, longer, and longest

My sister-in-law hand-selected a book for me to read on my New York-Los

Angeles flight,a post-Cold War spy novel. It turned out to be only so-so.

Commit this to memory: Use hyphens (-) to hyphenate words; use en dashes (–) to show ranges and to connect compound modifiers in which one of the elements is an open compound; and use em dashes (—) to separate subordinate clauses and to indicate abrupt changes in continuity. And see Chapter 12 for examples of each.

Apostrophe

Since the 80s, the Smiths have been one of my favorite bands. Its not that

they're more talented than any other band; its just that Morrisseys voice and

big hair make me happy.

Did you catch all these errors? I chose to correct *80s* with *'80s,* but some style guides call for *80's* — this is where house style rules. If you didn't get *it's,* twice, write this down: The only time you use *it's* is for the contraction of *it is,* like here. Everywhere else, you use the possessive pronoun *its.* It's important stuff.

Quotation marks

Do you know what the local paper said about my poem The Overeater? It

takes the cake . . . and the burger, and even the french fries.

The other paper wrote only the following: It's not all that.

Except for maybe the poem title, this one should have been easy. Note that dialogue punctuation should be within the quotation marks.

Question marks and exclamation points

"Huh?" she bellowed, "What did you say?"

"Thanks a whole lot!" I screamed, "Now the whole auditorium is listening!"

Exclamation points within running copy are few and far between. Be sure not to use a comma as well as an exclamation point; exclamation points and question marks trump commas and periods (which neatly avoids any doubled-up punctuation).

Parentheses

The covert operation nicknamed "Project Meatbeard" required us to gather

the following: 1) WD-40, 2) chewed gum, and 3) rotten eggs. Fortunately, each

was already under my bed.

Parentheses are cushions that enclose information within a sentence. Parentheses are also used to set numbers and letters apart from the text visually, as here.

Brackets

Alternative titles for the external profit report include *earnings statement* and

operating statement. (Note that profit reports distributed to managers inside a

business are often called *P&L* profit and loss statements.)   ⸢/⸣

When you've got information that's already tucked inside parentheses, and part of it needs to be tucked in a little further to set it off, brackets come in quite handy. For additional examples of how to use brackets, see Chapter 12.

Fun Times with Formatting

Formatting can be a bit like art class — you get to make lots of lines and squiggles and flourishes. Inner creative self, emerge!

Formatting examples

Boldfaced type

PROOFREADING MARKS
Core Symbols: Change words in the text
Punctuation Symbols: Change or insert punctuation
Format Symbols: Change the look or format of text
Layout Symbols: Change the page layout

Italic type

Enclosed is the most recent galley proof of On the Go-Go: My Butt-Shaking

Life in the '70s. Every time you see shimmery eyeshadow, please mark it

with stet.

Underlines or underscores

I typed www.mulletmarket.com into my browser, but it doesn't look like that's a valid Web site address. Where else will I find my mulleted true love?

Roman type

With the advent of **desktop publishing**, many younger writers began *self-publishing* their own works in <u>zines</u>. Suddenly, everyone I knew was claiming <u>to be</u> published!

Wrong font

Sometimes it makes sense to proofread a document a number of times, each time looking out for a different set of errors. For example, look for punctuation errors the first run, then expand to grammar and diction the second.

Formatting corrected examples

Boldfaced type

PROOFREADING M<u>ARKS</u>   (bf)|

Core <u>Symbols</u>: Change words in the text   (bf)|

Punctuation Symbols: Change or insert punctuation

<u>Format Symbols</u>: Change the look or format of text   (bf)|

Layout Symbols: Change the page layout

Let consistency in copy dictate which words should be boldfaced. If only one of many headers is not boldfaced, it's likely a mistake — correct it and move on.

Italic type

Enclosed is the most recent galley proof of <u>On the Go-Go: My Butt-Shaking</u> (ital)|

<u>Life in the '70s</u>. Every time you see <u>shimmery eyeshadow</u>, please mark it (ital)||

with <u>stet</u>.   (ital)|

Why italicize *shimmery eyeshadow,* again? That's right: Use italic to indicate words as words and letters as letters. Check and check.

Underlines or underscores

I typed www.mulletmarket.com into my browser, but it doesn't look like (underscore)

that's a valid Web site address. Where else will I find my mulleted true love?

This was an important mark back in the day, but the underscore is now relegated to the role of formatting Web site addresses. (And in some print media, such as magazine articles, you'd use it only if the entire URL — including *http://* — were included.)

Roman type

With the advent of **desktop publishing,** many younger writers began *self-* (rom)

publishing their own works in *zines.* Suddenly, everyone I knew was claiming (rom)

to be published! (rom)

When in ROM: Think of *ROM* as the great "Undo this!" sign to return boldface, italics, and underscores to regular Roman type.

Wrong font

Sometimes it makes *sense* to proofread a document a number of times, (wf)

each time looking out for a different set of errors. *For example* look for (wf)

punctuation errors the first run, then expand to grammar and *diction* the (wf)

second.

This is an easy one that needs little explanation, so I'll leave you be.

Looking Out for Layout

Good layout relaxes a reader's mind: New paragraphs make text orderly and digestible; in lists, consistent organization allows the reader to know the order of things; and dependable alignment creates a subconscious trust on the reader's part. You can help foster that faith.

Layout examples

Move left, right, up, or down

Proofreading Layout

As you read through a document, you will be taking in clues as to its layout or the way the information is consistently presented. For example, if you see that each heading but one is centered, the heading not centered is likely a mistake and will need to be corrected.

Correcting Layout

There is a proofreading symbol for   changes to the look or layout
      text   most
of   .

Center

The Wee Wee Man
'O wee wee man, but ye be strang!
O tell me where your dwelling be?'
'My dwelling's down by yon bonny bower;
Fair lady, come wi' me and see.'

Run in text

When proofreading, don't skip over the little words like *to, of,* and *is.*

Even when interchanged, these little ones can effortlessly disguise themselves.

Begin paragraph

"But what am I to do, Billy? How . . . how will I ever find a man as rugged and masculine as you?" she cried, shaking like a flower at his feet. "You'll just have to settle for second best, baby," he said, stomping off into the sunset, not suspecting the large sinkhole a few feet away.

Break or rebreak

"What do you call twelve blondes in a freezer?" asked Peggy in a self-deprecating tone.
"Why do you ask?" replied Buck, eyeing Peggy Sue's golden locks.

Bad break

If you are a self-con-

fessed word nerd, you might enjoy proofrea-

ding and copyediting.

Layout corrected examples

Move left, right, up, or down

Proofreading Layout

As you read through a document, you will be taking in clues as to its   (move left)
layout or the way the information is consistently presented. For example, if you
see that each heading but one is centered, the heading not centered is likely a
mistake and will need to be corrected.

Correcting Layout   (move left)
There is a proofreading symbol for changes to the look or layout   (move up)
text   most
of .   (move down)

Unless you are proofing, say, contemporary poetry, words out of line are usually in need of the move left, move right, move up, or move down actions.
Though it's difficult to explain, you'll know it when you see it.

Center

The Wee Wee Man
'O wee wee man, but ye be strang!
O tell me where your dwelling be?'
  ] 'My dwelling's down by yon bonny bower,[
Fair lady, come wi' me and see.'

Here, again, let consistency within the copy dictate the layout. Though in
poetry there are few rules for layout, if only one line is out of sync, it's likely
an error. If you aren't confident making a change, query it at the very least.
And do not go with the wee wee man. Ever.

Run in text

When proofreading, don't skip over the little words like *to*, *of*, and *is*. [run in]

Even when interchanged, these little ones can effortlessly disguise

themselves.

Good advice.

Begin paragraph

"But what am I to do, Billy? How . . . how will I ever find a man as rugged

and masculine as you?" she cried, shaking like a flower at his feet. "You'll   ¶/

just have to settle for second best, baby," he said, stomping off into the

sunset, not suspecting the large sinkhole a few feet away.

In dialogue, create a new paragraph when there is a change in the speaker.
And never warn a loser before he's about to step into a sinkhole.

Break or rebreak

"What do you call twelve blondes in a freezer?" asked Peggy in a self-dep- (rebreak)/
recating tone.
"Why do you ask?" replied Buck, eyeing Peggy Sue's golden locks.

A *double break* — an additional break in a word that already contains a
hyphen — means the layout should be adjusted. You want the word to break
only at its hyphen, if possible.

Bad break

If you are a self-con   (bb)/

fessed word nerd, you might enjoy proofrea   (bb)/

ding and copyediting.

Did this one confound you? Remember, consult the house dictionary for
acceptable breaks within words. They are often indicated as dots between
the syllables in the initial entry of the word.

My Hidden Agenda: Proofreading as Art and Science

If you didn't catch every mistake in the examples, don't get too freaked out. This stuff really does take practice. And the more you do it, the better you'll be at spotting these things — both the easy and the devilish.

Let me tell you a little something about proofreading tests, which you're bound to encounter when you start looking for work. You know those standardized tests that have become a bit controversial of late? SATs, GREs, and their initialistic ilk? They're controversial because the importance placed on them has led not so much to better teaching of the material within the test but to expensive test preparation and coaching services that teach you how to navigate through the tricky language of the test itself.

What does test preparation have to do with you? Well, there's an art of finessing the skills of copyediting and proofreading — you need to exhibit your talents through prettily scribbled symbols, and you must know your stuff. But there's a bit of science behind the development of these tests that's worth mentioning.

Here's the reality: The goal of most proofreading tests (and the examples in this chapter) is to cram in as many mistakes as possible — and to try to screw you up in the process. Actual proofreading projects are never rife with as many errors as the tests taken by would-be proofreaders (and the examples in this chapter). Never. Really. Take these tests (and the examples in this chapter) with a grain of salt — large rock-size salt. When you're finally sitting at your desk, excitedly starting your first proofreading job, you will enjoy it so much more than you ever could tripping over the often obvious errors in a test (and — say it with me — the examples in this chapter). Alas, for now, your job is to trip with skill and a smile.

Get your hands on as many proofreading tests as you can. How do you do this? Inquire directly to your favorite publishers about freelance proofreading opportunities. Most likely, they will send you a letter thanking you for your interest and enclose a proofreading test for you to complete and return. Do it, but make copies that you can reference for study later. And don't forget to ask for feedback on how you did — you're bound to learn something new.

Chapter 11

Watching a Proofreader in Action

*A*t my husband's birthday party last year, a friend of ours presented him with a large box. *Fantastic,* I thought, *it's a magic bathroom-cleaning machine.* No such luck. It turned out to be an ice-cream maker. My first thought was, *Huh? He doesn't make ice cream.* My second thought was, *Oh no, he's not going to be the one making the ice cream.*

The machine came with a few recipes that looked easy enough. And so, because it was a big birthday for him (I won't tell you which, but it comes between 34 and 36), I tried my hand at this thing they call cooking. Four hours and much spilled egg and scalded milk later, I had exactly one quart of cold, sweet soup. Not one to give up, I did what any resourceful homemaker would do: I checked out the Food Channel and watched a sauce pan–wielding chef — with a way snazzier kitchen and fancy chef's pants, to boot — make ice cream the right way.

Why am I telling you this? Because even if (as I hope) you've read the proofreading recipe book — the previous chapters of Part III — sometimes watching a pro at work is the best way to figure something out. I don't have any fancy proofreading pants, but I do have some experience in the field, and I'm happy to show you how I'd handle certain types of proofreading projects.

In each section of this chapter, I first present a brief writing example for you to read. I follow it with a fully proofread version (a *redline,* if you want to toss the lingo around) that includes some explanations from me as to why the corrections were made, as well as some queries that I'd suggest posing to the author or assigning editor. Let's get cooking!

Example One: Playing with Fiction

The original

It was a dark and stromy night. At least thats what the weatherman said it would be. Shelly speed along to the static of the radio, her eyes darting from the road to the flourescent clock on the dash board and back to the road. Now shed be walking into the party late and over-dressed.

She could of killed Mike for standing her up. She had waited until 8:0 p.m., just like he asked her to, 8:30 even, until the excuse's to her Mother ran out. When it was obvious he wasn't going to show she decided to driver herself to the party.

"You have another think coming if you think thisll keep me down," Shelley said allowed to the empty car. Olive a sudden, something darted from the shadows just outside the headlights of her Saaab Shelly reacted by drawing her arms to her face causing the steering wheel to slip and jerking the car into what would have been oncoming traffic, had there been any body else on the road. Underfoot, Shelly feels the rumble strips of the wrong side of the parkway and the dip of the small road side gutter. The car rolled for ever before coming to a stop, bumbing the thin trunk of a tree.

The Saab had landed perpendiculer to the road that lay quiet behind her, and there was trees prohibiting a clear view from the car. She looked the passenger seat in a quiet search for glass. Seeing nothing, she twisted her head towards the back seat. Again, nothing. But for the glove compartmen hanging a gape, there was little to in dicate that she had just run off the road.

Relizing that she wasn't hurt, Shelly was releived.

Thats when she heard it a faint tapping at the passenger door. Tap, tap. There it was again? Highly-panicked, she now heard the silence that was the car not starting, not making any niose what so ever. She violently turned the key again and again and again until it snapped with a metalic ping.

"Please leave me alone", she cried, "don't you see I'm in trouble here."

My suggested edits

It was a dark and stromy night. At least thats what the weatherman (tr)/ᵛ/

said it would be. Shelly speed along to the static of the radio, her eyes ⑨/

darting from the road to the flourescent clock on the dash board and (tr)/⌒/

back to the road. Now shed be walking into the party late and over- ᵛ/

dressed.

> The commas don't quite work in context. Em-dashes are great for offsetting changes in continuity, such as the one here.

She could of killed Mike for standing her up. She had waited until 've/⊤/

8:0 p.m., just like he asked her to 8:30 even until the excuse is to her Ø/ ⊤/M /⑨/

Mother ran out. When it was obvious he wasn't going to show she ⑩/↷/

decided to drive herself to the party. ⑨/

> When preceded by a personal pronoun—*my, his, our*—*mother* does not require capitalization. Try this when you're confused: Replace *mother* with a person's name. If there's no problem, keep it capitalized; if it sounds awkward, that's your indication to leave it lowercased.

"You have another think coming if you think thisll keep me down," ᵛ/

Shelley said allowed to the empty car. Olive a sudden, something darted ⑨/lou/All of/

from the shadows just outside the headlights of her Saab, Shelly reacted by ⑨/o/

drawing her arms to her face causing the steering wheel to slip and jerking ↷/

the car into what would have been oncoming traffic, had there been any ⌒/

body else on the road. Underfoot, Shelly feels the rumble strips of the ⑨/t/

wrong side of the parkway and the dip of the small road side gutter. The car ⌒/

rolled for ever before coming to a stop, bumping the thin trunk of a tree. ⌒/p/

> Understanding of the first part of the sentence is dependent upon the second part, hence a dependent clause. Be sure to connect dependent clauses with a comma.

¶The Saab had landed perpendicular to the road that lay quiet behind her, ¶/a/

> Whatever is happening to the alignment of this paragraph shouldn't be.

and there was trees prohibiting a clear view from the car. She looked the (align)/⌐ere/at/

passenger seat in a quiet search for glass. Seeing nothing, she twisted her

head towards the back seat. Again, nothing. But for the glove compart- ⑨/

> I prefer *toward* to *towards* in most cases. Not everyone does, though.

men hanging a gape, there was little to indicate that she had just run off t/⌒//

the road.

Relizing that she wasn't hurt, Shelly was releived. a/(tr)/(run in

> Compound modifiers in which the first word is an adverb ending in *ly* do not need to be hyphenated.

That's when she heard it a faint tapping at the passenger door. <u>Tap, tap.</u>

There it was again Highly panicked, she now heard the silence that was the

car not starting, not making any noise what so ever. She violently turned the

key again and again and again until it snapped with a metallic ping.

> Punctuation should typically be inside the quotation marks. This style is often called *punk-in*.

"Please leave me alone, she cried, "don't you see I'm in trouble here?"

Example Two: A Recipe for Disaster

The original

Classic Vanilla Ice Cream

A blend of purity and prefection, classic vanilla ice cream, heavily-scented with vanilla pods is the perfect conclusion to any meal. In flavored ice creams it serves as the base, upon which essences are added. It also accompanies other deserts, such as apple pie [pg. TK], and peach cobbler [pg 3], complimenting them like a white suit on a fat man. But vanila icecream, in it's purist form, is best enjoyed alone.

> *"My advice to you is not to enquire why or whither, but just enjoy your ice cream while it's on your plate—that's my philosophy"*
> *—Thornton Wilder*

Our recipe uses whole* vanila pods for an authentic flavour and color unattainable with vanilla extract alone.

Ingredients;

2 cups whole milk
4-6 vanilla pods, sliced lenthwise
1 cup sugar

Ten eggs, seperate the yolks from the whites
300 ml whipping cream, partly whipped
2 tbsp. Worcestershire sauce

Pour milk into pan, add vanilla pods, and slowly bring to a boil. Beat egg yokes in a mixing bowl, slowly adding suger. Beat until white. When the skim milk reaches a boil, slowly pour it over the egg yolks, whisking briskly.

Stir mixture with a spoon until custard begins to thicken. When it is thick enough, to coat the back of the spoon; strain it through a sieve into another mixing bowl.

After the mixture cools, fold in the partly-whipped cream. Add to an ice cream maker and churn until firm. Place in freezer until ready to enjoy. Serves 20.

**Store extra vanilla pods in your sugar jar. The sugar will absorb the vanilla's rich aroma. Use this sugar for future batches of ice cream.

My suggested edits

Classic Vanilla Ice Cream

A blend of purity and prefection, classic vanilla ice cream, heavily

scented with vanilla pods,is the perfect conclusion to any meal. In fla-

vored ice creams it serves as the base upon which essences are added. It

also accompanies other deserts, such as apple pie [pg. TK] and peach

cobbler [pg.3], complimenting them like a white suit on a fat man. But

vanila icecream, in it's purist form, is best enjoyed alone.

*My advice to you is not to enquire why or whither, but just enjoy your
ice cream while it's on your plate—that's my philosophy*

—*Thornton Wilder*

Our recipe uses whole* vanila pods for an authentic flavour and

color unattainable with vanilla extract alone.

Ingredients:

2 cups whole milk
4-6 vanilla pods, sliced lengthwise
1 cup sugar
Ten eggs, seperate the yolks from the whites
300 ml whipping cream, partly whipped
2 tbsp. Worcestershire sauce

Pour milk into pan, add vanilla pods, and slowly bring to a boil.

Beat egg yokes in a mixing bowl, slowly adding sugar. Beat until white.

When the skim milk reaches a boil, slowly pour it over the egg yolks,

whisking briskly.

Stir mixture with a spoon until custard begins to thicken. When it is thick

enough to coat the back of the spoon,strain it through a sieve into

another mixing bowl.

Margin notes:

TK basically means "to come." The publisher know this information is missing and is working on getting it. Just make a reminder note.

If you were copy-editing this, you would have much reason to urge the writer to change this metaphor. But since you're proofreading it, all you can do is shake your head.

Quotes are tricky. If you think it's wrong, at least query whether the error is intentional.

This asterisk refers to the pods, not the fact they're whole.

If you were copy-editing, you might suggest changing this ingredient to "10 egg yolks" because the recipe doesn't use the whites. In your proof-reading capacity, however, you may want to let this stand without comment.

Wow. How did the metric system sneak in here? If you're up for it, do the math and put down the correct measurement. If not, query it.

If you know an ingredient is a mistake, query it. Be tactful: "Seems incorrect, consider omitting."

You may want to query this because yolks get pale, not white.

Whoops. The ingredients list says it's whole milk. Query this.

> **Since ice cream modifies maker, hyphenate it so readers know the words go together.**

> **This doesn't sound right to you? It doesn't sound right to me, either. Query whether this recipe will, in fact, serve 20.**

After the mixture cools, fold in the partly whipped cream. Add to an ice cream maker and churn until firm. Place in freezer until ready to enjoy. Serves 20.

**Store extra vanilla pods in your sugar jar. The sugar will absorb the vanilla's rich aroma. Use this sugar for future batches of ice cream.

Example Three: Wonder of the Word

The original

Haigia Sophia

The architects Anthemius of Tralles and Isidorus of Miletus began work on the enormous chursh of Santa Sophia, properly known as Hagia Sophia, Church of the Holy Wisdom (FIGS. 3-13, 3–14) for Justinian in Constantinople in 532 a.d. Today, the church stands as a historical pinnacle of acheivement in world architecture. Consider its dimensions: 270 feet long by 240' wide with a 108-foot diameter dome. The top of the dome reaches a height of 60 meters. Hagia Sophia dwarfed all the buildings of its day, including such behemoths we discussed in chapter two as the Basilica of Constantine, the Baths of Caracalla, and the Pantheon. While it was completed in 537, Hagia Sophia was a work in progress for years to come—most notably, towering butresses were added to the exterior, and after the Ottoman conquest of 1453, it became an Islamic mosque, whereupon four Turkish minarets were added, greatly altering the original design put forth by ANTHEMIUS and ISIDORUS, who, no doubt, would have been astounded at the fact that their work was not only standing, but still significant almost a thousand years later. After having been secularized in the last century, the Hagia Sophia stands to-day as a museum and it is now one of Istanbul's most visited tourist attractions.

At its center, an enormous dome is held aloft by four arches, configured to form a square. The dome's weight is transferred down piers, enabling an airy, unobstructed interior. The walkways, the vistas, the threshholds and the delicate ormamented surfaces serve to hide the imense lines of structure, Much of interior, in fact, has no structural function. Rather, what visitors encounter inside is merely non-loadbearing decoration between the great piers.

The light in Hagia Sophia streams through 40 windows at the base of the dome, lending an etherial illusion of it being lit not from without, but within.

Blending Greek Theology, Roman scale, Near East tradition and Eastern Christian mysticism, this monuments to Holy Wisdom proves formidable even by today's standards, while not using todays principle building materials: steel and concrete.

<PLACE GRAPHIC OF HAGIA SOPHIA HERE, CAPTION TO READ: *3-13 Exterior of Hagia Sophia, Constanople (Istanbul)*>

<PLACE GRAPHIC OF A SAILBOAT HERE, CAPTION TO READ: *3-14 Plan (left) and section (right) of Hagia Sophia. (Redrawn after a sixth-century manuscript.)*>

My suggested edits

Hagia Sophia

The architects ANTHEMIUS OF TRALLES and ISIDORUS of MILETUS began work on
the enormous church of Santa Sophia, properly known as Hagia Sophia,
Church of the Holy Wisdom (FIGS. 3-13, 3–14) for Justinian in
Constantinople in 532 a.d. Today, the church stands as a historical pinnacle of achievement in world architecture. Consider its dimensions: 270
feet long by 240 wide with a 108-foot diameter dome. The top of the
dome reaches a height of 60 meters. Hagia Sophia dwarfed all the buildings of its day, including such behemoths we discussed in chapter two as
the Basilica of Constantine, the Baths of Caracalla, and the Pantheon.
While it was completed in 537, Hagia Sophia was a work in progress for
years to come—most notably, towering butresses were added to the exterior, and after the Ottoman conquest of 1453, it became an Islamic
mosque, whereupon four Turkish minarets were added, greatly altering
the original design put forth by ANTHEMIUS and ISIDORUS, who, no doubt,
would have been astounded at the fact that their work was not only
standing but also still significant almost a thousand years later. After having
been secularized in the last century, the Hagia Sophia stands today as a
museum and it is now one of Istanbul's most visited tourist attractions.

At its center, an enormous dome is held aloft by four arches, configured
to form a square. The dome's weight is transferred down piers, enabling
an airy, unobstructed interior. The walkways, the vistas, the threshholds,
and the delicate ornamented surfaces serve to hide the imense lines of
structure. Much of the interior, in fact, has no structural function. Rather,
what visitors encounter inside is merely non-loadbearing decoration
between the great piers.

Margin notes (left):

If you're not sure whether these should be hyphens or en dashes, take a look at the labels on the pictures they reference.

If the dates are A.D. and there aren't any B.C. dates with which to confuse them, they don't need a designator.

It doesn't matter whether *feet* is spelled out or the apostrophe symbol is used, but it should be consistent.

Not only should always be followed with *but also*.

It's tough to know what to do with a sentence like this. Sometimes it's best to just point out a run-on and suggest breaking it up or suggest the copyeditor or author sees fit.

The light in Hagia Sophia streams through 40 windows at the base of the ⓢⓟ

dome, lending an etherial illusion of it being lit not from without, but e/s

within.

Blending Greek Theology, Roman scale, Near East tradition and Eastern ⓛⓒ/∧

Christian mysticism, this monuments to Holy Wisdom proves formidable ⟋

even by today's standards, while not using todays principle building ∨/a/⟋

materials: steel and concrete.

<PLACE GRAPHIC OF HAGIA SOPHIA HERE, CAPTION TO READ: 3⋅13 ½

Exterior of Hagia Sophia, Constanople (Istanbul) tin/⊙

This picture does not belong. You can simply write "*fix picture*" here.

<PLACE GRAPHIC OF A SAILBOAT HERE, CAPTION TO READ: 3⋅14 *Plan* ½

(left) and section (right) of Hagia Sophia (Redrawn after a sixth-century ⟋/ⓛⓒ

manuscript)> ⓣⓡ

How'd You Do?

Did you overlook some mistakes in this chapter? Don't sweat it. These examples give you a sense of the kinds of errors to look out for when you're on the job. If you're considering working in publishing, you'll be glad to know that many of the mistakes incorporated into this chapter were lifted directly from proofreading tests I've taken in my lengthy career as a proofreading-test thief.

TIP

It's important to test yourself as often as possible by doing the type of work I've just shown you. I recommend periodically applying for jobs, even when you don't want them, and asking to take proofreading tests. Doing so definitely hones your test-taking skills and may improve your all-around job skills.

Now, if you're wondering whether watching the cooking show on ice-cream manufacturing helped improve my skills and demonstrate how supportive I am of my husband's sweet tooth . . . if I ever dust off the ice-cream maker, we will see.

Part IV
Adding to Your Repertoire

The 5th Wave   By Rich Tennant

IT SAYS,"BREAK GLASS," BUT IT DOESN'T SAY WHAT GLASS!

TRY THE DOOR AGAIN!

MAYBE THE WHOLE THING IS SUPPOSED TO COME OFF THE WALL.

"AIM THE HOSE"? AIM IT AT WHAT?!

LET'S GO OVER IT ONCE MORE— SLOWLY!

I COULD BREAK A WINDOW! THAT'S GLASS!

FIRE EXTINGUISHER

ROOM 101

Descriptive English Grammar

In this part . . .

The chapters in this part help you take your skills to the next level. First, I present a punctuation and usage primer that introduces you to some of the most common errors you'll encounter on the job. Then, I present an anatomy lesson on books and magazines so you can understand the parts of a publication.

Doing your job well sometimes requires making judgment calls, so next I delve into the all-important balancing act between following the rules and allowing some leeway for an author's personal style.

I also show you what a style sheet is, how to create and use it, and why it should be your new best friend. Plus, I discuss one of the more technical aspects of copyediting: formatting a document in preparation for layout.

Next, I tackle a subject that has changed the publishing world radically in recent years: electronic editing and proofreading. I consider Chapter 17 required reading for anyone serious about a copyediting or proofreading career, and you should too.

Chapter 12

Boning Up on Punctuation and Usage

In This Chapter

▶ Reviewing punctuation

▶ Catching common spelling and usage errors

*I*n this chapter, I put you through a boot camp of sorts — one intended to get your brain revved and ready to catch some of the more common errors you're likely to encounter when copyediting and proofreading. I focus on punctuation, spelling, and word usage, and I toss in a few grammar reminders for fun.

I wrote this chapter assuming that you're bringing some knowledge of grammar to the table. But if you're hankering for a grammar review (and even seasoned editors and proofreaders need one from time to time), I recommend that you pick up one of the following:

✔ *Woe is I: The Grammarphobe's Guide to Better English in Plain English* by Patricia T. O'Conner (Riverhead): You'll actually enjoy reading this great primer, which has accessible explanations.

✔ *The Gregg Reference Manual,* 9th Edition, by William A. Sabin (Irwin/McGraw-Hill): This is a business style manual with a wonderful glossary of grammatical terms in the back.

A Punctuation Primer

This section reminds you how to use the main punctuation marks. Treat these guidelines as just that: guidelines. Check out your favorite style guide for more detailed explanations.

Apostrophe

It would shock you, the examples of apostrophe transgression you can find just on the way to work in the morning: *Bagel's and Cream Cheese*, *Its Going to Be a Hot One!*, *Baker and Son's*, and on and on.

Contrary to popular usage, apostrophes are not used to pluralize normal old nouns: *taco's, dog's, bottle's* — all wrong! Apostrophes are used to form possessives of singular nouns (*the editor's book, the baby's bottle*) and plural words (*the girls' room, the buses' routes*). The main exceptions to the rule (and there are always exceptions!) are individual lowercase letters (*mind your p's and q's*) and abbreviations that have periods or both upper- and lower-case letters in them (*Ph.D.'s, PhD's*).

Brackets

Brackets (sometimes also called *square brackets*) are used to enclose comments, clarifications, or corrections added by someone other than the original writer, as well as to supply missing letters or words within quoted material. Consider these examples:

> *"I think the next project [her new screenplay] will be the most challenging one yet," she said.*

> *"The clinical trial showed that the combination of medications has a 92 percent success rate in people who don't have heart problems." [Emphasis is mine.]*

They come in handy if you need to insert a parenthetical reference within text already enclosed by parentheses. For example, the year range in the following sentence is a parenthetical reference within a parenthetical statement:

> *(Albert Einstein [1879–1955] studied the violin during his childhood.)*

Brackets also enclose the expression [*sic*], which means "thus" and is used to indicate that an error in the quoted material was present in the original:

> *One posting read, ironically, "I would definately [sic] recommend this editing course to others."*

Colon

Colons are used to introduce information in a sentence:

> *Jason could draw three things well: flowers, 3-D letters, and little devil people.*

There were only two ways I could compete with him: practice drawing or break all his pencils.

When a colon introduces an independent clause, the first letter in that clause can either be capitalized or not.

For me, artistic expression is liberating: smashed pencil boxes can be considered art.

For others, artistic expression is a way to show off: They draw fancy figures all day long to impress others.

It's all a matter of preference and style. Always check your house style guide.

Most house style guides direct you to capitalize the word after a colon if it's the first word of an independent clause. However, the 15th edition of *The Chicago Manual of Style* has thrown a wrench in that convention; it says to capitalize the first word of an independent clause after a colon only if two or more related independent clauses follow the colon.

Comma

The comma is the most versatile of the punctuation marks. Because it is so common, we sometimes overlook its value. But in the publishing industry, the comma is critical. Writers, magazines, and newspapers are all judged on comma usage at some time or other.

While we all use commas more often than other punctuation marks, I urge you to use them sparingly. If a sentence makes sense without a comma, it's usually better to leave it out.

But keep in mind that authors definitely get a say in how to use commas. For example, when you work on fiction, an author may want to leave commas out of a desperate and breathless and dangerous fight scene because some frenzied scenes want to stay frenzied while commas would slow those scenes down. You don't want to star in your own fight scene with a frustrated author. And on the flip side, if an author really wants to use an unnecessary comma, and if that comma doesn't interfere with the sentence's meaning, leave it alone.

Commas in compound sentences

When two independent clauses are joined with a conjunction, use a comma:

Sean stood at the blackboard trying to recall the equation, but his nerves had erased that memory.

Keep in mind that some editors choose to leave the comma out if the independent clauses are short and joined by *and*.

If one clause cannot stand alone, don't use the comma:

Sean stood at the blackboard and tried to recall the equation.

Commas in a series

Usually a comma is used to join each element of a series, including the last two. The final comma before a conjunction in a series is the *serial comma*: Think *lions, tigers, and bears.* Always use the house style guide as your indication of whether a serial comma belongs in the document or not.

Be sure not to place the serial comma in the middle of compounds. You don't want *For breakfast today we have pancakes, bacon, and eggs, and sausage and biscuits.* Instead, you want *For breakfast today we have pancakes, bacon and eggs, and sausage and biscuits.*

Some house styles recommend omitting the last comma in a series if its omission will not be confusing. But keep in mind that some sentences will still require it. For example, if the last two items in the series could be mistaken for a single compound phrase, a comma is necessary. Otherwise, you may end up with something inaccurate (and perhaps tabloid-worthy):

In Karen's acceptance speech, she thanked her parents, Justin Timberlake and Dr. Ruth.

Commas after introductory phrases

If an introductory phrase is short (three words or less, typically), you don't need to set it off with a comma:

At lunch Joe burned the roof of his mouth on an over-microwaved zucchini slice.

If the introductory phrase is longer, use a comma.

When Joe wolfed down an over-microwaved zucchini slice, he burned the roof of his mouth.

If the introductory phrase is one word, and if that word is an adverb (or you want to emphasize it), use a comma.

Suddenly, his palate felt like crisp bacon.

Commas in interjections and side explanations

When a sentence is interrupted by a phrase that isn't essential to the meaning of the sentence, set off the phrase with commas on each side.

Gregg, a famous suck-up, brought Ms. Goldin a crate of oranges from Florida.

Ellipses

An ellipsis indicates missing material or an incomplete thought; it can also denote hesitation and uncertainty. Two schools of convention govern your every decision about ellipses: the three-dot method and the three- or four-dot method. They roll out like this:

✔ **The three-dot method:** Easy enough — you always use three dots no matter what your dotty heart desires. No more, no fewer. Why not use this method all the time? Because some editors and publishers just don't like it.

✔ **The three- or four-dot method:** This method is preferred by a majority of editors. The difference here is that you use a period followed by ellipsis points if the previous sentence is a complete sentence. In other words, in this situation, you have a total of four dots: the period, which should be saddled up next to the end of the sentence, and the three ellipsis points.

Regardless of your method, I have two important reminders about ellipses:

✔ Turn off your computer's little ellipses auto-format thingamajig. Editors don't like it, so you shouldn't like it.

✔ Put a space before and after the ellipsis points, as well as between each point, unless house style indicates otherwise.

Em dash

Em dashes — so called because they are the width of the character *m* — are used for emphasis or interruption. They can be used on their own or in pairs to offset a word or phrase:

Many people seek help from naturopathic medical professionals — those who emphasize using diet, exercise, meditation, and other tools for improving health.

A vast amount of serotonin — about 95 percent of the body's total — is produced in the digestive system.

The double hyphen (--) is sometimes used in place of the em dash. You may notice that word-processing programs automatically convert double hyphens into em dashes for you. However, since the programs aren't infallible, some stray double hyphens may remain, so if you're copyediting on hard copy, you'll want to mark each em dash no matter how it appears in the text. The production editor will then make the global change to convert everything to proper em dashes. If you're proofreading, you need to make sure the change has been made and note any stray double hyphens that need to be corrected.

(If you're copyediting electronically, just do a global search-and-replace to convert all double hyphens to em dashes — or vice versa, if that's what the production editor wants.)

Some styles call for em dashes to have spaces on either side. These are called *floating* em dashes. If there are no spaces around them, the em dashes are referred to as *squeezed*.

Em dashes also precede quotation attributions:

> *Poetry is a deal of joy and pain and wonder, with a dash of the dictionary.*
>
> — Kahlil Gibran

 You may encounter a supersized first cousin of the em dash if you work on texts that include bibliography sections. The *3-em* dash (which is the width of three *m*'s in the corresponding font) most frequently appears in a bibliography when an author's name is cited more than once. Repeat listings by that same author feature a 3-em dash rather than the author's name again.

En dash

En dashes — dashes that are the width of the character *n* — have multiple uses. They're used to connect two items (usually numbers) that designate a range:

> *We submitted chapters 10–12 well after midnight.*
>
> *I left at halftime with the score stuck at 3–1.*
>
> *The January–February issue is due on newsstands tomorrow.*

They take the place of hyphens when one part of an open compound is made up of two words:

> *The author is a Nobel Prize–winning physicist.*

In the above example, *Prize* and *winning* are joined, but *Nobel* is just floating out there. The en dash works a little harder than a hyphen to show that the word *Nobel* is included in the open compound.

And en dashes may also be used to indicate that tension or opposition exists in a relationship, or to show a direction of movement:

> *The article supports the tax–spend hypothesis: Tax revenues determine government spending.*
>
> *The New York–Washington, D.C. run takes about three hours by train.*

Admittedly, the idea of tension can be difficult to pinpoint. Definitely check what the house style or the preferred style guide has to say about en dashes.

Exclamation point

Exclamation points should be used sparingly (except in dialogue). Their purpose is emphasis, but they all too often equate to overemphasis. In teaching this principle, F. Scott Fitzgerald said, "An exclamation mark is like laughing at your own joke."

When an exclamation point is used in dialogue and ends a sentence, don't put a period after it:

> *Curtis had had enough and snarled, "Fish out your stinkin' oranges, and take 'em back to Disneyworld!"*

Hyphen

Don't let the hyphen's diminutive size fool you. It's the lynchpin holding together your copyediting or proofreading career.

Hyphens link compound modifiers in cases where the meaning would not be clear without them:

> *Bobby took a fast-acting pill.*

Without the hyphen *(Bobby took a fast acting pill)*, some readers may think Bobby took a drug (that works immediately) that helped him audition for *Hamlet*.

 Open compound modifiers with adverbs ending in *-ly* do not need hyphens. The reason is that *-ly* adverbs always alert the reader that they modify the words immediately following them — without exception. There is no way to misread *a quickly moving van*. You know it's a van and it's moving quickly. Notice the difference with *a fast moving van*; you may think the author is talking about a moving van that is speeding along. In this case, you hyphenate fast-moving to convey that it's just a regular van.

Hyphens are used to separate telephone, Social Security, and other numbers:

> *212-555-1212*
>
> *123-45-6789*

Hyphens are used with some prefixes to form compounds. Check your preferred dictionary and house style to determine if a hyphen is necessary in, say, the word *co-worker*.

Hyphens join the words in multiword expressions that are to be read as a single unit, such as fractions and some compound nouns:

> *We bought three-quarters of a tank of gas.*

> *It was driven by a nine-year-old.*

Hyphen usage can vary between genres. For technical documents, you don't hyphenate a compound after the verb: *He's people oriented.* For narrative manuscripts, that same guy is bound to be *people-oriented.*

Much of hyphenation is open to interpretation, so whatever you do, make sure to pick one style and stick with it through the book or document for consistency. Keep track of every hyphen situation and refer to your trusty notes.

Parentheses

Parentheses enclose asides or information that offers some sort of explanation:

> *I drove through the night (on caffeine pills and black coffee) and arrived before dawn.*

> *Police found a box of "Espresso Mix" (chocolate-covered espresso beans) beneath the passenger seat.*

Parentheses enclose numbers for clarity:

> *At three dollars ($3) a gallon, we should have flown.*

> *Add two (2) tablespoons of cocoa powder.*

When parentheses follow a phrase or clause that requires a comma, always place the comma after the parentheses, not before:

> *When Joy got to Jacksonville (my hometown), she headed straight for the water.*

A rare exception to this rule is in numbering elements in a series:

> *I had to remember to (1) wake up my brother, (2) wake up my mother, and (3) shake the sand out of my shoes.*

Period

A period marks the end of a sentence, of course. It also marks the end of an abbreviation. When an abbreviation ends a sentence, one period suffices:

Monitor sizes range from 15 in. to 21 in.

For a very brief moment in time, people were avoiding placing periods after Web site addresses when the addresses ended a sentence. The fear was that someone might think the period belonged to the URL. Heavens! Trust me, people are smarter than that. Use the period. (While I'm on this note, when a URL breaks at the end of a line and does so at a period in the URL, the period should be moved to the start of the new line so the reader knows it's part of the address.)

Put the period inside parentheses when they house the entire sentence or phrase. Put the period after the closing parenthesis when the phrase is part of the sentence. In some cases, like these examples, you can choose either structure:

Everyone acted like Mr. Riebe's job was fascinating (but it wasn't).

Everyone acted like Mr. Riebe's job was fascinating. (But it wasn't.)

By the way, the convention of using two spaces between sentences has gone the way of the manual typewriter. It was useful when printing was less precise than today's laser-precision standards, so commas and periods were often difficult to tell apart. Adding the extra space between sentences made it clear where one ended and one began. Now that everything you read is 300 dots per inch and better, we don't need the extra spaces.

Question mark

Question marks are used to indicate a question in dialogue:

Raymond asked, "What's so fun about sitting in front of a computer?"

Question marks are also used to end sentences that are direct questions:

Does this sound "fascinating" to you?

And question marks can be used mid-sentence:

Why did I let him come speak to the class? she wondered.

Quotation marks

Quotation marks are used for direct quotations, of course:

"Come back when you guys come out with an affordable 64-bit processor," taunted John.

They are used with words that are newly coined and just entering the language:

> *The staffers felt "plutoed" when the new president brought his own PR firm into the project.*

They may be used for words or phrases used in a one-off way that is understandable given the context:

> *Lizette sprained her "mousing" hand.*

And they do the trick when a writer wants to distance herself from a word:

> *She called it "neo-abstract," whatever that is.*

Titles of works such as articles, chapters, essays, poems, and short stories usually get quotation marks:

> *We were supposed to be preparing a report on Auden's "Lullaby," but we couldn't stop talking about "Funeral Blues."*

Semicolon

Semicolons are placed between two independent clauses when they aren't separated by a conjunction such as *and* or *but:*

> *I preferred the presentation by Dionne's dad; he's a clarinetist.*

Semicolons are used to separate items in a series when they have commas or other punctuation within them:

> *All I remembered was that one kid, whose name I can never remember, started screaming; another kid threw a melted popsicle at him; and before anyone could stop laughing, the principal walked in.*

Single quotation marks

Single quotation marks are used for a quote within a quote:

> *Jay explained, "When Buddy opened the van door, he couldn't think of anything to say, so he just blurted out, 'Say, what's going on here?' "*

One more thing. See where the single quote and the quotation mark are next to each other at the end of the sentence? I inserted a space between them to give them a little definition. A little identity. Without it, a reader may not notice that there are two distinct marks in that little clump. Some style guides call for this space (usually a hair space), and some don't.

Slash

Slashes should be used sparingly. They are seen more often in technical writing than in fiction:

> *Average highway performance: 36 miles/gallon*
>
> *By the end, my vision wasn't exactly 20/20.*
>
> *Fold in 1/2 cup of chocolate liqueur.*

Often, an en dash can replace a slash:

> *2007–2008 subscription* instead of *2007/2008 subscription*

Your Hit Parade: Spelling and Word Usage Errors

Trying to fit all the crimes committed against the English language into the few pages of this chapter would be like trying to stuff a locker room's worth of dirty gym clothes into the coach's briefcase.

Commonly mispelled words: Er, make that misspelled

Have you ever been writing, come up with the perfect word, and been unsure of the spelling? She *alluded* to his earlier plastic surgery, or she *eluded*? Did the truck have five *axels* or five *axles*? Let us pour over a few of the trickiest words and even admire a few bastardized cousins. Ugh, I meant *pore* over them, of course:

- ✔ **Absence:** Never *absense* or *abcense,* or someone may suspect you of having too much absinthe.

- ✔ **Abundance:** *A bun dence*? No, no, *a bun dance.* Cha-cha-cha!

- ✔ **Accessible** (and, while we're at it, **collectible**): No matter how much everybody wants these words to be *accessable* or *collectable,* they are what they are. Please respect them for it.

- ✔ **Accommodate:** This word is big enough to accommodate two sets of double letters.

- **Achievement:** Yes, the *ie* is after a *c,* but the two gangs are held apart by the *h,* so the old rule doesn't fly here. Remember this: *eve* is smack-dab in the middle.

- **Ad nauseam:** It's Latin, folks. Latin. So no *ad nauseum* to any degree.

- **Alcohol:** Not *alcahol* or *alcohole,* no matter how much alcohol you've had.

- **Apology:** Think *polo,* one *p* and *olo.*

- **Apparent:** Not *apparant* or even *apparrent;* just imagine your *parent*s.

- **Atheist:** You may be the athiest person in the whole bunch, but for the love of no gods, please spell it *theist.* And it's not *Christain,* either (though, to be fair, that's usually a typo).

- **Business:** *Busyness* and *bussiness* are not your business; instead, get busy with *busi.*

- **Cemetery:** This is so commonly misspelled as *cemetary* that you may not even know it's incorrect. It is. Please . . . use three *es.*

- **Committee:** You don't need a committee to tell you that it's two *ms,* two *ts,* and two *es.*

- **Conceive, deceive, perceive,** and **receive:** Repeat after me: "*I* before *e,* except after *c,* or when sounded like *a,* as in *neighbor* and *weigh.*" Thank you.

- **Definitely:** Definitely not *definately* or *definitely.* Definitely.

- **Desperate:** Just commit this one to memory. Or, going out on a limb, think *E! E! Rat!* (Hey, I tried.)

- **Eighth:** This one about makes me blind, but *ghth* is pretty fun to say.

- **Embarrass:** Two *rs* and two *ss,* but only one *m; em-barr-ass.*

- **Exercise:** I still have trouble with this one, I'll admit. Though you're bound to see *exersice, excercise,* and *exercize,* it's pre*cise*ly *exercise.*

- **Fluorescent:** From *fluorospar,* not *flour. You owe (uo)* it to yourself to get it right.

- **Friend:** You've a friend 'til the end with the *ie* in this word.

- **Harass:** I've been harassed with *harrass,* but this word's only big enough for one *r.*

- **Hors d'oeuvre:** While it's a fancy French term for appetizers, don't get too fancy with the spelling. Also, pluralizing these appetizers *hors d'oeuvres* is common in American English, despite the French rolling their eyes and gasping *non*!

- **Immediate:** Use two *m*s, immediately!

- **Independent** and **independence:** Nobody wants *ants* at their Independence Day picnic. Nobody.

- **Liaise** and **liaison:** *i, a, i,* like a mariachi band.

- **License:** Only in the United Kingdom is it *licence;* here, both the noun and verb are *license.*

- **Maneuver:** All those vowels can seem confusing, but let *mane* or *a-e-u-e* serve as reminders.

- **Millennium:** I'm happy this milestone's behind us, because I don't think I could take another *millenium* or *milennium,* thank you. Two *l*s, two *n*s, O.K.?

- **Misspell:** This word and, ironically, *grammar* inevitably end up on the top ten list of misspelled words. If you commit nothing else to memory, get these two down pat.

- **Necessary:** You have no idea how necessary it is that you not spell this one *neccessary* or *necesary.*

- **Occasion:** Two *c*s and one *s*. You'll have occasion to say it with me: "See-see-and-ess!"

- **Omission:** Take all those *ommissions* and omit the extra *m*; think of it as your (o)mission.

- **Possess:** Four, count them, four *s*s.

- **Practice:** Practice this one over and over again, if necessary, and notice that there is nary an *s* in the whole slew of letters.

- **Presence:** Declare your independence from *precense* and *presense*; the ending is *–ence.*

- **Privilege:** *Privilige* and *priviledge* are your privilege, but they're still wrong. Think of *ivi* and the ending *–ege.*

- **Recommend:** I don't recommend trying two *c*s; instead, use one *c* and two *m*s, the end.

- **Restaurateur:** Though this word is a relative of *restaurant,* it's not *restauranteur.* It's on the *n*-diet.

- **Seize** and **seizure:** What was that I said earlier? *I* before *e*? Forget that with these two words; it doesn't apply. *Seize* the inconsistency and use *e* before *i*.

- **Separate:** Sometimes, to remind myself of this spelling, I spell *desperate* and do the opposite. Here's a tip: One se*para*tes things into *parts.* That help?

- **Sufficient:** Suffice it to say that this ends in *–cient*, like *ancient*.

- **Surprise:** Not *suprise* and definitely not *surprize*; remember the *rpr* surprise inside.

- **Threshold:** This is a toughie, but hold it back at just one *h*.

- **Tomorrow:** The sun will not come out *tommorrow*; *orro*, all right?

- **Unfortunately:** It's not so difficult when you break it down: The word is *unfortunate* with *–ly* attached. Fortunately, that's easy enough.

- **Vehicle:** I see a lot of *vehical*, but it doesn't look right, does it? I should be seeing a lot of *i-c-l-e*.

- **Weird:** Another rebel to the *i* after *e* rule, but weird as it is, don't fall prey to *wierd*.

- **Withhold:** Unlike *threshold*, there are two *h*s smack dab in the middle here.

In Appendix A, I list these and even more commonly misspelled words so you have a handy reference.

Think you've found a misspelled word? Beware: You may have been duped by a devious variant, an acceptable spelling that's second to the standard. Heed this, though: Choosing a nonstandard variant can make your writing sound affected or veer into the territory of spellings used only in technical texts. Going with the first word listed in a house dictionary is the best default.

Here are a few examples for your gray (or is it grey?) matter to consider:

The word is . . .	*Now meet the variant*
all right	alright
ax	axe
catalog	catalogue
gauge	gage
gray	grey
liquefy (and rarefy, for that matter)	liquify and rarify
minuscule	miniscule*
OK (or O.K.)	okay
Till	til or 'til

* I admit, miniscule is cringeworthy, and I'd rather it be considered a frequently misspelled word. Fact is, it's listed in many dictionaries. Go figure.

Word usages that everybody (but you) gets wrong

Some things are inevitable: taxes, death, *affect/effect* mishaps. Wait, that last one is preventable. And there's so much more of this stuff that's easy after it's pointed out to you. Just let me pull on this big foam "We're Number One!" finger, and I'll get pointing.

Accept, except

Accept means *to receive* or *admit; except* refers to an exclusion:

> *Tami was accepted to Columbia University.*

> *Bruce was rejected by all schools except Yokelville College.*

Adverse, averse

Adverse means *unfavorable,* generally referring to a thing or action; *averse* means *opposed to* or *reluctant,* generally referring to a person:

> *Haili faced adverse conditions in pitching her book to the number-one publisher.*

> *Shane was averse to pitching his book to the number-100 publisher.*

Affect, effect

Affect as a verb means *to influence* or *to have an effect on* someone or something; *effect* as a noun is a result of that influence:

> *The book affected her greatly.*

> *The book had a tremendous effect on her.*

Here's a great way to remember the difference between these troublesome twos: *affect* = Action, and *effect* = rEsults. In most contexts, this is all you need to remember.

However, because life is never simple, *affect* can also be used as a noun to mean *an emotional display*:

> *Michael read the same book without affect.*

And *effect* can be used as a verb meaning *to bring something about*:

> *Technology has finally effected the transition to electronic books.*

All ready, already

All ready expresses a state of complete readiness; *already* expresses time adverbially:

> *She was all ready to get going on her proofreading career.*

> *She talked to people who were proofreading already to get some tips.*

Altogether, all together

All together implies a gathering together of people or things; *altogether* means *in all* or *all told*:

> *They hid all together from their angry boss.*

> *Altogether, their boss isn't as angry today as he was yesterday.*

Allude, elude

To *allude* to something is to make an indirect reference to it; to *elude* someone (a pursuer, a cop) or something (a danger, a threat) is to escape from the person or situation:

> *Amy alluded to her beauty more than once in her flirtations.*

> *After suspecting Amy was flirting with him, he did everything he could to elude her.*

A concept or word can also *elude* someone, as in *The right phrase for my character eluded me.*

allusion, illusion

An *allusion* is an indirect reference to something; an *illusion* is a misconception:

> *Pete's boss screamed, "Your strong-man tactics have no place here," an allusion to Pete's earlier stint in the circus.*

> *Pete has no illusions about how tough it will be to get back into shape.*

Any way, anyway

Any way means *in any manner*; *anyway* means *nevertheless*:

> *Debbie was determined to finish the puzzle in any way possible.*

> *Debbie warned him about the complexity of the puzzle, but he went ahead and delved in anyway.*

Assure, ensure, insure

Here's a one-two-three punch: *assure* means *to put one's mind at ease*; *ensure* means *to guarantee*; and *insure* means *to provide* or *to obtain insurance* for something:

> *Lisa assured him that insuring his possessions now would ensure he would be reimbursed for lost or stolen items later.*

A while, awhile

You probably have never thought about this, but *while* is a noun referring to a period of time. In most cases, if you see the preposition *for* before this word, *a while* is what you want (as *for* is preceding the noun *while*). *Awhile* is an adverb that means — quite literally — *for a while*:

> *While he waited for a while, and waited awhile, he never waited for awhile.*

Between you and me

Between you and me, I see the incorrect *between you and I* more times than I care to admit. *Me* is the correct pronoun in this expression . . . always.

Biannually, biennially, bimonthly, biweekly, fortnightly, semiannually, semimonthly, semiweekly

Say them all in order as fast as you can, and then consider if you can say for certain what any of them mean.

We have the words *biannually* (meaning *twice a year*) and *biennially* (meaning *once every two years*). But, unfortunately, we don't have similar pairs of words to cover months and weeks, so *bimonthly* and *biweekly* do double duty. In other words, *bimonthly* can mean *twice a month* or *once every two months,* and *biweekly* can mean *twice a week* or *once every two weeks.* In publishing, you want to use the *bi-* words when you mean *twice a* and use the *semi-* words (*semimonthly, semiweekly*) when you mean *every two.*

To make things easy, you can also avoid these terms altogether and use *twice a year, twice a month,* and so forth.

Blatant, flagrant

Blatant implies noticeable and obtrusive; *flagrant* is a bit stronger and implies obvious and over the top:

> *Jodie is a blatant liar who has a flagrant disregard for the law.*

Blatantly obvious is redundantly redundant.

Boom, boon

A *boom* is both a loud sound and a period of rapid growth or expansion; a *boon* is a timely benefit or turn of fortune:

> *When times were good, population boomed.*

> *Low mortgage rates were a boon to new homebuyers.*

Capital, capitol, Capitol

Capital refers to a seat of government and can also be used in the context of money. The building that houses a legislative body of government is the *capitol.* Capitalized, the *Capitol* is the building that houses the U.S. Congress:

> *Needing to raise capital, Heather visited the state capitol to raise awareness of the issue and, that failing, worked her way up to the Capitol.*

Cite, sight, site

Use *cite* when you mean to quote or mention a source as an authority or proof; use *sight* when you mean something seen or the power of seeing; and use *site* to refer to a specific location:

> *Kristin cited Whitman's comments at the sight of multitudes on the ferry as we passed the site of the Statue of Liberty.*

Complement, compliment

Complement means *to go well together;* *compliment* is *to praise:*

> *Trisha complimented Tom on his tie that complemented his shirt.*

Compose, comprise, consist, constitute

To say that the United States is made up of 50 states, you can say it *is composed of* them, that it *consists of* them, or that it *comprises* them:

> *The U.S. is composed of 50 states.*

> *The U.S. consists of 50 states.*

> *The U.S. comprises 50 states.*

What you can't do is use *comprise* or *consist* in the passive — no *be consisted of,* no *be comprised of.*

To shift the focus from the whole to the parts, you can use *constitute,* which means *to form* or *make up*:

> *Fifty states constitute the U.S.*

The no-passive rule applies here too: no *be constituted of.* It is also not correct to write *Fifty states comprise the U.S.*

Consul, council, counsel

If you will be proofing legal documents, sit up straight and pay attention: A *consul* is an official in the foreign service of a country; a *council* is a group or committee, usually one that makes decisions; and a *counsel* is an attorney or advisor and, as a verb, can mean *to advise*:

> *Before working on the book, Piroska was consul general of Hungary, working with a council of editors and a legal counsel to counsel the general populace on how to write clearly.*

Continual, continuous

Continual suggests repeated though not nonstop action; in contrast, *continuous* suggests nonstop and uninterrupted action:

> *Ben is a continual pest.*

> *It snowed continuously for 14 hours.*

Convince, persuade

Convince means *to make someone believe something to be true*; *persuade* means *to influence* or *to win over.*

> *Dugans convinced her that he knew what he was talking about and persuaded her to give him money for his advice.*

Currently, presently

Currently means *now*, at the present time; *presently* can mean *now* but also means *soon* or *before long.* To avoid confusion, use *currently* when you definitely want to mean *now*:

> *Dave currently needs help, and Denise insists she will be with him presently.*

Disinterested, uninterested

Disinterested means *impartial*; *uninterested* means *bored* or *not interested*:

> *The jury should be a disinterested panel.*

> *The jury member was clearly uninterested as she snapped her gum and filed her nails.*

e.g., i.e.

Why English continues to be peppered with the likes of *e.g.* and *i.e.,* I'll never figure out. Until we rid ourselves of *exempli gratia* and *id est,* think of their use this way: *e.g.* = for example (think: for **e.g.**sample) and *i.e.* = in other words (**i**n oth**e**r words):

> *After getting up to snuff with grammar (e.g., spelling, punctuation, syntax), Shana decided to hop to it with a job (i.e., become a proofreader).*

Elicit, illicit

Elicit means *to coax* or *bring forth*; *illicit* means *illegal*:

> *News of the illicit affair elicited shrieks of delight from the paparazzi.*

Emigrate, immigrate

Emigrate refers to departure from a homeland; *immigrate* refers to arrival in a new homeland. The tricky part? They can be followed by *from* or *to,* depending on context. When focusing on life or conditions in the old country, say *Magda emigrated from Poland to the United States* or *She immigrated to the United States*; when focusing on life or conditions in the new country, say *Magda immigrated to the United States from Poland* or *She emigrated to the United States.*

Eminent, imminent

Eminent means *famous and respected* and *clearly obvious,* and *imminent* means *about to take place*:

> *He had a reputation as an eminent scholar of Spanish history.*
>
> *They all agreed on his eminent suitability for the job.*
>
> *The release of his first book is imminent.*

Fewer, less

The basic rule is to use *fewer* for things that can be counted in discrete units (think numbers) and to use *less* for everything else (think quantities):

> *Because fewer people attended the rally, the organization raised less money than ever.*

But the complete rule is more complicated than that. Most of the time, you use *less* for rates, weights, temperatures, speeds, money — anything that can be said to be below a benchmark. For example, consider temperatures. Even though you measure temperature in discrete units (degrees), you would say that it's *less* than 90 degrees outside, not *fewer* than 90 degrees. That's because 90 degrees is the benchmark measurement that the temperature falls below.

Flaunt, flout

Flaunt means *to show off ostentatiously*; *flout* means *to ignore or disregard contemptuously*:

> *Michele flaunted her three-carat ring.*

> *Michele flouted rules against wearing expensive jewelry.*

Flounder, founder

Flounder is a verb that means *to move clumsily or awkwardly*; the verb *founder* means *to encounter trouble, to collapse,* or *to sink below the surface*:

> *When Bria realized she had stepped into quicksand, she floundered trying to regain her footing.*

> *When he failed to make the sharp turn, Derrell started to founder and eventually lost the race.*

Hanged, hung

Lots of people have hanged themselves with this one. The past tense and past participle of hang is *hung*:

> *Leora hung the pictures on the wall.*

> *Leora has hung the pictures on the wall.*

Easy, right? Well, then there's the pleasant topic of executions by hanging. In this case, the past tense and past participle is *hanged*:

> *Leora hung the pictures on the wall, and they hanged her for it; yes, she was hanged.*

Historic, historical

Historic refers to an important event in history; *historical* connotes something dealing with the subject of history:

> *Martin Luther King gave his historic "I Have a Dream" speech in 1963.*

> *Bob had a dream that he won first place in a historical trivia contest.*

Imply, infer

Imply means *to suggest indirectly*; *infer* means *to conclude or deduce*. Think of it this way: *Implying* is usually done by the speaker or writer, and *inferring* is usually done by the listener or reader:

> *Donna implied that a divorce was imminent.*

> *Ian inferred from the phone call that a divorce was imminent.*

Irregardless, regardless

Regardless of its widespread use, *irregardless* is not acceptable in standard English. The correct form is *regardless,* or you can slip in the similar-sounding *irrespective* — they'll never even notice.

Its, it's

This one's so high on my list, I'm sure you'll hear this lesson again. *Its* indicates possession, just like fellow pronouns *his, hers,* and *theirs. It's* is a contraction of *it is.* Really, it is:

> *Kathy couldn't believe its deep red color and tantalizingly tart taste. "It's the best apple I've ever tasted!"*

Lay, lie

Nobody gets this one right without the little ditty "Lay = place, lie = recline." *Lay* means *to put, to place,* or *to prepare,* and each of its past and perfect forms is *laid:*

> *He lays the book on the table.*
>
> *He laid the book on the table.*
>
> *He has laid the book on the table.*
>
> *He had laid the book on the table.*

Lie means *to recline,* and its present perfect and past perfect forms are both *lain,* but — here's where the confusion comes in — its past tense form is *lay:*

> *He decided to lie down on the bench.*
>
> *He lay down on the bench.*
>
> *He has lain on the bench for three days now.*
>
> *He had lain on the bench for a week when a cop gave him a citation and forced him to move.*

Lead, led

Lead is a verb meaning *to guide; led* is its past-tense form. Here's where it gets stupid: *Lead* the metal is pronounced the same way as *led,* the past-tense form of the verb:

> *He led the protestors past the lead-pencil factory, and who was leading the group? That pencil-necked editor we love!*

Lets, let's

Pay close attention: *Lets* is the present tense singular form of the verb *to let,* meaning *permit, allow,* or *make possible. Let's* is the contraction for *let us*:

> *Winning this game lets us go to the finals. Let's go, team!*

May be, maybe

May be, two words, is a verb phrase that indicates a possibility; *maybe,* the single word, is an adverb that means *perhaps*:

> *There's a chance that I may be moving in with your parents.*
>
> *Maybe I'll live in the park instead.*

Nauseate, nauseous

Think of *sicken* and *sick*; one is a verb and the other is an adjective:

> *The smell of sulfur nauseated the workers.*
>
> *The nauseous stench seemed to be coming from the basement.*

Generally, the adjective *nauseated* is linked with a verb like *feel* or *become*:

> *The nauseous stench made me feel nauseated.*

Precede, proceed, proceeds

Precede means *to come before, proceed* means *to move forward,* and *proceeds* refers to a net amount of money:

> *His test preceded the release of the answer key, but he proceeded with taking the test anyhow, even though the proceeds from the sale of the answer key went to a good cause.*

Predominant, predominate

Predominant is an adjective that means *more dominant,* or *having superior qualities; predominate* is the verb:

> *The predominant interior designer in the country designed my house.*
>
> *In my living room, gold wallpaper predominates.*

As a bonus, the adverbs *predominantly* and *predominately* are interchangeable, although *predominately* is used less frequently.

Prescribe, proscribe

Prescribe means *to recommend a remedy* or *to advise authoritatively,* and *proscribe* means *to denounce* or *to prohibit:*

> The witch doctor prescribed magic herbs for his migraines, but his doctor proscribed the taking of them.

If you see "proscribe against" in a document you're editing or proofreading, delete "against" because it's redundant.

Principal, principle

A *principal* is a leader (and he wants to be your *pal*), or in financial transactions, it's the initial capital of an investment; a *principle* is a truth or tenet:

> The principal is a good woman who follows the principle of goodwill toward others.

Raise, rise

The verb *raise* is a transitive verb, which means it must be followed by a direct object; *rise* is intransitive, which means it doesn't require a direct object:

> James raised the window with one hand.

> The window rises very easily.

Stationary, stationery

Stationary is an adjective that means *immobile,* while *stationery* is a noun that you write on. If you can't move, you are *stationary,* and if you want to share it with the world, you write it on *stationery.*

That, which

A word of warning: This is general information and may be contrary to information you find in your house style guide. Generally, *that* is preferred when introducing an essential (or restrictive) clause:

> The book that Elaine wrote over the summer turned out to be all right.

Which is preferred when introducing a nonessential (or nonrestrictive) clause:

> The book, which Elaine wrote over the summer, turned out to be all right.

Their, there, they're

They're easy to explain: *Their* is a possessive pronoun, like *his, her,* and *its*; *there* indicates direction, like *here* (see a similarity in the words?); and *they're* is a contraction of *they are*:

> *Over there, my neighbors built a gold-plated garage; now they're destitute. Their house has been repossessed.*

We're, were

We're is the contraction of *we are*, and *were* is . . . well, it's the past second-person singular, the past plural (for all persons), and the past subjunctive of *to be*. But don't let that scare you: If you can replace it with *we are*, you want *we're*; for everything else, you want *were*:

> *We were going to Hawaii for vacation, but we're going instead to Providence.*

Who, whom

Here's the easy way to solve this one, once and for all: If you can replace the word with the subjective *I, we, he, she, it,* or *they,* use *who.* If you can replace the word with the objective *me, us, him, her,* or *them,* use *whom.* For example, "*Who* or *Whom* left their shoes in the hallway?" *She* did, so it's *Who* for this sentence. But "For *whom* or *who* does the bell toll?" It tolls for *her,* so it's *whom* for this sentence.

Want me to boil it down even more? If you can substitute an *-m* pronoun (*him, them*), use the *-m* pronoun *whom.* Otherwise, use *who.*

Don't like this rule? I'm not so fond of it myself. And neither are the more relaxed style guides. Don't sweat this one.

Who's, whose

Who's is the contraction of *who is; whose* is possessive:

> *Who's the one responsible for leaving her shoes here?*
>
> *I want to know now: Whose shoes are these?*

If you have survived reading through this entire list, you are better prepared to proofread than I was . . . last week, when I began researching these shyster-y words.

A Grab Bag of Other Common Errors

Following are a handful of language issues that crop up all the time and are easily remedied:

- **Confusing pronoun references and incorrect pronoun case:** A pronoun substitutes for a noun, of course. In *She took a picture and sent it to her mother,* the noun is *the picture* and the pronoun is *it.* Easy enough.

  A pronoun becomes confusing when a reader is forced to guess what *it* refers to:

  Ella never discussed what happened to the car during her vacation to California, where she learned to walk on her hands for minutes at a time. This has become quite the topic of discussion in our circle.

  What does *This* mean? What happened to Ella's car? Or that Ella can walk on her hands for minutes at a time? One possible rewrite is *Ella's refusal to tell us about the car has become quite the topic of discussion in our circle.*

  Just a wee bit more on pronouns. I hear a lot of this abuse in conversation: *Her and her sister enjoy eating crushed ice.* Here is an SAT plural-subject trick: If you break down the sentence into *She enjoys eating crushed ice* and *Her sister enjoys eating crushed ice,* you will more clearly hear the error — the sentence should read *She and her sister enjoy eating crushed ice.*

- **Errant or missing capital letters:** Capitalization varies by house style, so be sure to check the reigning guide in your publishing house or organization before you get started. Here's when capital letters are usually required:

  - The first letter of every sentence. *The first letter of every sentence.*

  - Proper nouns. *Sarah brought a Scrabble game to my sister Sam's house.*

  - Nationalities. *While in Europe, I like to eat French food, wear Italian leather, and date Spanish men.*

  - Brand names. *I rode my Vespa to the Piggly Wiggly and bought a Kodak Instamatic camera.*

  - Titles of books, plays, works of art, and so on. *That strange film* Eyes Wide Shut *was based on the novel* Traumnovelle, *I hear.*

  - Some acronyms and initialisms, such as abbreviations of organizations. *Some PTA presidents cited high SAT scores as a benchmark for superior school systems.*

When *mother, aunt, uncle,* and so on are used to directly address a person, they should be capitalized as proper nouns. For example, *After school, my father told me to go to bed,* but *After school, Father told me to go to bed.*

The words *earth, moon,* and *sun,* as well as the names of the seasons — *spring, summer, winter,* and *fall* (or *autumn*) — are not capitalized. Nor are the names of decades, such as *the fifties* or *the eighties.* Unless beginning a sentence, names like *iWon, eBay,* and *iMac* should not be capitalized. (Avoid using them at the beginning of sentences, if you can.) Some last names of European origin may contain particles that are not capitalized, unless they are used alone: Sunny *von Bulow* as opposed to *Von Bulow.*

✔ **Essential and nonessential clauses:** Essential clauses and nonessential clauses both convey additional information about a word or phrase in a sentence. The principal difference is that a nonessential clause can be eliminated without changing the overall meaning of a sentence, while removing an essential clause alters the meaning of a sentence.

Consider this example:

The copyeditor, who is an essential part of the editing team, works with the editor to perfect a manuscript.

Here, the removal of the nonessential phrase — the words offset by commas — wouldn't change the essential meaning of the sentence, which is that the copyeditor works with the editor to perfect a manuscript.

However, take a look at this sentence:

Copyeditors who always make or beat their deadlines make editors very happy.

If the essential clause *who always make or beat their deadlines* was removed, the meaning of the sentence would be changed. This would imply that the mere presence of copyeditors makes editors happy, regardless of anything else — wishful thinking.

✔ **Inconsistent parallelism:** Be sure that sentences containing a series or other matching elements are grammatically equal. Consider this example:

We planned to read a few manuscripts, go to the beach, and dinner.

We planned to dinner? How 'bout:

We planned to read a few manuscripts, go to the beach, and eat dinner.

✔ **Sentence fragments and run-ons:** In some cases, house style may allow for fragments (such as in *For Dummies* books). But run-ons are usually a no-no, except perhaps if a fiction author uses them to create a distinct voice.

Assuming that you need to correct these errors, here's an example of what you're looking for:

Copyeditors should attempt to correct all errors found within a document. For example, sentence fragments and run-ons.

The second is a fragment — and a very common error. Here's an easy change:

Copyeditors should attempt to correct all errors found within a document, such as sentence fragments and run-ons.

✔ **Subject and verb agreement:** The subject(s) and verb(s) of a sentence must agree in number and person. Consider this example:

The copyeditor and the editor is working together on the manuscript.

If that doesn't sound grating, read it again — out loud and at the top of your lungs. The subjects are joined by *and* and require a plural verb. The sentence should read as follows:

The copyeditor and the editor are working together on the manuscript.

Chapter 13

Dissecting Books and Magazines

. . . .

In This Chapter

▶ Getting familiar with a book's many parts

▶ Studying the anatomy of a magazine

. . . .

*N*o one likes an appendectomy except for the doctor getting paid to perform it. And while you're sitting there in your hospital gown waiting to go into the operating room, it's comforting to realize that, with all that could go wrong, your doctor knows more about the human body than just the appendix.

The more you know about a subject, the better equipped you are to deal with its nuances, and the kingdom of copyediting and proofreading is by no means exempt from nuance. To be well rounded in the publishing industry, you've got to be able to wield terms like *table of contents, bibliography,* and, well, *appendix.*

In your many years of reading — for school and for fun — you have undoubtedly encountered all the sections of a book and magazine. But as a consumer, you may have had little reason to pay attention to the parts I discuss in this chapter. For instance, I bet you've never read an entire copyright notice. Who would? Most likely, you flip right past that page. And the half-title page of a book? Who cares — you already know the name of what you're reading! But now, in your role as copyeditor or proofreader, you have to view the structure of a book or magazine through a whole different lens, and the parts other than the story or subject matter itself take on a whole lot more importance.

In this chapter, I help you get familiar with the language of the book and magazine publishing industries. Armed with this knowledge, you'll have no problem communicating efficiently and accurately with a production team. Your ability to "talk the talk" like a copyediting or proofreading pro — from your first day on the job — inspires confidence in those around you, which may lead them to take more risks with you. (Translation: more work and better assignments for you.)

You don't need a doctorate in etymology to understand publishing terminology. Even more encouraging, the terms I discuss here are standard to the industry, so you'll be understood no matter which publisher(s) you work with.

So get your scrubs on — it's time for an anatomy lesson. We're going to lift the dressing off some things you've scratched the surface of a thousand times before. We'll start by peering at a book's front matter, back matter, and everything in between. Sexy.

Unwrapping a Book's Front Matter

I hope you don't have your sights set on designing a book's cover. Graphic artists, both freelance and those working for publishers in-house, generally work their special magic with the cover text and art — you won't be much (if at all) involved with the cover. Though you may be asked to copyedit or proofread back cover copy, the areas of your jurisdiction as copyeditor or proofreader usually begin with what is known in the industry as *front matter*.

Generally, front matter consists of these elements:

- Marketing pieces such as ads and bits of praise (*blurbs*) for the author and/or book
- The title and half-title pages
- The copyright page
- The table of contents

Depending on the book's content, you may also find an introduction or preface, usually written by the author, and/or a foreword, usually written by a well-known contemporary of the novelist or a renowned industry guru or specialist. Acknowledgments pages often come in the front matter too.

Ads and blurbs

Ah, the all-important marketing message. A lot of fiction publishers have now taken to placing ads on the inside of the front cover or the first page of the book. Here, the publisher is taking a personal interest in the reader — and his next book purchase. Where better to capture the attention of the reader with enticing ads for books by the same author or of the same genre?

Next come the shiny and sometimes grandiose accolades for book and author. If you're proofreading, you give the newspaper reviews and praise from the author's contemporaries the once-over — the last thing you want is typos or other errors mucking up the kudos. After making it to production, believe me, the author deserves to bask in the spotlight. Just the fact that he's written this book means you've got work to do . . . so hail to the author!

Title and half-title pages

At first blush, the difference between these parts of the book may be somewhat confusing. But trust me: These two pages are distinct from one another. The half-title page includes the title, and that's it. The title page contains a lot more information than that. The industry standard is for the title page to include the following:

- ✔ The title
- ✔ The subtitle, if there is one
- ✔ The edition
- ✔ The author(s) name(s)
- ✔ The author(s) affiliation(s) if you're working on a textbook
- ✔ The publisher name and location

If space allows, you may even find the copyright notice tagged onto this page. (I cover copyrights in the next section.)

Placement of the pages follows a particular sequence established by the publisher. Usually, the half-title page appears first. It may be placed on a right-facing page and be the first page of the book, or it may appear immediately following the ads and blurbs. If the publisher wants to get really fancy schmancy, it may try to make the half-title page stand out more by including an elaborately designed page or a blank page just before the half-title page. This page is called a *frontispiece.*

The title page usually comes second in the sequence and is also placed on a right-facing page. Often the title page appears on the third page in the book and may be placed just after a *card* or *series* page. The card page lists other works by the same author; the series page lists works from the same series that are offered by the publisher.

Some books may also include a page just before the beginning of the first chapter that also features the title of the book. This practice is common if the author's story spans several "books" or "parts" which are to be combined under one title.

Necessary legals: The copyright page

From a legal standpoint, the copyright page is arguably the single most important page in the book. But you don't need to be a legal eagle to eagle-eye this page; the publisher provides the legalese for the copyright notice.

If the book is being published by a large publishing company, the copyright notice is likely to have been written and reviewed by not one or even two people, but by a whole team of corporate attorneys. But, even though 20 well-dressed and seasoned attorneys may have collectively written and reviewed the copyright notice, don't assume it's error free.

Whether you're copyediting or proofreading, you need to review this page. But what are you looking for exactly? The notice should begin with a copyright symbol (©), but the spelled-out word *copyright* is also acceptable. You may bump into both the symbol and the word, even though both are not necessary. The copyright symbol is immediately followed by the year the material was copyrighted and the name of the person or entity holding the copyright. Next, the publisher should include a blurb known as the *copyright notice,* which includes a few standard lines about who the copyright belongs to and the protections the copyright offers. Go grab a book — go! go! — and check the copyright page to get an idea of all this.

Are all these legal terms and rules making you nervous? Well, relax. Relative to the body of the text, the work here is fairly superficial. Whether you're the copyeditor or proofreader, you make no major changes to the legal terminology. Most of the legal responsibility falls to the author and the publisher, and all you need to do is spot if a certain item in the copyright has been omitted. If you suspect there is an error or an omission in the notice, pose a query to the assigning editor and move on.

Two other important items need attention whether you're a copyeditor or proofreader: the Cataloging in Publication record (known as *CIP data*), if there is one; and the International Standard Book Number (ISBN). The last thing you want is an author's name misspelled in the data or an ISBN with a missing digit!

In addition to checking the language of the copyright page, you also want to check its placement. Believe it or not, even the placement of the copyright is dictated by law, so make sure it appears prior to the fifth page in the book and immediately after the title page. Although some publishers place the copyright notice on the title page, you'll find that the copyright makes its appearance on the reverse side of the title page in most cases. The author may also include his credits and acknowledgments on the copyright page; this is not dictated by law but is an option left up to the editor's, author's, or publisher's discretion.

Seeking out copyright infringement and other infractions

As you grow into your role as copyeditor or proofreader, you want to familiarize yourself with the basic tenets of copyright, libel, and slander laws — publishers and those who love them will love you for it. Because you are one of the last people to review a work with a critical eye, you have the power to spot potential problems. Many a copyeditor has saved the author and publisher a lot of headaches and millions of dollars in lawsuits.

But how? Even though publishers are careful about lawsuits and possible slanderous material and many times have book manuscripts reviewed by a lawyer (called *vetting*) for any potentially libelous information, you should always be on alert for copyright infringement and statements that could be deemed slanderous. Make no mistake: Most authors have no

intention of lifting text from other publications without giving credit and do not set out to slander anyone. Sometimes they just don't realize that they are using a copyrighted work, or they're unaware of the implications. Other times, they just plain forget to provide the editor with the information necessary to properly credit a source. In the author's defense, there's a lot that goes into writing a book, and if all goes well, the necessary information will be placed in a list of credits or acknowledgments that the author provides to the editor. If it doesn't go well, you can help spot the omission and bail the author out.

For tips on spotting plagiarism and/or slanderous language, see Chapter 5.

ToCs for you and me

If you truly want to sound like a seasoned editor or proofreader, muster up your best blasé behavior and refer to the table of contents as the *ToC* ("tee-oh-see").

First things first: Not all books contain a ToC. So if you find yourself frantically searching and failing to find one, furiously flipping through the first five or six pages of a book with one hand and ready to speed-dial the publisher with the other, stop it now! Only if what you're looking at is a nonfiction or specialty book do you need to sound the alarms.

If the book you are copyediting does include a ToC, the editor should place it as early as possible in the front matter. The placement takes into consideration the fact that the reader should not have to fish through many pages of introductions to find the ToC.

An author-provided ToC should list the elements in the front matter; the chapter titles and subtitles, if appropriate; and the back matter, such as appendixes and the index. If you're the copyeditor, you won't have the page numbers on the ToC, but by the time the book is ready for a proofread, the numbers should be there. And if not, it is up to the proofreader to insert them.

A proofreader's role in checking the ToC is very important. You need to check page numbers, chapter numbers, and — very important — chapter titles. You must make sure the chapter titles on the ToC reflect the chapter titles in the text, including the capitalization. If they don't, be sure to query as to which is correct. If you proofread an educational or specialty book, there may be additional heads in the ToC that need the same attention as the chapter titles.

Give the ToC a lot of TLC. It deserves special, nuzzly consideration as its accuracy is critical to the work.

Introductions, prefaces, and forewords: So many ways to begin

Confused about which terminology to use for the introductory statement? Ever wonder why some books have an introduction while others have a preface and also, maybe, a foreword? You're not alone.

While the term *introduction* is often used interchangeably with *preface,* these elements are not wholly the same — in fact, the objective for each is quite different. Authors and even seasoned copyeditors may be hard pressed to make the proper distinction, so don't despair if you were unaware of this fact until now. (Now you can police the correct usage of each term and spread the word about correct usage to others!)

Each introductory statement has its own nuanced meaning and use. To make appropriate use of the headings, keep the following rules in mind:

- ✔ The **introduction** is usually written by the author (or, if a book consists of contributions by different writers, the editor) and offers background information on the subject matter of the book.
- ✔ A **preface** is also usually written by the author but describes the objective or reasons for writing the book.
- ✔ A **foreword** is not usually written by the author. Instead, it may be written by a contemporary of the author — generally someone who is well known and/or writes a lot of books from the same genre.

Baring a Book's Back Story

Not all books include indexes, appendixes, glossaries, notes, or bibliographies. But if you work on nonfiction manuscripts, especially educational or specialty texts (like science publications), you can expect to see these elements quite frequently.

If you're copyediting, you're not usually responsible for editing an index because this element is created late in the production process, after your participation in the project ends. However, if you're proofreading, the index is definitely part of your territory. As proofreader, you go through the index with a fine-tooth comb. Your house style documentation (see Chapter 14) should include information about the format of index entries.

Appendixes

You won't commonly find appendixes in works of fiction. However, if you copyedit or proofread educational texts or works of a particular specialty, expect to be knee-deep in them.

The style and format of appendixes differ depending on the content, the type of book, and the publisher. As always, the assigning editor counts on you — the intrepid copyeditor or proofreader — to ensure uniformity. The most important thing you can do during your copyedit or proofread is ensure that the appendixes appear in the proper order and have a consistent format. (And keep in mind that if there's an *Appendix A,* it had best be followed by *Appendix B.*)

Glossaries

Ah, the glossary . . . Brings back memories of elementary school vocabulary quizzes, doesn't it? Sigh.

Not all books have them, but if yours does, the glossary will contain definitions of words the author thinks the reader ought to know to fully comprehend the story or content in the book. As copyeditor or proofreader, your main concern is to check for proper alphabetization and consistency of overall page format and format of the definitions. As copyeditor, ensure the definitions are straightforward and simple to understand. It wouldn't make any sense for the definitions in the glossary to be so complex that they need their own glossary, right? And make sure, too, that the part of speech of words and their definitions match — no "flusterated: someone who is flustered and frustrated." As proofreader, if you find entries that don't meet these criteria, query away.

Notes and bibliography pages

As I explain in Chapter 5, a note can take the form of a *footnote* (located at the bottom of the page where an item is being discussed) or an *endnote* (located at the back of the book). What's in a note? One of two things: reference information that tells the reader where the author got his information, or some extra content for the reader who can't sleep until she knows even more about the topic at hand.

A *bibliography* is a comprehensive list of sources that the author used while creating the book.

The style of editing used for a particular book — such as APA, Chicago, or MLA (see Chapter 5) — determines how notes and the bibliography are handled. Each style has its own rules for indentation, capitalization, order of information, and punctuation.

If you're proofreading notes and bibliographies, you have to make sure that all the necessary information is included and presented in the right order and right style. Here's what makes the job challenging:

- ✔ Typically the typeface is smaller than the rest of the book.
- ✔ There are a lot of numbers (dates of publications, volume numbers, page references).
- ✔ You have to pay careful attention to the multitude of names (authors of the publications) and titles of sources.

But if proofreading these elements is a challenge, copyediting notes or a bibliography can be downright daunting. The author provides the information for the notes or bibliography. If the author is diligent, your job shouldn't be too tough. But if the author is less than perfectly organized, well . . . let's just say you may be spending some quality time on these pieces.

Taken at face value, the bibliography has the appearance of being a fairly easy edit because each entry is short and amounts to only about two or three lines of text. However, within each grouping of text lay potential pitfalls. You need to put your powers of concentration on high, and don't give up! Like most things I cover in this book, copyediting the bibliography becomes easier with practice. Scout's honor.

There's nothing more frustrating than discovering you need to revisit a section of text because you began editing using the wrong guidelines, so before you pick up that red Ticonderoga pencil, prepare a plan of attack. You need all the ammunition you can get your hands on for this task. Review your handy-dandy house style sheet and dust off that style manual — you're going to need them both!

Examining Everything in Between

After you copyedit or proofread a text for grammar, syntax, meaning, and all the rest, you need to revisit the middle section of the book to check for uniformity of page format.

In the publishing world, page format is known as the *typographical style.* Because typographical style can vary by book and from one publisher to the next, you want to check with your editor for direction before you begin marking your edits.

This round of editing or proofreading requires a change in focus. You want to remain just as vigilant and detailed as ever, but you need to take a few steps back to look at the bigger picture. No, keep going . . . farther, farther — until you no longer see individual letters and words on the page but are viewing blocks of text surrounded by white space.

Although each book you edit may have a different typographical format, rest assured that there are a finite number of format errors. With a little experience and practice (and this book to jump-start the learning process), spotting these errors becomes second nature in no time. I go over some of the more common typographical errors in the following sections.

Heads

The term *heads* can refer to two types of elements:

- ✔ Running heads, which are found at the top of the page and made up of the book title or chapter title and page numbers (*folios*)
- ✔ Chapter headings and subheadings, which are part of the body of the text

Running heads

Even as technology pushes publishing companies to experiment with increasingly diverse and creative typographical formats, tradition holds fast when it comes to running heads. The most common practice in the industry is to place the book title on the left-hand (*verso*) page in the running head and the chapter title on the right-hand (*recto*) page.

Page numbers often appear in running heads as well (although they may appear in the *feet,* which I discuss in a moment). Some publishers prefer placing page numbers on both left- and right-hand pages. Others may include them only on odd or even pages. See the upcoming "Folio" section for more details.

Chapter headings and subheadings

White space and headlines are commonly, and judiciously, used to break up blocks of text into neat parcels. Tricks of the trade that set headings and subheadings apart from the body of the text include varying the font face and size or using small caps, all caps, italic, or boldface type.

Different levels of headings are set in different styles to denote a hierarchy. (See Chapter 16 for specifics about how to designate these styles using typecodes.) As a copyeditor, your job may require that you make decisions about when to use the various levels of headings to help organize the text in the most logical way. As a proofreader, your job most definitely includes ensuring that the various levels of headings and subheadings are represented consistently on the page.

Feet

The term *feet* refers to the *footer* — any text placed at the bottom of the published page. Not all books have feet, but those that do may place page numbers and/or footnotes in that area. As with endnotes or a bibliography, footnotes must be proofread very closely for adherence to the particular style of the publisher.

If you're proofreading a book whose feet contain footnotes and page numbers, watch for a common error: footnotes overwriting page numbers.

Folio

Speaking of page numbers . . . When you proofread a book, you have to pay attention to every one of them. In book parlance, the page number is called the *folio.* You must check every folio for sequence and uniformity. In addition to the numbering itself, you need to notice if the folio appears in the same place on each page, and you need to know whether it should appear only on even-numbered or odd-numbered pages.

The text of a book almost always begins on page one, and page one will always be a right-side (*recto*) page. This means that throughout the book, all the recto pages will be odd numbers. All the left-side (*verso*) pages will be even numbers.

Arabic numerals are the norm for the folio in the body of a book. But when it comes to the front matter, there are many different acceptable formats. Sometimes, the pages that make up the front matter do not have page numbers themselves. Usually, numbering the pages of the front matter becomes necessary when the front matter contains content such as an introduction, a preface, or a foreword. One way to differentiate the pages of the front matter from the body of the book is to use lowercase Roman numerals (*i, ii, iii,* and so on) in the front matter. However, some editors use Arabic numerals throughout a book, beginning the numbering with the front matter.

Your responsibility as copyeditor or proofreader is to flag any inconsistencies in numbering format or style. Also, should edits require that pages be deleted or added, you need to mark the pages appropriately for the editor.

Margins

Obviously, margin sizes vary depending on the publisher and the type of book. Publishers are always trying to find the perfect balance between margin size and text for easier reading. (We voracious readers can certainly attest to the negative effects of having too much text and too little white space on a page.) The white space allotted for the margins should create a Zen-like balance between margin and text. Readability is key. Ohmmm . . .

As with style and formatting, the assigning editor should provide guidelines on the page setup. Margins are almost never exactly equal on all sides. The header margin may be smaller than the footer (or vice versa). And in most publications, the *gutter* margin (the side of the page that is bound in the book) is wider than the outside margin, which ensures that the type can easily be seen and read after the pages are bound.

Proofreaders are expected to ensure the uniformity of margin size and the alignment of text (and, of course, the alignment of the running heads and feet contained in the top or bottom margins).

Left behind: Widows and orphans

As you delve deeper into typographical style, you will feel more confident about your ability to spot problem areas. High on your list of important things to remember is that publishers are very concerned with the aesthetics of the printed page. Until you have a lot of experience, spotting inconsistencies can be more instinctual, and if you review the pages for uniformity, you instinctively know to flag anything that looks out of place — like widows and orphans. Find it in your heart to help them.

A *widow* refers to a line of text at the top of a page or column that is — you guessed it — hanging there all alone without anyone to keep it company. The line of text is likely to belong to the last sentence on the preceding page or in the preceding column and, due to margin constraints, does not fit on the preceding page or in the preceding column. A similar lone line can occur at the end of a page or column; this is your *orphan*.

If you run your eyes along each page, searching for format errors, widows and orphans are easy to spot. Just remember that each page should have a clean, concise appearance and should include at least a few lines of text, even if you're reading the last page in a chapter. Flag down and save any line of text from the loneliness that comes with standing alone on either the top or the bottom of a page. Aside from being visually jarring to the reader, a string of text hanging out alone on a page may also be misconstrued by the reader as a header.

Exactly how does an editor make space for widows and orphans? There are a few tricks: Editors can take space from the bottom margin, edit a paragraph to lose a line, or visually adjust the space above and below a head to pull up the text.

Piecing Together a Magazine

In the magazine world, *book* is slang for the magazine itself. The usage is telling: It hints at the difficulty of producing issue after issue chock-full of enough content to fill an actual book. Obviously, no two magazines are structured exactly the same, and scholarly journals are very different animals from consumer magazines. In the sections that follow, I explain the pieces of a magazine that you're most likely to encounter, focusing primarily on consumer mags.

For an overview of how a magazine is produced, be sure to check out Chapter 2.

The cover

You may not be able to judge a book by its cover, but consumer magazine publishers hope you judge their products by the covers. They know they may get only a brief glance from you while you're waiting in the checkout line, so the cover has to scream "Buy me!"

The cover of any magazine conveys its tone and advertises its wares to its target audience. The elements that in-house designers and marketing and sales people use to manipulate the cover include the following:

- ✔ **The logo:** A magazine's logo is designed to fit the mission of the magazine and usually appears on the cover in the same spot for each issue.

- ✔ **Coverlines:** These are the headlines found on a magazine's cover. In consumer magazines, you see certain words and phrases used over and over in coverlines, such as *sex, lose weight fast,* and *reduce stress.* Celebrity names and timely events also get prominent play in coverlines. (Timeliness is important in this industry; current events should still be current by the time the magazine hits the newsstand.)

  If you really want to talk the talk, refer to the coverlines at the top of the magazine cover as *rooflines.*

- ✔ **Cover art:** The cover art should have something to do with the coverlines or should at least reflect the magazine's mission. The cover art may also include a *burst:* a seal- or star-like image containing text like *Plus: 19 Hot New Gadgets!*

- ✔ **UPC/label box:** Many consumer magazines create two slightly different covers for each issue: one for subscribers and one for people who will pick up the magazine at their local drugstore. The latter will feature a box on the cover that contains a UPC code for easy scanning at the checkout counter. The cover for subscribers may instead have a blank box on the cover in which the delivery address can be printed (or a label affixed).

- ✔ **Spine:** This term refers to the bound edge of the magazine. The spine is the part that shows when you line up your *National Geographic* collection chronologically on your bookshelf. Generally, the spine contains the date, issue, name of the magazine, and sometimes some fun summary of the topic in that issue.

  Magazines that are bound using *saddle stitching* (staples or stitches through the fold) don't have a spine. That's why your chronological collection of *People* doesn't look so impressive on your bookshelf.

Some publications print both in the United States and overseas, resulting in yet another cover tailored to the other readership. As a copyeditor or proofreader, you're responsible for checking the magazine cover. (That's not often the case with books, as I explain earlier in the chapter.)

When copyediting and proofreading, be especially careful with the cover and spine. You never want to miss an incorrect month, year, or volume number printed on the spine, for example. And if the coverlines include page numbers, make sure, make sure, make sure the page numbers indeed match the articles. One more thing: Often treated as a sort of hybrid of editorial and marketing content, the cover can bend the house rules a bit, such as using numerals instead of spelling out single-digit numbers.

The front matter

Referred to as the *front of the book* (or *FOB*), the first third of a magazine contains elements such as these:

- The table of contents
- Letter from the editor
- Letters to the editor
- Boilerplate
- Masthead page
- Ads

Depending on the magazine, you may also find a contributing editors' page containing brief biographies and photos of writers who contributed articles for that particular issue.

ToC

Yup, it's that ToC (table of contents) again. All magazines contain them, and they're located in the first few pages (perhaps after a grandiose gatefold perfume ad). Depending on the magazine, the table of contents can include all matter in the magazine as it appears in the issue, or it can be arranged by type of matter, such as features, regular columns, or reviews.

The ToC page may also feature headlines for stories available only on the Web, directing the reader to visit the Web site (and thereby ensuring the marketing department gets its kudos).

At a magazine, copyeditors are more likely to be the ones who check for internal consistency of page and title references across the magazine after the layout has been finalized; proofreaders may see only the text of articles before they're laid out, or may see page spreads out of sequence as each department turns in the pages it's responsible for.

If a magazine's ToC lists the volume and issue numbers, make sure these are correct.

If a magazine features pictures in the ToC, you need to ask whether the page number listed with the picture should be the one the related article starts on, or the one on which the picture actually appears. (I prefer to use the page number that starts the article, but I'm not your editor!)

Letter from the editor

Usually, the top editor — an editor-in-chief or managing editor, for instance — writes a brief introduction to the issue, often contained within one page and always in the same spot each issue. This can be an article addressing concerns within the scope of the magazine's topic or an editorial expressing the views of the editor within the context of a particular feature. Here, an editor can express herself in her own language, be creative, and talk about the things she feels are important, all tied into the magazine's mission.

Letters to the editor

These are reader response letters sent to the editor or the magazine, wherein readers praise and punish the magazine for its last few issues.

If you are asked to edit or proofread letters to the editor, take a look at the "signature" of each letter to make sure the cities and states are listed consistently . . . and that the cities actually exist somewhere. Believe me, it has happened that a city called "Xanadu" slipped into publication. Funny, readers.

Boilerplate

The boilerplate is a box or section placed somewhere in the opening pages that contains any combination of the following:

- Publisher details, like the name of the publisher and locations of its various offices, as well as whether the publication is published weekly, monthly, or on some other schedule.

- Issue details, such as the volume number and ISSN (International Standard Serial Number issued by the Library of Congress to magazines, newspapers, annual publications, and journals).

- Fine-print legalese, like notes to the postmaster in case of incorrect addresses, permissions statements and information on where to obtain reprint permission, advertising opt-out information for subscribers, subscription and advertising rates, and any other tiny things you probably don't want to read.

The boilerplate is called this for a reason: After it's created, the standardized text within the boilerplate rarely changes — unless, say, the headquarters move into another building.

Masthead page

The masthead contains the details of ownership and list of staff — it acknowledges the management, creative staff, editors, and marketing people involved in the publication. In some magazines, the editorial and business mastheads are combined; in others, they are separated. The boilerplate can sometimes be found on the masthead page.

Mastheads do change. Usually, somebody on the business end will make sure the lists are correct, but always proofread the masthead for correctly spelled titles, consistent spacing, and the like.

Ads

Let's be frank: How many magazines can the average person really read? Now, look at the magazine section of any bookstore: How many of those titles do you think will be around in, say, a year or two? One reason so many consumer magazines fold is that the business is just not very lucrative. There are limited streams of revenue. Subscriptions and single-issue purchases aren't even the half of it. Literally. The bulk of a magazine's revenue comes from — shocker! — advertising.

Logically, then, magazines are chock-a-block with ads. Advertising departments tend to solicit ads from companies that reflect the mission and target audience of that magazine, though this isn't always the case (hey, money talks). Take a peek at a magazine like *Sports Illustrated,* and you'll see shiny faces of athletes hawking the latest got-to-have sneakers, ripped fitness types swearing by a vitamin supplement's benefits, and photos of contraptions designed to make you sweat. (You may even see ads for "sex enhancers" for the midlife-crisis crew.) It's unlikely that you'll see ads for Betty Crocker cake mixes or astrophysics software.

Copyeditors and proofreaders rarely deal with advertisements, unless an ad is being designed in-house, which tends to happen only with very small, often local publications.

The meat of a magazine

People don't pick up and purchase a magazine for the front matter. No, we pay for the juicy articles between the covers.

Referred to as the *well* or *feature well,* the middle section of a magazine contains many types of articles, oftentimes separated into *departments,* or columns contained in each issue. (For example, a department may be *Beauty Under $20* or *New Makeup Revue,* and each issue features something new within the topic.)

There is no standard for the number or length of articles contained within a magazine, but there are strategic decisions behind the placement of articles within a magazine. For example, the article considered most important to the issue will likely be found toward the middle of the issue, in the middle of the well.

Shorter, easier-to-swallow articles are referred to as *briefs.* Briefs are those one-page snippets tucked between articles, and they give the reader a quick something to read while on the bus. They tend to be 200 words or less but still reflect the tone of the publication.

Longer topical articles are referred to as *features,* and they can span a number of pages to cover a subject. Features are usually advertised on the magazine cover in bigger, bolder fonts. Writers can get pretty creative in features, taking time with descriptions of people and places. Usually, visually appealing graphics and photos accompany these articles, and pull quotes may be used to draw a reader in.

I'm sure you've read an article that requires you to turn to the back of the magazine for the rest of the story. When an article continues on nonconsecutive pages, this is called a *jump.*

A feature article may contain any number of the following elements:

- **Head and deck:** You know what a headline is, but did you know the extra line of information following a headline is called a *deck*? This subheading is also referred to as the *tagline.*

- **Pull quote:** The pull quote, also called a *blurb,* is a sentence excerpted from the body of the article and emphasized in larger type to draw the reader's attention.

- **Caption:** This is a phrase or sentence that accompanies a picture or image associated with an article.

- **Sidebar:** Often seen in feature articles, the sidebar is a smaller story related to the article but separated from the copy by a box and often has its own headline and deck.

- **Graphic elements:** Charts, graphs, pictures, drawings, or any other images associated with the article fall into this category.

As a copyeditor or proofreader, you need to look at each of these elements, making sure that captions correctly match their images, pull quotes match the article, and everything seems coherent as a piece.

If any features *jump* to another page, make sure there are *continued* lines indicating this fact to the reader. Oh, and make sure that the text carries over to the jump page or pages intact — even one missing word can throw the reader for a loop.

The back story

The *back of the book* (or *BoB*) refers to the final third part of the magazine, often heavy on advertising. What else will you find here? You will certainly find all those *jump pages,* or pages containing the remainders of feature articles. You will also see yet more departments and columns, often designed to accommodate jump pages, and *fractionals* — ads that take up less than a full page.

Also, almost every consumer magazine has a *back page* — a page on a theme that is consistent issue to issue and is usually located opposite the inside back cover.

Chapter 14

Balancing Between Style and Rules

*W*hen you first start copyediting or proofreading, you may curse the whimsical gods of Style and Rules. Just about every rule has an exception. Or ten. For every style deemed standard, some know-it-all will claim to know it better and that you need to work based on her style. The possibilities are truly dizzying and can be tough to remember.

Fortunately, you don't have to. The reason seasoned copyeditors and proofreaders don't spend their work days yelling "Fie!" and shaking their carpal-tunneled fists at the heavens is this: You don't need to know every specialized style and rule and every idiosyncratic exception. You just have to know where to *look* to figure them out. For this reason, you need a comprehensive arsenal of resources. In this chapter, I show you what you should have in your arsenal.

After I help you stock your shelves (or hard drive) with the appropriate resource materials, I then explain why the rules you find in those resources aren't hard and fast. A little creature called *house style* can always trump another resource, so I introduce you to this fella as well.

Arming Yourself with Resources

Fret not: Despite the language I'm using, copyediting and proofreading don't always constitute an all-out battle. If you're not a war-mongering type, think of the resources I introduce here not as weapons but as members of a loyal posse that you can count on to get you through any pinch. I promise you'll feel far more editorially confident surrounded by your go-to peeps.

Webster's and other dictionaries

Let me start by introducing you to your best-est of friends. He's the most popular kid in school: class president, quarterback, and prom king, all wrapped up in one bright-red book cover. His name is *Merriam-Webster's Collegiate Dictionary,* 11th Edition (Merriam-Webster). But his friends — which you most certainly will be — call him *Web 11.* This is the dictionary most commonly used by publishing houses, and if you buy the 11th edition, you get a year's free subscription to the online edition (www.m-w.com), which has the advantage of frequent updates.

Unless you focus on British copyediting and proofreading (see Chapter 6) or on specialized clients (such as the Outdoor Writers of America, which uses its own glossary of terms), you will probably use *Web 11.* However, you should certainly ask all new clients their preferred dictionary.

Webster's has become synonymous with *dictionary* in the United States, and the name is in the public domain. Be aware that not every *Webster's* is a Merriam-Webster. But some of the others are highly reputable as well. For example, *Webster's New World Dictionary,* 4th edition (Wiley) is the official dictionary of the Associated Press and is used by many magazine publishers as well as newspapers. Another dictionary used and preferred by many copy-editors, particularly for the usage information, is the *American Heritage Dictionary of the English Language,* Fourth Edition (Houghton Mifflin).

Fortunately for you, the Webster family doesn't get jealous, so it's okay to have a few other friendly dictionaries around. I recommend that you have access to the following:

- *The Oxford English Dictionary* **(Oxford University Press) *(OED).*** The *OED* is a 20-volume set that sells for nearly $1,000. Instead of coughing up that kind of dough (and shelf space), you may want to opt for a sub-scription to its online edition ($295 annually, $29.95 monthly). Or you can get a print copy of *The Compact Oxford English Dictionary* — less tout-worthy as a revered editorial accoutrement, but smaller than a barn and, at roughly $30, way more affordable than the original.

  Back in the day, the *OED* came with its own magnifying glass. Now, thanks to the online edition, you can simply adjust the font size on your screen. If you pay for the subscription you get access to the ongoing project underway, the third edition.

- *Random House Webster's Unabridged Dictionary* **(Random House).** This is a good option for a one-volume unabridged dictionary and is also available free online at www.dictionary.com.

- **Google.com.** Google has plenty of splendid uses, and you can add "dictio-nary" to your list of them. In the Google search field, type "define:" and the word in question — no space after the colon ("define:utilitarian"). The search engine churns out multiple definitions from multiple sources.

Chicago and other style and usage guides

You've made all the right friends in the dictionary crowd, and now it's time to decide who will get invites to your gala style-guide soiree. If you know what's good for you, you'll make *The Chicago Manual of Style,* 15th Edition (University of Chicago Press) your guest of honor. This book is your bread and butter; it's your most important friend after your dictionary — *unless* you don't want to work in book publishing. If your focus is magazines, academic journals, corporate publications, or any other type of writing that doesn't appear in a book, you're likely to need another style guide as your date.

Here's a guide to the guides so you know what you need to accomplish any given job. First I list the style name and then the publication it's based on.

- ✔ **AMA:** *American Medical Association Manual of Style* (Lippincott Williams & Wilkins).

- ✔ **AP:** *The Associated Press Stylebook and Libel Manual* (Perseus Books): This is the style bible for the vast majority of newspapers, making it an indispensable resource for anyone who wants to proofread or copyedit for them.

- ✔ **APA:** *Publication Manual of the American Psychological Association* (American Psychological Association).

- ✔ **CSE:** *Scientific Style and Format: The CSE Manual for Authors, Editors, and Publishers* (Council of Science Editors).

- ✔ **Chicago or CMS:** *The Chicago Manual of Style,* 15th Edition (University of Chicago Press).

- ✔ **Garner's:** *Garner's Modern American Usage* by Bryan A. Garner (Oxford University Press). This is *the* usage bible nowadays.

- ✔ **GPO:** *United States Government Printing Office Style Manual* (U.S. Government Printing Office).

- ✔ **Gregg:** *The Gregg Reference Manual,* 9th Edition, by William A. Sabin (Irwin/McGraw-Hill). This manual is a favorite of business writers and has a great glossary of grammatical terms.

- ✔ **MLA:** *MLA Style Manual and Guide to Scholarly Publishing* (Modern Language Association of America).

- ✔ **NYT:** *The New York Times Manual of Style and Usage* (Three Rivers Press). It ain't just for *The New York Times. Time* magazine uses it, as do many other periodicals.

- ✔ **Turabian:** Kate Turabian's *A Manual for Writers of Term Papers, Theses, and Dissertations* (University of Chicago Press). It's mostly just a simpler version of *The Chicago Manual of Style,* streamlined for the undergrad world.

✔ **WiT:** *Words into Type* by Marjorie Skillin and Robert Gay (Prentice Hall). This manual touts material similar to CMS, with additional insights on grammar. Its popularity has remained surprisingly strong despite the lack of an updated edition since 1974, because its advice is so timeless. The only really outdated stuff is in the typography section.

More resources

Eureka! You're about to discover a wealth of resources better than gold for copyeditors and proofreaders. Luckily, you don't have to boil down and lug these insightful doubloons.

Whether the resources are print- or Internet-based, I've provided URLs to ease the process of researching and securing them, in the order of ones I've found most helpful:

✔ **American Copy Editors Society (www.copydesk.org):** The American Copy Editors Society (ACES) provides copyeditors with a full spectrum of services — a current job bank, directory listings and access, bulletin boards, an e-mail address (@copydesk.org), and educational conferences. Membership is $55 per year. Its goal? "To provide solutions to copy desk problems, through training, discussion and an awareness of common issues."

✔ **Copyeditors' Knowledge Base (www.kokedit.com/library.shtml):** Katharine O'Moore-Klopf has spearheaded quite a resource for copyeditors, one that you can even contribute to. Her how-to's start with helping people become copyeditors and then move right through improving existing skills, sharing tools and tips, networking within the copyeditor community, and ultimately finding work.

✔ **Editorial Freelancers Association (www.the-efa.org):** The EFA is the largest and oldest national professional organization dedicated to supporting editorial freelancers, and its members include experienced editors, writers, indexers, and translators touting the full gamut of specialized experience. Don't live in NYC? Neither do half the members. If you're outside the New York tri-state region, you even get $15 off the $120 annual membership fee.

✔ **Deanna Hoak's blog on copyediting (http://deannahoak.com/category/blog/copyediting/):** Deanna Hoak is an award-winning freelance copyeditor specializing in fantasy and science fiction. Plus, she's a hoot. Witty and brilliant: an invaluable combo for budding copyeditors.

✔ **The Editorium (www.editorium.com/freebies.htm):** Editorium is a small company that creates many programs to help automate editing tasks in Microsoft Word, including this generous collection of free programs and macros of use to all kinds of editors and writers.

- ✔ **The Copy Editor Job Board (`http://jobs.copyeditor.com/home/index.cfm?site_id=502`):** This free job board from *Copy Editor* newsletter features freelance and in-house opportunities. You can peruse job postings, or you can post your own profile for employers and recruiters. You can even set up job alerts. You'll get a daily or weekly e-mail whenever a new job is posted within your stated expertise.

- ✔ **Refdesk.com (`www.refdesk.com`):** This comprehensive site seems to make good on its claim that it's "The Single Best Source for Facts."

- ✔ **Copyediting-L: Stalking Danglers Around the World (`www.copyediting-l.info/`):** The founders of Copyediting-L describe it as "a list for copy editors and other defenders of the English language who want to discuss anything related to editing" — and they mean anything: style sheets and issues, driving philosophies, resources, electronic versus hard-copy editing, freelance pros and cons, checklists, and advice on every genre of copyediting from people in the field. This is quite a helpful community for beginners and experts alike. Ask questions (that haven't yet been answered — check the archives) or weigh in through surveys such as "What do you think of dots in phone numbers?" It's all free. Subscribers even get blog promotion, along with a presence in — and access to — the Directory of CE-L Freelancers.

- ✔ **AskOxford.com (`www.askoxford.com`):** Got questions on English grammar, spelling, and usage? Find answers here. You can also search a dictionary of words, names, or quotations.

- ✔ **Getting the Most Out of Your Copyeditor: The Style Sheet, Parts One and Two:** These two articles were commissioned by American Book Publishing and written by Bonnie Darrington. They provide a good inside look at what publishers hope to get from their copyeditors, and they double as checklists for how copyeditors can deliver on those ideals. Find Part One at `www.positivearticles.com/Article/Getting-the-Most-Out-of-Your-Copyeditor--The-Style-Sheet--Part-One/1694` and Part Two at `www.positivearticles.com/article.php?id=1749`.

- ✔ **The American Society of Indexers (`www.asindexing.org/site/publishers.shtml`):** The American Society of Indexers is the only professional organization in the United States devoted solely to the advancement of indexing, abstracting, and database building, and it offers a hearty section of resources regardless of membership.

- ✔ **Wikipedia's entry for copyediting (`http://en.wikipedia.org/wiki/copy_editing`):** This is a live document that grows with every new entry from people in-the-know about copyediting. Contents span "Changes in the profession" to "Traits, skills and training," as well as excellent reference sources and links.

- ✔ **Copy-Editing Corner (`http://copyeditingcorner.blogspot.com`):** This is an informative blog about the many issues copyeditors face and the many resources and real-life experiences that can help.

- ✔ **DMOZ's copyediting section (`http://dmoz.org/Arts/Writers_Resources/Copy_Editing`):** DMOZ is an open directory project that lists lots of "Copy Editing" links; it's a copyediting resource for copyediting resources.

- ✔ **Common Errors in English (`www.wsu.edu/~brians/errors/errors.html`):** Paul Brians has compiled an exhaustive and enlightening list of words and phrases that writers — and people of all kinds, including, probably, you — frequently misuse.

- ✔ **Modern English Grammar (`http://papyr.com/hypertextbooks/grammar/`):** This is a collection of grammar insights from Daniel Kies, of College of DuPage's Department of English. It's the equivalent of years' worth of courses.

- ✔ **Hazel Tank's Word Lists: Medical Transcription Central (`www.prenhall.com/medtransoriginal/wordlist/index.html`):** Here you find word lists galore — and not your everyday collections. Hazel Tank has compiled a wealth of specialized jargon and all its hyphenation and assorted word-list issues that editors hope you'll unearth and note on your style sheets. Peek in for cryptic terms covering "Alternative Medicine" and "Fungus Among Us" to "Military Jargon" and "Creepy Crawling Critters."

- ✔ **The Eggcorn Database (`http://eggcorns.lascribe.net`):** The Eggcorn Database is a one-of-a-kind collection of misheard words and phrases, a lexical account that's not meant to ridicule the errors but to document them. The site explains: "They tell us something about how ordinary speakers and writers make sense of the language." (Or mistakenly make nonsense of it.)

- ✔ **Testy Copy Editors (`www.testycopyeditors.org/phpBB2`):** This is a lively and current online forum for copyeditors and their gripes. Okay, there are insights, too, but often in the context of where the problems are, be they in grammar or job opportunities.

- ✔ **The Slot (`http://theslot.com`):** Bill Walsh's *The Slot: A Spot for Copy Editors* has some great history of copyediting as well as a lively blog. Walsh is copy chief of the national desk of *The Washington Post,* and although this site has no affiliation with the *Post,* the good writing and organization reflect an impressive standard.

The Unbreakable Rule: Rules Can Be Broken

Don't get me wrong: I still don't want to see you wearing white after Labor Day, especially not accompanied by black dress socks and sandals. Please. Some rules are for the world's greater good.

In the fashionable publishing world, however, anything goes (birthday suits included if you work at home). The only rule that's usually followed is this: The author sets his own style and rules, so long as the author has the credentials and mastery to make it work.

Don't unilaterally cram an author's work into a grammatical rule, especially while proofreading or copyediting novels (or any genre for smaller publishing houses). See the section on authorial voice in Chapter 4 for more information, including why I've dubbed it "The most important section in this book." At the very least, your queries should be open to discussion. If authors stay consistent in their alternative techniques, they can and should have carte blanche when it comes to style and rules.

The hard part is recognizing when a new author should have carte blanche because his wayward writing just works somehow. It's sometimes tempting for us as astute copyeditors and proofreaders to exert our astuteness onto a manuscript. Yes, we strive for invisibility, and we try to keep the authorial tone, but dang if I'm, er, *we're* not getting credit for knowing that something is a copy error.

So keep a loving editorial eye out for the little author. Let Stephen King and his 100-million-copies-sold misspell every word if he wants. Let Arundhati Roy, author of the beautifully written *The God of Small Things,* break every rule and sentence into fragments willy-nilly. And don't forget to let emerging authors have enough leeway to become the next King or Roy. You both will be glad you did.

Realizing When House Style Reigns Supreme

Even Stephen King would be in for a big surprise, however, if he were to write a *For Dummies* book. In branded publishing, brand is king, even over King. The house style guide is created by the publishing house to best build its editorial brand, and that trumps all. No matter how much King may prefer using *etc.,* his Dummies editor would have to insist on changing it to *and so on* for the sake of brand-building consistency throughout the many books in the series.

This hierarchy of house style over author style is unique to branded publishing. Yes, some of the more behemoth and self-important publishers fancy all of their varying books branded to them, and therefore fancy themselves as keepers (and creators) of house style guides that reign over author style, but that's only until one of their best-selling authors threatens mutiny over heavy-handed manuscript changes.

Can a proofreader or copyeditor advocate and eventually have house style overridden in these environments, too? Yes, but it's not a good *yes*. If you're knowledgeable enough and authoritative enough, you may possibly be able to usurp style power from your powerful and proud employer, but do you really want to risk the damage that trying may cause? My advice? If preserving author style is a priority, bite your tongue until you're back to working in kindred environs.

With the majority of publishers in the world, house style is under author style in the hierarchy, but it's still very important. It's the guide that your publishing house created/cherishes/expects you to use on its books, unless some vital author exception is needed. If an in-house editor doesn't provide you with the house style guide, ask for it. Use it. Honor it until death/the end of the editing job do you part. And even then, don't part too far from it because you'll need it for your next job with that publisher.

Committing a Few Rules to Memory

Most rules are rife with exceptions in this industry, but a few are so standard and ubiquitous that they're well worth memorizing. The time you spend now will be saved tenfold on each new copyediting or proofreading job.

Treating numbers

Numbers are fun! If you didn't detect any sarcasm in that statement, you may be one of the specialized few eager and able to copyedit or proofread texts about math and science.

The rest of us know those manuscripts officially as gobbledygook. I'm well-schooled and financially literate, but marathon chalkboard formulas and 18-digit numerals — even repeating ones — give me math vertigo. Or at least that's what I feign to get out of reading or copyediting them.

Here's what you can't feign: knowing the basic rules about incorporating numbers into *narrative* (nontechnical or humanistic) manuscripts and into *technical* (scientific) manuscripts. Definitely ask about house style for your particular project because variant, hybrid treatments are common. But a few rules are usually common to both genres and are worth committing to memory for that reason:

✔ Never begin a sentence with a numeral. This rule is absolute, no matter what genre you're working in. Spell out the number or reword the sentence.

✔ Style all numerals of the same class or type consistently in the text.

✔ Avoid using two unrelated numerals in a row: *In 2007 40,000 people will become millionaires, and I plan on being one of them.* Fix this problem by rewording the sentence: *I plan on being one of the 40,000 people who will become millionaires in 2007.*

✔ Always use a numeral before an abbreviated unit of measurement, such as 8 oz. or 7 lbs.

✔ Write a percentage as a numeral followed by the word *percent.*

Numbers in narrative documents

Narrative or nontechnical documents typically don't have many numbers in them, so the numbers are more frequently spelled out than in technical documents. You may find that these conventions hold true for most narrative projects:

✔ Spell out numbers from one to one hundred.

✔ Use numerals for page numbers, chapter numbers, years, and dates.

✔ Spell out large numbers but only if they can be spelled out in two words: *fifty-nine thousand; three million.*

Numbers in technical documents

Technical documents typically have the pleasure of being rife with numbers. Hence, editors usually prefer numerals to spelled-out numbers because they're easier to find, easier to read, and less space-consuming. Here are two rules that are fairly standard in technical copyediting and proofreading:

✔ Spell out numbers from one to nine.

✔ Spell out all units of measurement.

When correcting numerals that you want spelled out, you can circle the numeral and then circle an "sp" in the margin. However, you risk that a *compositor* (the person preparing the laid-out text for publication) will misspell the word. It's always safer to spell the word out.

Using special display type consistently

Special display type constitutes anything that deviates from good ol' fashioned straight text. To keep special text through design attributes consistent, it's important to set (or learn) style rules that govern the full gamut of special display.

Italics

Some authors *really* love using italics for emphasis. If an author needs to italicize a word for emphasis, maybe the author just hasn't found a strong enough word. However, this use of italic is acceptable. Also acceptable uses: to denote thoughts, imagined speech, remembered speech, foreign terms, words used as words, letters used as letters, and sounds used as sounds. *Vrooooooom, vrooooooom* — let's drive on over to the section on SMALL CAPS.

Small caps

If your author is John Irving–esque, you may encounter small caps used to render a yelling character's words, reminiscent of the book *A Prayer for Owen Meany.* But in general, small caps are usually limited to these instances:

- ✔ Signage and inscriptions (T-shirts, bumper stickers, billboards, and so on)

- ✔ Acronyms such as INTERPOL and UNICEF (but not FBI because you don't say "FBI" as a word — not in public anyway).

- ✔ Time and time periods (B.C., A.M., P.M., and so on), though definitely refer to the publisher's house style guide for the definitive answer on these instances.

Boldface

Boldface works well in headings. (Doesn't it? See above.) Occasionally you find authors using it for emphasis, but that looks amateurish. Do yourselves both a favor: Nix boldfaced type in that instance.

Chapter 15

Creating and Using the All-Important Style Sheet

. . . .

In This Chapter

▶ Documenting your every decision

▶ Using style sheets to everyone's advantage

▶ Tasting some samples

. . . .

The style sheet is all-important, exhaustive — and great for you. Not great like a steamed broccoli floret when you're trying to round out your diet. Great like a bacon double cheeseburger on *Sundays-don't-count-on-my-diet* days. Great like Santa seeing, tallying, and rewarding your every good editorial deed. If the style sheet could slow-dance, your heart might swoon right into a marriage proposal.

In this chapter, I walk you through who uses a style sheet, what should be on it, and how to use it. I also offer samples that you can feel free to use as starting points for your own style sheets. While some of the information here is specific to copyeditors, I encourage you to read it even if your goal is to become a proofreader. As proofreader, you're among the style sheet's most valuable audience members, and you may appreciate its performance all the more by getting a behind-the-scenes tour of how it was created.

What's the Big Deal about the Style Sheet?

If you're working on any document that's more than a few pages long, here are some of the things a great style sheet can give you:

- ✔ **Consistency:** Copyeditors have to make myriad judgment calls because every document is unique, and whatever choices are made must be implemented throughout. Documenting each style decision is the best way for the copyeditor to stay consistent and for the proofreader to check that consistency.

- ✔ **Efficiency:** When it comes to saving time, the style sheet pays off exponentially for everyone involved. Whether you're the copyeditor or proofreader, you won't have to look up the same word multiple times — nor will the author, in-house editor, caption writer, indexer, designer, or anyone else lucky enough to have the style sheet.

- ✔ **Clarity:** Immediately after copyediting or proofreading a manuscript, you're probably clear on how to handle certain conventions — for example, all state names absolutely have to be abbreviated instead of spelled out. But two weeks later, when you're reviewing the document again after the author has made revisions, will you remember each convention? Like a toothsome trail of copyediting bread crumbs, your style sheet safely leads you back to even the most cryptic of editorial decisions.

Copyeditors, Know Your Audience

Yes, your audience will ultimately be droves of adoring readers who feast on the error-free publication you help to create. And yes, you should know this audience, as I discuss in Chapter 4.

But when you're trying to decide what to include on your style sheet, you must also have a different audience in mind: your fellow players in the stages of production — all the people who'll subsequently work with your copyedited manuscript, relying on your expertise, cross-checking your expertise, and sometimes unwittingly undermining your expertise if your style decisions aren't clearly communicated to them.

All these players are concerned with the general well-being of the product, but each of them has a few particular concerns. In the following list, I explain some considerations you can give them on your style sheet to assuage those concerns before you pass the manuscript along:

- ✔ **The author:** He cares most about the Style Notes (or General Notes) section of your style sheet because his greatest concern is that you override the house style in every instance where author style should be maintained (see Chapter 14). For example, each time you decide to let The Author capitalize Words That Wouldn't Normally Be Capitalized for the sake of the story, you need to note that decision on your style sheet. Otherwise, those exceptions will most likely be "fixed" by people working on the manuscript after you.

✔ **The proofreader:** Depending on your work situation, more than one proofreader may work on your document. If you're copyediting a book, up to four people could proofread the manuscript, with each proofreader doing a separate check of either the manuscript's first pass or second pass (see Chapter 2). Proofreaders are mostly concerned with the Word List (or Alpha List) section of your style sheet because they're hoping you've conscientiously caught and confirmed the spelling and usage of every word that may possibly be wrong.

✔ **The compositor:** This person, also called the *typesetter,* focuses mostly on the Design Memo (or Typography or Typesetter Notes) section of your style sheet. The compositor typesets each pass of the document based on the design specs (created by the designer) and your typecoding throughout the manuscript (see Chapter 16).

✔ **The production editor:** If you're working on a book, this person roots for you and for every section of your style sheet because every section affects the manuscript's ultimate success. (See Chapter 2 for a discussion of what a production editor does.)

These are all discerning audience members, but don't start getting stage fright. They're all on your team, working toward the common goal of a clean, reader-worthy document.

The tone of your style sheet should exude expertise and confidence, but also accessibility. Some copyeditors suggest that you convey your style decisions as if you were speaking to an auto mechanic — someone who's very capable but very inexperienced when it comes to editorial style.

Deciding What to Put on Your Style Sheet

In this section, I put together a few simple rules to help you decide what to list on your style sheet, along with details of just about every section that you could possibly include. With this info, you'll have all you need to win over your audience and get a standing ovation at each project's curtain call.

Recognizing a judgment call

The style sheet entry possibilities are endless, but the golden rule governing them isn't. Remember this little precious nugget: Every time you make a judgment call about any aspect of the document, enter it onto your style sheet. Noting your decisions helps keep them consistent throughout the document and helps keep them intact while the document is being tweaked by the rest of the production players.

Do you need to note a typo on your style sheet? No. There's no judgment call involved. You correct the typo on the document page, and you're a hero. Same goes for misspelled terms. Exceptions exist but, again, they're all governed by that golden rule: If you've made a judgment call, include it in the style sheet.

For example, if you found the word *recieved* in a manuscript, you'd fix the spelling error and move on — no need to enter it on your style sheet. However, if it were part of the phrase *a well received manuscript,* then the word also involves hyphenation, which often warrants a style decision on your part. If house style is to hyphenate compound adjectives, you'll likely fix it and add *well-received* to your style sheet in two places: as an example under punctuation to be used as a guideline for other compound adjectives in the manuscript, and also in your Word List section so that all instances get changed and those changes are maintained throughout the production process. If your decision is to leave the hyphen out of *well received,* as the author has it, you definitely have to alert others to your decision or else they'll follow house style and make the correction.

Now here's where budding copyeditors often falter, and where you're not going to: You have to remember to make an entry on your style sheet whether or not the house style is to hyphenate compound adjectives. Why? Because you care. And caring copyeditors know that other people working on the document will question the same thing (*Do I hyphenate this compound or not?*).

Similarly, if you think a word is misspelled in the manuscript but end up finding it in the dictionary, add it to your style sheet anyway. Just because the word turned out to be spelled and used correctly, that doesn't mean you won't question its nuances in the manuscript's future. It also doesn't mean you'll be the only one who questions its spelling and usage. It's always better to be safe than sheepish. Have confidence in your questions — and in your consideration for those who may have those same questions themselves.

Noting essential issues

Every document is unique, but you can bet your bottom dollar that a few issues arise again and again whether you're copyediting books, Web sites, or technical manuals. Stay on red alert for the following essentials:

 ✔ **Numbers:** You'll be surprised at how many numbers find their way into even the most narrative of manuscripts. With house style firmly in hand, you'll decide and document on your style sheet how they're styled in sums of money (60 cents or $0.60), four-digit numbers (8000 or 8,000), dates (11 February 1998 or February 11, 1998 or 2/11/98 or . . .), and cross-references (pp. 291–298 or 291–8). You'll also note the range of numbers to spell out (usually one through nine or one through ninety-nine).

✔ **Special display:** Boldfaced and underlined text may appear in designed headings, thanks to your typesetting codes (see Chapter 16). But the bulk of your special display decisions will involve the use of italic. Will you italicize all foreign words (even though italic is rarely used for some Spanish words, such as España)? Will you use italic to express sounds, remembered speech, and thoughts? *Will I, for that matter? It appears so.* And how about using italic to denote letters as letters (such as the letter *s*), words as words, emphasis — *emphasis,* TV shows, and magazines? Song titles, too, or should those be in quotes? With house style as your guide, it's up to you to suggest what's best for the book and to note it on your style sheet.

✔ **Reference sources used:** If you find yourself delving into any source other than the house-specified dictionary and style manual to make your style decisions, it's always good to note where you confirmed a definition, style, or historical fact — whether it's a hardcover tome, online database, *New York Times* best-seller, or obscure leaflet. This documentation helps if you have to further research the issue moving forward or if someone is conscientious enough to want to double-check your work.

✔ **Punctuation:** Some copyeditors divvy punctuation decisions into individual style-sheet sections (Acronyms, Dashes, and so forth), but there are a *Chicago Manual of Style*'s worth of potential issues and a dwindling supply of trees. I recommend consolidating your punctuation choices under the heading of Punctuation and bulleting each issue underneath it. Common punctuation decisions include the following:

- Will you use serial commas (here, there, and everywhere)?

- How will you treat possessives of pronouns ending in *s*?

- Are you using three-dot ellipses only? Or should your style include four-dot ellipses?

- Will you place a comma after *Hence* or *Thus*?

- Will you allow sentences ending in prepositions to maintain the narrator's conversational tone or the author's conversational style?

You may also have to address acronyms, quotation marks, and hyphenation (Oh my!), as well as abbreviation and capitalization. Just follow the yellow brick road and jot down any punctuation ambiguities you see along the way. (For helpful reminders about how to use punctuation, click your heels three times and see Chapter 12.)

✔ **Design notes:** This section may also be labeled Typography or Typesetting codes. No matter what it's called, it always consists of the same information: the keys to all the design codes you've added to the manuscript (assuming this is part of your job). Each code (or tag) improves organization by adding emphasis through design. Common codes include CT (Chapter Title), CN (Chapter Number), FMH (Front Matter Head), BMH (Back Matter Head), A (First-Level Heading), B (Second-Level Heading), and NL (Numbered List). See Chapter 16 for a full discussion of typecodes and their usage.

✔ **Word list:** In this section you note not only every word involving a style decision, but also every word that you weren't sure was being used correctly — even if it ended up being correct. Because you took the time to look the word up in the house dictionary, do your proofreaders a favor and let them know you did so in your style sheet. There's a good chance they'll have similar questions, so you'll save them a trip to the dictionary.

Your dictionary also comes in handy with word issues involving continuity. For example, if a book manuscript is set in the 1930s, you want to note and confirm the author's incorrect reference to a UFO — because the first recorded use of that term in English didn't appear until 1953.

Alphabetize this section. Doing so helps prevent the same word from being included twice with different spellings, and it helps you double-check words in a flash. Alphabetizing correctly is so important that copyeditors also refer to the Word List as the *Alpha List*. (If you're not sure how to alphabetize certain entries, such as names that begin with numerals, follow the alphabetization guidelines in your house style guide.)

Listing additional issues

All publishing projects more than a few pages long benefit from a style sheet, but not all projects require the same style sheet sections. You have to note only what you find and only what isn't addressed by house style. In the previous section, I list style sheet categories you're more than likely to require for every project. Here, I note other possibilities that may or may not be applicable depending on the specifics of your document:

✔ **Locations:** Some copyeditors include all nouns (people, places, and things) in the Word List section, but if you find a lot of locations in your manuscript — whether they're real or fictitious — it's best to give them their own section.

✔ **Characters:** If a book or short story has fewer than five characters, you could tuck them into your Word List, too, but boy is it handy to refer to a single list of characters as the author introduces you to each new one. Don't forget to add an *a.k.a.* if a character has a nickname or an alias.

✔ **Foreign terms:** Especially if your document is academic or otherwise specialized, you may want to pull foreign terms out of your Word List and give each type its own convenient section (Italian Terms, Hebrew

Terms, and so forth). Foreign terms that have Anglicized their way into your house dictionary don't have to be set in italic, and they can remain in your Word List section.

✔ **Tables:** House style may state how to style tables. If not, maintain consistent styles for column heads and table notes throughout your manuscript by including them on your style sheet and citing an example.

✔ **Lists:** Whether lists are embedded in the narrative or extracted in outline form, you may need to decide how to mark each item. Asterisks or letters? Numbers or bullets? Note that you aren't making design decisions here; if house style specifies how to treat the type of list in question, you don't need to note anything on your style sheet. But if you're making a judgment call about how to treat a certain list, note your decision on the style sheet. See Chapter 16 for details on dealing with lists.

✔ **Small caps:** If there's any question whether to use small caps in a given circumstance, note your decision on the style sheet. (Small caps are often used for AM and PM; for slogans; for logos, emblems, and signs; and for newspaper headlines.)

✔ **Treatment of Web sites:** Do you include the "http://" or start URLs off with "www"? Should you bypass the period at the end of a Web link that ends a sentence because readers may mistakenly type it into their Internet browsers? (I'd advise you to include the period and give the readers some credit, but if house style doesn't address this issue, ask the assigning editor what to do.)

✔ **Footnotes:** Provide style samples of footnotes used in the manuscript, preferably one for each type of source credited (such as book, periodical, and Web site).

✔ **Bibliography:** Same for the bibliography section: Provide one style sample for each genre referenced.

✔ **Captions:** Do you end captions with periods? Do you write them in the present tense? Do you use labels of *left* and *right* even if there are only two people in the photo? If any of these decisions are left up to you, include them on the style sheet.

✔ **Special symbols:** Unless you're copyediting math or science books (in which case this section may be substantial), the only special symbols you're likely to come across are diacritical marks (é, ñ, and so forth). Noting "European diacritics" is usually all it takes to keep these symbols consistent and easily confirmed.

Wherever possible, show your style choices instead of telling them. Using specific examples from the manuscript illustrates your style sheet entries. Instead of noting just "en dash for dualisms," add the phrase that inspired your style decision (for example, *their love–hate relationship*).

Also, to save time later, you may want to note the page number where a word or style issue first appears, especially if you think there may be a future question about it. Even if you're copyediting electronically and plan to use the global search feature (see Chapter 17) for changes document-wide, noting these page numbers on your style sheet may still come in handy.

Proofreading Your Baby

I know, I know. Like you need more work to do. But your copyediting career could very well be done with if you don't. Remember, the style sheet is your most vital and most visible of documents. Your employer or client knows this. And your employer or client knows that you know this. So any mistake that you miss on the style sheet is ten times the red flare of missing something in the document.

Word travels as fast as your style sheet gets forwarded. If you're working on a book, it's seen and scrutinized not just by your assigning editor but by the author, the compositor, the proofreader, and anyone else these folks think may get a big ol' guffaw at reading a typo on your style sheet.

Don't cower in fear — just be extra thorough about proofing your style sheet because the stakes are so darn high. Searching for spell-check marks isn't enough. You want to catch an "on" that should be an "of" and an "it's" that should be an "its." You want to catch a misspelled book title or author's name. You want to be sure your epic-length "Alpha List" is correctly alphabetized right through to its *zebra-striped* stockings.

Sampling Style Sheets

All style sheets come with leeway regardless of genre. I've seen different section names, orders, and hierarchies, but these samples are good reference points. Just keep in mind that each document is unique, and each style sheet should be, too.

Figure 15-1 shows a sample style sheet for fiction, Figure 15-2 a sample style sheet for nonfiction, Figure 15-3 a sample style sheet for a specialized manuscript, and Figure 15-4 a sample style sheet for a Web site.

Style Sheet for *Fiction Book Title*
Copyeditor: Jane Copyeditor (jane@janecopyeditor.com)
Date: 4/11/07

REFERENCE SOURCES USED:
Merriam-Webster's Collegiate Dictionary, 11th ed. [*W11*]
The Chicago Manual of Style, 15th ed. [*CMS*]
Words into Type, 3rd ed. [*WiT*]
International Trademark Association Checklist (www.inta.org)
Internet Movie Database (www.imdb.com)

NUMBERS:
Spell out numbers up to one hundred, except in specific dates ('60s, 1980, August 10), times
(3:01; *but* six P.M.), dollar amounts ($20 million), and with percent (15 percent)
Spell out numbers in dialogue; use numerals in narrative
Age: nine years old; a nine-year-old

GENERAL NOTES:
* Americanize spelling; use *W11* first-listed spelling (see word list below for specifics)
* An adverb ending in "ly" followed by a particle or adjective is always open: i.e. "highly publicized" *not* "highly-publicized"
* Compound adjective takes hyphen only when needed for clarity: "sorry-ass bicep" (p. 6), "four-act dramas" (p. 12), *but* stainless steel knife (p. 15)
* Compounds with *well, ill, better, best, little, lesser,* and *least* are hyphenated before the noun, open after the noun, and open if modified by an adverb
* Italics for thoughts, remembered speech, words as words, emphasis, TV shows, magazines, sounds
* Song titles in quotes
* Small caps for A.M., P.M.; also signs (REGENT THEATRE; WELCOME TO ACTORS CONNECTION)
* Use serial comma
* Comma before terminal *too*; around internal *too*
* No commas around names with Jr. or Sr. ("Martin Luther King Jr. is…") (per *Chicago Manual* 8.55 and author's preference)
* Initials: T. S. Eliot; FAO Schwarz
* Possessives: Atlas's, The Jones's, *but* Jesus', Moses'

WORD LIST:
afterglow (n.), 53
ball breaker (n.), 71
The Bright Beacon [newspaper], 222
caller ID, 2
child care (n.); child-care (before noun), 8
crème brulée, 93
Donegan's [w/apostrophe], 82
dominoes, 152
farther [for distance; otherwise "further"], 123
gateposts, 92
geode (n.), 174
grownups (n.), 52
7-Up, 51
Sheetrock [trademark], 18
soulless (adj.), 338
sunroof, 12
1040s [forms], 21
toodle-loo, 152
trash cans, 65
Williams-Sonoma [*not* William], 141
woohoo [exclamation], 221
X-ray (adj.); X ray (n.), 72

LOCATIONS:
Albuquerque, 13
Baton Rouge, Louisiana, 56
Delhi, CA, 45
East Hill Farm, 196
L.A. [city], 5

CHARACTERS:
Chuck Tucker [fireman], 214
Cindy Ivy Vahane, 32
Devalle Ann Crumb [*aka* Great Aunt Dev], 167
Gregory Etheart [*aka* G], 11
Poddonbook [cat], 11
Violet Tesori [*known as Vi to her family*], 5

DESIGN KEYMARKS:
FMH—Front Matter Head, pp. v, vi
CN—Chapter Number, 1, 8, 29, 46, 63, 84, 90, 98, 123, 139, 204 (11 chapters total)
CT—Chapter Title, 1, 8, 29, 46, 63, 84, 90, 98, 123, 139, 204 (11 chapters total)
BMH—Back Matter Head, p. 501

Figure 15-1:
A sample style sheet for a work of fiction.

Style Sheet for *Nonfiction Book Title*
Copyeditor: Joe Copyeditor (joe@joecopyeditor.com)
Date: 4/11/07

REFERENCE SOURCES USED:
Merriam-Webster's Collegiate Dictionary, 11th ed. [*W11*]
The Chicago Manual of Style, 15th ed. [*CMS*]
Words into Type, 3rd ed. [*WiT*]
Bartlett's Familiar Quotations, 17th ed.
The World Factbook, 2003
Internet Movie Database (www.imdb.com)
Publication Manual of the American Psychological Association. 5th ed. [*APA*]

PERMISSIONS/CREDITS:
4 lines of poetry from *God's Silence* by Franz Wright (MS p. 29)
Illustration from Kevin Slavin (MS p. 212)

NUMBERS/DATES:
15 April 2001
See pp. 245–322 (en dash, repeat all digits)

STYLE NOTES:
• Serial comma (*town, city, and state*)
• Americanize spelling; use *W11* first-listed spelling (see word list below for specifics)
• Abbreviate U.S. but all other acronyms without periods
• "their" after "anybody" and "everybody"
• lc party (*Republican party*)
• All narration describing surveillance in past tense
• Foreign phrases and terms in italics (unless in Webster's)
• Hyphen: compound military titles (*Lieutenant-General John Rosa*)
• Spell out numbers up to nine

TYPESETTING TAGS:
[CN] chapter number
[CT] chapter title
[CST] chapter subtitle
[CEP] chapter epigraph
[CES] chapter epigraph source line
[A] first-level head
[B] second-level head

FOOTNOTES:
R. Graves, *Title of Book* (City: Publisher, date), 78
C. Soler, "Title of Article." *Publication Name* (date): 12-16

BIBLIOGRAPHY:
Graves, Rebecca. *Title of Book*. City: Publisher, date.
Soler, Christopher. "Title of Article." *Publication Name* (date): 10–21.

FOREIGN LANGUAGE TERMS:
allons-y, 94
fou, 13
merde, 135
zut alors, 46

Figure 15-2:
A sample
style sheet
for a work of
nonfiction.

WORD LIST:
dot-com, not dot.com or dot com
9/11 attacks
OK, not okay
online, not on-line
10-Adam-12
Web site, not website or Website

Style Sheet for *Scholarly Biblical Studies Monograph*
Copyeditor: Ann Delgehausen, Trio Bookworks (ann@triobookworks.com)

PRIMARY REFERENCES:
The Chicago Manual of Style, 15th edition
Merriam-Webster's Collegiate Dictionary, 11th edition
The SBL Handbook of Style

TYPESETTER NOTES:
Tags
[A] A-head
[B] B-head
[CBib] Chapter biblical reference
[CN] Chapter number
[CT] Chapter title
[EXT], [/EXT] Extract
[PN] Part number
[PT] Part title

Overall
1. Four illustrations appear in the German edition. Their locations are now identified in the manuscript.
2. Biblical translations are numbered lists; keep an eye out for imported style problems.

STYLE:
1. Greek transliterations: (a) English word first with Greek in italics inside parentheses immediately afterward as often as possible. (b) if Greek should be first, follow immediately with English in roman inside parentheses and quotation marks at first use within a chapter. More than one English word is fine, of course. If we follow this practice, a glossary will not be necessary.
2. Use *SBL* biblical abbreviations, even in running text.
3. Series of biblical citations: (a) "*par/r.*" used to indicate that there are parallels (b) semicolons okay within parentheses (c) use "and" in place of last semicolon in running text.
4. "Matthew"/"Mark"/"Luke": Use quotation marks when names are used to represent the authors of these documents.
5. Use serial comma.
6. Works by other authors that [Author] *discusses* have a footnote after the author's name in the running text and then in-text page numbers in parentheses following each quotation. Volume numbers are provided in the in-text citations.
7. Extracts must be at least six manuscript lines long.
8. Personification of the text is allowed (e.g., "The text wants to emphasize . . .").

TERMS AND NAMES:

apocalyptic (n., ch8)	Gentile Christian (adj., ch7)	realia (n., ch9)
Body of Christ (as community, ch8)	Messiah (Jesus)	realpolitik (ch22)
church, the (ch8)	New Testament (and First Testament)	Roman empire
Decalogue (ch7)	Pharisaism (ch1)	Scripture (ch2)
Flood, the (ch3)	Pharisee	Western world (ch9)

GREEK AND HEBREW TERMS:
All Greek and Hebrew terms should be translated upon first use in a section.

anaideia, persistence (ch23)	*ketubah*, what is owing to her (ch09)
daneion, loan (ch25)	*zedaka*, "alms" (ch19)

NOTES:
• Short-title style throughout (taking bibliography into account), not only after a first full reference
• Used full main title, not an abbreviation, for short titles

BIBLIOGRAPHY:
• German edition first, then English for English translations of German originals
• Deleted German translations of English-original works
• Short publisher names; kept ampersands in publisher names where appropriate

This style sheet has been substantially reduced in length by the author and reformatted by the publisher. It is printed with permission. To see a fuller version of this style sheet in its original form or to look at other style sheets by Trio Bookworks, go to the Editing section of www.triobookworks.com or e-mail Trio at baz@triobookworks.com.

Figure 15-3:
A sample style sheet for a specialized manuscript.

Style Sheet for *BigCorporation.com*
Copyeditor: Your Copyediting Business Name
Contact: Your business e-mail and phone number
Date: 04/11/07

NOTES:
As instructed, I've fixed all errors and implemented all style decisions directly onto the site pages in the staging directory (BigCorporation.com/staging) for your review.

PRIMARY REFERENCE SOURCES:
• *Merriam-Webster's Collegiate Dictionary*, 11th ed. [*W11*]
• *The Associated Press Stylebook and Libel Manual*
• *Wired Style*, 1999

NUMBERS/DATES:
• $15 billion
• 10–15 men (en dash)
• Spell out one through nine and first through ninth
• Always use numerals in scores (a 6–3 victory)
• March 12th, 1973

PUNCTUATION:
• Use serial comma (*cake, cookies, ice cream, and candy*)
• Capitalize both parts of a hyphenated compound in headlines (Mass-Produced Mania)
• Omit second part of hyphenated expressions (three- to four-minute intervals)
• Do not enclose slang terms in quotation marks
• Ellipses: In all instances denote with three dots—with one space before and after each dot.

SPECIAL DISPLAY:
• Use capitals for emphasis and not italics
• Italicize words used as words, but use quotation marks around letters used as letters. (He never pronounced the "r" in *beer*.)

SPECIAL SYMBOLS:
• Leave off diacritic marks (manana, cafe, ubercool)
• Use % instead of percent

TREATMENT OF WEBSITES:
• No period at the end of URLs in context
• Cut http:// from URLs
• Add "www." to URL even if the URL works without it, too

CAPTIONS:
• Use a complete sentence or a tagline (name and title)
• Don't use a period with a tagline
• Keep caption in present tense

TYPESETTING TAGS:
[A] A-level head
[B] B-level head
[BL] bulleted list
[NL] numbered list
[TT] table title
[TCH] table column head
[TB] table body
[EX] extract
[FGC] figure caption

Figure 15-4:
A sample style sheet for a Web site.

WORD LIST:
email, not e-mail
e-zine
homepage, not home page

PCs not PC's
preenrollment
website, not Web site or Website

Putting the Style Sheet into Action

Whether you're the copyeditor who created the style sheet or the proof-reader benefiting from its thoroughness, never underestimate the power of proximity. The closer you are to your style sheet, the quicker you may be to use it. If you're copyediting or proofreading electronically, have your style sheet file open and adjacent to the document, if your screen is big enough to show the split. If you're working on hard copy, keep the style sheet within arm's reach at all times.

As a proofreader, you want to review the style sheet as soon as you get a project. Become familiar with what's on it so you know what to look for from the minute you start the job. And if the length of the document is substantial (you're working on a book manuscript, for example), review the style sheet periodically (between chapters, perhaps). Don't let yourself get to the end of a proofreading job and then discover you've missed something that was spelled out on the style sheet. Maybe you've got house style memorized, but you still have to make sure the copyeditor hasn't identified exceptions. For example, if an author doesn't want to use the serial comma, you'd hate to find that out after you've marked corrections throughout the document.

While proofreading, you may identify terms or other items that you think should be added to the style sheet for the benefit of anyone who will see the document after you. You can certainly make those additions, and you want to identify them so the copyeditor or assigning editor knows to use the updated version of the style sheet going forward.

Chapter 16

Formatting a Manuscript

. . . .

In This Chapter

▶ Understanding what typecoding is

▶ Designing for emphasis

▶ Knowing the basic codes

▶ Preparing for pesky exceptions

. . . .

*I*f you want to copyedit book manuscripts, part of the job is to identify and mark the parts of a manuscript (such as titles, headings, lists, block quotes, and tables) that need to be displayed differently from the body text. Why do you have to do this job? Because the text needs you! You swoop in wearing a cape and save the manuscript from looking like one long block of grayness. You've got the moxie and the means it takes to add visual emphasis to the various elements within books.

Before we delve into how to mark these display elements, I need to clarify some terminology. Let me start with the familiar word *formatting*. We use this word whenever we change the standard typeface by, for example, using bold-faced or italicized type. But the term also applies to the process of identifying the display elements in a manuscript.

After you identify an element that requires special display, you use *typecoding* or *tagging* to communicate to the compositor (typesetter) how to treat that element. (Don't know who the compositor is? Check out Chapter 2.) These terms are closely related. The word *typecoding* is used when you mark a hard-copy manuscript with the appropriate codes to identify display text, and it's sometimes used when the process takes place in an electronic file. But most people in the publishing biz use the word *tagging* to mean typing display codes into an electronic file (and the codes themselves, when placed in an electronic file, are often called *tags*).

Don't know what these mysterious codes are that I'm yammering about? Don't worry — I show you examples of codes in this chapter and explain why and how they're used.

Typecoding, tagging, codes . . . if the terms seem too technical to be any fun, please believe me when I say that formatting a manuscript is a creative process. Artistic, even. You're going to love the codes when you see how much work they save you.

Knowing Just Enough about Design and Composition

Let's take a lightning-quick design tour. This section is like the first hour of a Design and Composition 101 course. You need only the first hour because even the second hour features way more design and composition info than most copyeditors really need to know. Lots of scholarly copyeditor-types will tell you differently, but even the most noxious of naysayers would have to admit: Although it's *nice* for a copyeditor to know a pica from third base, it's by no means necessary.

Peruse a book or article and notice how any special elements are set apart from the regular text. You'll find they're set apart through varying design attributes, such as different font types and sizes; through different-sized margins or different alignments (all the way to the left of the page, or centered, or to the right); and through different many-other-things, all of which you don't need to know.

Here's what you do need to know:

- ✔ **How to notice anything in the manuscript that needs to be set differently from the standard manuscript text (for emphasis, for organization, for display).** Some display elements are obvious, but some aren't. For example, if a manuscript comes to you with headings all in the same font, same size, no distinctions, as a copyeditor, you have to use your judgment to determine which should be a level-one (main) heading, which should be level two (a subhead), and so on. (Obviously, if you have doubts, you need to query.) If there's a list, you may have to study house style to figure out if it should be a bulleted list, numbered list, or checkbox list (and again, query if in doubt).

- ✔ **How to relay that difference to the compositor.** That's what the rest of this chapter is about.

Trust your designer. She knows that 6 picas = 1 inch = 72 points, and she will decide to design your book's chapter titles in, say, 28-point ITC Franklin Gothic Heavy, small caps, indent 5 picas, leading 38 points b/b above and below. Your job is much simpler: Just find the chapter title in the manuscript and code it with a [CT].

In case the compositor doesn't know what [CT] stands for — or more likely, what a less common code stands for — you also note in your style sheet what each of your codes represents ("[CT] chapter title").

That's it. Same goes for all the other special elements of a manuscript or article, and all their accompanying codes.

Meeting the Basic Codes

Most manuscripts require only a short list of codes, but you don't need to memorize even the most basic ones. The publisher will have its own list for you to use; just keep it handy for easy reference. As I explain in the next section, codes may be enclosed in square brackets or angle brackets when typed into an electronic document. On hard copy, you normally circle the code letters instead of enclosing them in brackets.

Following is a list of the most common codes:

- **[CN]:** Chapter number
- **[CT]:** Chapter title
- **[CST]:** Chapter subtitle
- **[CEP]:** Chapter epigraph
- **[CES]:** Chapter epigraph source line
- **[PN]:** Part number
- **[PT]:** Part title
- **[A] or [1]:** First-level head
- **[B] or [2]:** Second-level head
- **[C] or [3]:** Third-level head
- **[D] or [4]:** Fourth-level head
- **[BL]:** Bulleted list
- **[NL]:** Numbered list
- **[CL]:** Checkbox list
- **[MCL]:** Multicolumn list
- **[EX] or [EXT]:** Extract (block quotation)
- **[PX]:** Poetry extract
- **[TT]:** Table title
- **[TCH]:** Table column head
- **[TB]:** Table body
- **[TFN]:** Table footnote
- **[FN]:** Footnote
- **[FGC]:** Figure caption
- **[FGN]:** Figure number
- **[PC]:** Photo caption
- **[PN]:** Photo number
- **[FMH]:** Front matter head
- **[BMH]:** Back matter head

Placing Codes or Tags

While the codes themselves may differ slightly from publisher to publisher, their placement on a hard-copy page or in an electronic file will likely be the same no matter who you're working for:

- ✔ **On hard copy:** When you copyedit on hard copy, a code that is circled goes just to the left of the element to be coded. For example, you would write CST at the beginning of a chapter subtitle and circle the code. With some elements (lists, for example), you have to show where the element begins and ends using angled L-type marks. Look at the section "Hard-Copy Typecoding Sample" toward the end of the chapter to see what I mean.

- ✔ **In an electronic file:** Tags (codes that are typed into electronic files) are placed at the beginning and end of an element that requires display, and they are enclosed within either square brackets or angle brackets. The tag that indicates the end of the element to be displayed must have a *virgule* (forward slash) in front of the letters — that's how the compositor identifies it as an end code. So, for example, you would type [CST] or <CST> in front of a chapter subtitle and [/CST] or </CST> at the end. Check out the section "Electronic Tagging Sample" at the end of the chapter to see tags in action.

When you tag an electronic file, you have a great time-saving tool at your disposal: the macro. A macro is a shortcut that lets you hit one key or click on one icon on your toolbar and execute a series of commands that would otherwise give your fingers cramps. Macros are lifesavers for inputting tags. If you haven't used them before, type "create macros" into the Help menu in Word, or Google "macro" and the name of your software to find instructions for setting them up.

Taking Special Care with Extracts

Extracts — block quotes — require a little extra attention because they're quite common in nonfiction and textbooks, they vary according to their content, and they're often tucked inconspicuously into the running text. It's your job to recognize and rustle them up into display text whenever you feel they'd be better off as designed elements.

You should have no trouble noticing when a quote in the text is way too long to stay there. Anything more than 40 words — about three lines — is too long to be readily followed by readers. In an electronic document, you block it out like so:

As CEO Howard Lackey was always so fond of saying each morning upon entering my office: [EX] "Ah, Andrew, as you can see by my leaden eyes, I was again up late last night doing things that even young chic bachelors like yourself could never dream of. Let me remind you of my 24-hour routine, again. Sleep for eight seconds, get up to see why my beautiful twin baby girls are crying, try every possible solution twice until they stop crying, go back to sleep for eight more seconds."[/EX]

So it may be designed something like this:

As CEO Howard Lackey was always so fond of saying each morning upon entering my office:

> Ah, Andrew, as you can see by my leaden eyes, I was again up late last night doing things that even young chic bachelors like yourself could never dream of. Let me remind you of my 24-hour routine, again. Sleep for eight seconds, get up to see why my beautiful twin baby girls are crying, try every possible solution twice until they stop crying, go back to sleep for eight more seconds.

Don't forget to use your proofreader marks (see Chapter 9) to delete the quotation marks.

Epigraphs

Like extracts, epigraphs are quotations that need to be set off from the main body of text. But here's the difference: An epigraph is set apart no matter what its length because it serves the purpose of setting a theme for a proceeding chapter or section. The epigraph is usually attributed to someone, and both the epigraph and its source should be set apart from other paragraphs by the author. Most epigraphs are chapter epigraphs, so look for 'em right after the chapter title.

Here's how you might tag an epigraph in an electronic file:

[CEP]It's not wise to violate the rules until you know how to observe them.[/CEP]

[CES]T.S. Eliot[/CES]

Don't assume the author knows best in this case. Sometimes authors stray from standard quotation attributes, folding the source line into the running text even when the quotation's function is really that of an epigraph. It's all right to extract this into a standard chapter epigraph: *As T.S. Eliot once said: "It's not wise to violate the rules until you know how to observe them."*

Verse extracts

Also known as a *poetry extract,* the verse extract looks a lot like a block quote except with different alignment and line breaks in the final design. If you're trying to determine whether a piece of text should be a verse extract (rather than a regular extract), here's one clue: Keep an eye out for the slash (/) in running text because sometimes it denotes a poem's line break. Here's an example of how a verse extract may be coded in an electronic file:

> I know she reads poems by Maxwell Delacorte to calm her nerves, so I slipped her a note with a few of her favorite lines tucked in: [PX]"share your address with me and i shall send you sound remedies, / prescripts for serenity, potions for city scribes plagued by / commotion, pinned down in antipodes, pining for butchery / when all that she really needs are soothing soliloquies, / background amenities to set her swift mind at ease."[/PX]

If you delete the quotation marks and insert the [PX] tags as I show here, the compositor will be sure to set the lines apart from the text, to the effect of something like this:

> I know she reads poems by Maxwell Delacorte to calm her nerves, so I slipped her a note with a few of her favorite lines tucked in:
>
> > share your address with me and i shall send you sound remedies, prescripts for serenity, potions for city scribes plagued by commotion, pinned down in antipodes, pining for butchery when all that she really needs are soothing soliloquies, background amenities to set her swift mind at ease.

Letter extracts

If at all possible, gently but persistently nudge editors, authors, and the copyediting deities into allowing you to set off run-in text letters as extracted block quotes. You and I want it set off as displayed text, readers want it as displayed text, the deities — they definitely want it. But authors and the editors who blindly love them often push to keep short letters and short letter excerpts nestled into text.

If you can't get the letter extracted, remember that, as run-in text, the letter's first line begins with open quotation marks (usually the salutation), and each new paragraph begins with open quotation marks. No closing marks appear until the very last line (usually the signature).

For example, here is a letter as run-in text:

"Dear Vendela:

"I am enthralled with your frantic schedule, and with your ability to persevere through even the most frenetic of social settings. We've got to party together. Or scheme together. Or collaborate over lunch and change the world by dinner's aperitif.

"All right, let's just go see the new Jude Law movie. He's dreamy.

"Your friend in waiting,

"Samantha"

And here is its more preferable rendition as soon-to-be displayed text — a most beautiful block quote, *sans* quotation marks:

[EX]Dear Vendela:

I am enthralled with your frantic schedule, and with your ability to persevere through even the most frenetic of social settings. We've got to party together. Or scheme together. Or collaborate over lunch and change the world by dinner's aperitif.

All right, let's just go see the new Jude Law movie. He's dreamy.

Your friend in waiting,

Samantha[/EX]

Extracts even I haven't thought of yet

Every single book or article you edit will surprise you, and you will be astounded by the design elements. You may have an extract that includes a bulleted list. Or an author who wants to use different fonts for different extracts (Luci writes a note in Geneva font, Jay writes a note in Helvetica font). Sometimes you just give up and note to the designer that an element should look "different" or have "special formatting."

The list of possibilities is probably endless, and I'm endlessly curious about them! Please send me examples as you discover them; e-mail tags@SueGilad.com, and I'll be sure to thank and credit you on the book's free newsletter and Web page at www.SueGilad.com.

I've seen — and successfully extracted to safety — e-mails, notes, and various facts and figures desperately wishing they were formatted as tables. I'm eager to hear about your own gallant rescues of other extracts trapped in the running text!

Highlighting Text in Boxes, Sidebars, and Other Cheaters

A book's design will often include a variety of ways to emphasize text other than extracts and lists. For example, the design specifications may include boxed elements, sidebars, pull quotes, margin notes . . . a laundry list of possibilities. If you're working on a book that's part of a series, the house style guide may include guidelines for when to use each option. If you don't have such guidelines, your challenge is to use your editorial judgment to suggest design elements that best bridge any divide between what the author wants to communicate and what the reader takes in.

For example, maybe within the running text you identify a tip that has the potential to change the reader's life (and you know that the author is trying to change lives). The design specs may allow you to code a boxed element to highlight the tip so the reader can't miss it. The result may be something like Figure 16-1.

Figure 16-1: An example of a boxed element.

THE TIP THAT WILL CHANGE YOUR LIFE IN TEN SECONDS OR LESS:
Do this and this and this and this and this and this and this and presto!

If the tip is long enough, perhaps it would do better as a sidebar, which often runs along the side of the running text — see Figure 16-2. (In this book, sidebars are actually boxed elements; they don't run beside the body of the text. Just goes to show that every book design is different.)

Running text running text.

THE TIP THAT WILL CHANGE YOUR LIFE IN TEN SECONDS OR LESS: Do this and this and this and this and this and this and this and this and this and *presto!*

Figure 16-2:
An example
of a sidebar
design.

Keep in mind that the amount of leeway you have to identify and code these types of elements will vary. (Whoever has the final say regarding a book's design — the production editor, the acquisitions editor, or the designer — that person isn't you.) Sometimes you'll have detailed guidelines that you'll be expected simply to implement; in that case, if you find a gem you think should be highlighted but that hasn't been identified in the specs, your job is to flag it for the production editor and suggest what you think may work. Other times (the fun, creative times), you'll be the one to identify all the different parts of a manuscript that may need special treatment (and in this case, the designer will finalize the specifications after you've worked your magic). The production editor will tell you at the start what is needed for a project — and if he doesn't tell you, ask.

Creating Lists

No matter what type of project you're working on, chances are you'll run across a list. It's up to you to identify when lists may work best as run-in texts and when they may need to be elevated to display status. (You then flag each instance for the production editor to review.)

If your publishing house style doesn't address this topic specifically, your best bet is to get your math on. Count three, maybe four, items in a run-in sentence, and then cut that litany off. If the author hits five, there's a good chance you'll serve the reader better by pulling the information from the text and highlighting it as a list, especially in nonfiction and academic texts.

These lists must then be coded in order to appear on the page as bulleted, numbered, or unnumbered lists. Occasionally, you may even see a list requiring check boxes or warranting two or three columns side by side. (Multicolumn lists are double the editorial pleasure because they can also be bulleted, numbered, or unnumbered.)

Bullets versus numbers

A house style manual (see Chapter 14) may specify when to use bullets and when to use numbers in lists. And an author may identify lists and present them as bulleted or numbered in the original manuscript. If you aren't given these sorts of guidelines, your job is to identify text that needs to be set as lists and then suggest to the production editor and designer what type of list you think each should be. (The final decision rests with them.) My advice is stick to bullets no matter what the content of the list is and no matter how many items it contains, unless it falls under one of these exceptions:

✔ **List entries are sequential.** In this case, you've got to do things in a particular order (or else your recipe for Chicken Cacciatore is going to taste a lot like something you don't want to be tasting).

✔ **List entries have some hierarchical order of importance.** If "The Top 10 Steps You Can Take Toward Financial Freedom" starts with the most important thing and ends with the least important of the ten, numbers make sense.

✔ **The author subsequently refers back to one of the items in the list.**

What if I were to note that a few of my favorite things are: traveling, surfing, symphonies, chocolate, chick-flicks, and bumper cars? You bet — bullets, my friend. You could go with an unnumbered list, but bullets seem to be all the rage, as are their many spin-offs: the checkmark, the *x,* the box, the arrow, the diamond.

Let's go back to that paragraph and code both lists. As an equal-opportunity copyeditor, I'll even make the first one unnumbered and the next one bulleted.

What if I were to note that a few of my favorite things are: [UN]traveling, surfing, symphonies, chocolate, chick-flicks, and bumper cars?[/UN] You bet — bullets, my friend. You could go with an unnumbered list, but bullets seem to be all the rage, as are their many spin-offs: [BL]the checkmark, the *x,* the box, the arrow, the diamond.[/BL]

If your list does warrant numbers, and the number of your list items hits double or even triple digits, be sure to align the items properly. Hard-copy heroes will write and circle the instruction "Clear for 10s." This means that when the page is typeset, the space allotted from the number to the first word in the sentence will be based upon the last numeral rather than the first if a numbered list goes into double digits. (Most lists don't go into triple digits, which is why you don't see "Clear for 100s.") If you work on electronic files, you may be expected to align the numbers yourself by using tabs.

For example, this list is incorrectly aligned, according to most house styles:

1. First item

10. Tenth item

100. One hundredth item

I'd like to be the first to welcome you to the correctly aligned list:

  1. First item

 10. Tenth item

100. One hundredth item

 Remember to carefully proofread your lists, too. It gets tricky because the capitalization and punctuation of list items depend on a few different factors. If even just one of the list items is a complete sentence, then all the list items get the complete-sentence treatment: a capital letter kicking it off and a period ending it. However, if all the list items are single words or fragments, then each item may begin with a lowercase letter (except for proper nouns, of course) and end with no mark, or perhaps a comma or semicolon. An exception is if the manuscript features many lists, and some of the lists feature complete sentences. Many publishers treat lists consistently throughout the manuscript.

Lists complications

I'm always amazed how authors come up with new kinds of lists. You may encounter a bulleted list within a numbered list within a sidebar. You can't prepare for every exception. All you can do is be prepared to suggest new list treatments in such situations.

Rare tags

Some tags rarely show up except in specialized texts. I offer a handful here:

- [A"]: A-head in notes section

- [BL2]: Second-level bulleted list with a bullet

- [BLSEC]: Second-level bulleted list without a bullet

- [CBib]: Chapter biblical reference

- [CED]: Cedilla (as in gar[CED]con to tag *garçon*)

- [EQ]: Equation

- [SE]: Special element (for times when you need to just invent a tag and label it *special*)

- [TSQ]: Table squib (for a line that sometimes appears beneath a table title, above the table body, such as "Research conducted under NBDL standards")

Lists within lists? For the record, do try to avoid them whenever possible. And then try one more time. If the house style doesn't address two-tiered lists, and if you absolutely can't avoid them, your best option is to number the outer list and use letters for the interior list.

Hard-Copy Typecoding Sample

Colored pencil? Check. Printed copy of the manuscript? Check. Let the hard-copy typecoding begin.

As I explain in the earlier section "Placing Codes or Tags," codes are penciled in on the left margin of the manuscript or article, and you don't need to include end/closing tags. For extracts, you can just box them in by their left-hand corners. In the sample that follows, I don't include tags denoting the body text (the default), but some publishers may require them.

Ready? Here we go.

(CN) 5. (CT) Shiny Happy Scribes

(CST) Writing for the Fun of It

(CEP) Action is eloquence.

(CES) William Shakespeare

When Will Shakespeare says take action, you take action. He knows that half the battle of writing is just sitting down — finally — and typing/dipping the feather into the inkwell. So dip. You'll be happy you did.

How happy? Well, a completely fabricated study I'm about to cite found the return on writing effort to be astonishing, as clearly mock documented in Table 7.

(TN/TT) Table 7. Happiness Returns on Writing Effort

(TCH) Minutes Spent Writing   % increase in happiness

15	25
(TB)	50	90
74	950*

(TS) Source: Joe Imagination, *His Fake Book* (New York: No Publisher, 2009)

(TFN) * Retest results showed an even higher increase

What synonyms for happy did those percent increases elicit from study participants? The top five most frequently used adjectives were

ecstatic

jubilant

(NL) rosy

right-as-rain

blissful

① Participants Find Benefits Beyond Happiness

② The Case of Sarah Smiley

Ms. Smiley experienced happiness from writing, yes. But researchers were convinced her run-of-the-mill bliss had blossomed into unfettered euphoria when her response to a yes-or-no question was:

(EX) *Yes and no is my answer, and no and yes and yes is my answer, in addition to my answer being both no and yes, because truly I am euphoric with — and unfettered by — all answers. You can try to fetter me. But you'll fail.*

② What Ever Happened to the Happy Brothers?

They're still happy. With nothing but heightened happiness ahead.

Electronic Tagging Sample

I've been peppering you with electronic style tagging throughout this chapter, but here's a chance to see a bunch of those savvy little on-screen codes working in cahoots. In the sample below, there are no tags denoting the running text because it's the default setting.

[CN]5[/CN] [CT]Shiny Happy Scribes [/CT]

[CST]Writing for the Fun of It[/CST]

[CEP]Action is eloquence.[/CEP]

[CES]William Shakespeare[/CES]

When Will Shakespeare says take action, you take action. He knows that half the battle of writing is just sitting down — finally — and typing/dipping the feather into the inkwell. So dip. You'll be happy you did.

How happy? Well, a completely fabricated study I'm about to cite found the return on writing effort to be astonishing, as clearly mock documented in Table 7.

[TN]Table 7.[/TN] [TT]Happiness Returns on Writing Effort[/TT]

[TCH]Minutes Spent Writing % Increase In Happiness [/TCH]

[TB] 15   25

50   90

74   950* [/TB]

[TS] Source: Joe Imagination, *His Fake Book* (New York: No Publisher, 2009) [/TS]

[TFN] * Retest results showed an even higher increase [/TFN]

What synonyms for happy did those percent increases elicit from study participants? The top five most frequently used adjectives were

[NL]ecstatic

jubilant

rosy

right-as-rain

blissful[/NL]

[1]Participants Find Benefits Beyond Happiness[/1]

[2]The Case of Sherry Smiley[/2]

Ms. Smiley experienced happiness from writing, yes. But researchers were convinced her run-of-the-mill bliss had blossomed into unfettered euphoria when her response to a yes-or-no question was:

[EX]Yes and no is my answer, and no and yes and yes is my answer, in addition to my answer being both no and yes, because truly I am euphoric with—and unfettered by—all answers. You can try to fetter me. But you'll fail.[/EX]

[2]What Ever Happened to the Happy Brothers?[/2]

They're still happy. With nothing but heightened happiness ahead.

Chapter 17

Editing and Proofreading Electronically

*I*t all started with a stick and a patch of dirt. Some clever ancestor of ours discovered how to draw a picture that could be viewed by his knuckle-dragging pals. Then came cave paintings, rock chiseling, and painted pottery. When papyrus hit the scene, it pretty much blew everything else out of the water. Well, what paper did to cuneiform on tablets, the computer is doing to paper.

Welcome to the digital age, where it should come as no surprise that a trade as solidly rooted in tree pulp as publishing may soon become paperless. And whether you consider yourself one of the technology illuminati or just fortunate enough to have mastered the reheat button on the microwave, electronic editing may well turn out to be your medium of preference — and could make you your publisher's preferred copyeditor or proofreader.

If you have always associated the written word with the feel of paper in your hands, it may be difficult at first to get used to the fact that, yes, you can read and comprehend written words made out of pixels. Not to worry. Like anything new, it just takes a little practice. Making fire was once considered difficult . . . and look how you mastered the stove top.

Choosing Your Computer Wisely

You don't need to throw out any red pencils, erasers, and sticky notes you may have bought in anticipation of your new career. But if you hope to work from home, whether as a freelancer or as a staff member with telecommuting privileges, you must also invest in the most important tool of all: a computer.

(If your goal is to work in-house for a publisher, you can probably skip straight to the section "Keeping Your Body Happy," because you should have a lovely perk called an Information Technology department to select, set up, and maintain your computer for you.)

Laptop versus desktop

If, like me, you love being able to take your work along with you anywhere, one of your first orders of business will be to invest in a laptop computer. Having a laptop allows you to plop down at any java shack or park bench and exercise the right to be a freelancer or telecommuter. With computer components getting smaller and smaller, the weight of a laptop is getting down to that of a hardcover book. So, if your dream is to get paid to read while sitting in your Barcalounger, today's technology can make your dream a reality.

Using a laptop tends to be harder on your body than using a desktop computer. The reason? When you attain the optimum keyboard placement for your arms and hands, the laptop's screen will be too low. When you position the screen to the proper height, the keyboard will be too high for your hands to be properly positioned. In this chapter, I give lots of advice for making your workspace ergonomically appealing. With a laptop, you may have to just do the best you can.

If you're a masochist or homebody (or perhaps just require a bit of extra discipline), you may want to work at a desk, which means you probably want a desktop computer. If that's your choice, you should definitely invest in accessories that make your workspace friendly to your body. Treat your weary hands to some support in the form of ergonomic wrist rests, and splurge on a firm but cushiony back support and foot rest. (Think of all the money you'll save on chiropractic visits.) Then spend the time to set up your office space in a way that's least stressful on your various parts. I talk much more about how to make yourself comfortable in the upcoming section "Keeping Your Body Happy."

We all scream for wide screen

Slurp that carrot juice, because you're going to need those orbs in your skull to be in tip-top condition for all the reading you'll be getting paid to do.

If you don't want your eyes to take a beating, keep in mind that not all computer monitors are created equal. Most computer manufacturers offer a fairly wide selection of monitors, and you want to have a good one. Not to worry if you don't know a pixel from Pixy Stix. In general, all you need to know about pixels is that you want a whole lot of them! The more of them, the better the picture.

If you'll be doing most of your work at a desk and you have loads of space, you would do well to invest in a larger monitor. It doesn't have to be sports-bar big, but I suggest 17 to 21 inches if your desk can hold it. If space is tight, consider getting a flat-screen monitor; it costs more but takes up lots less room.

If you really want to flex your tech-savvy muscles, get one of those wide-screen monitors that can display two pages side by side. That feature really comes in handy when comparing two versions of a document or when you want to keep your document on screen while going online to check a Web site.

A friend of mine from the photography industry let me in on a trick he uses. A lot of monitors have a color adjustment control, and if you turn down the blues a bit, your eyes won't get tired as quickly.

Keeping Your Body Happy

Lots of professions are associated with injuries. You don't have to be a kick-boxer to get aches and pains from the work you do. The more scientists study injuries in the workplace, the more we learn about the harmful effects of repetitive motions. Computer use is a relative newcomer in the field, affecting the wrists, back, shoulders, and precious, precious eyes. For a crash course in minimizing stress on your body, plant your feet on the floor and read on.

Sit up straight, dear

You want to maintain neutral posture when sitting at your computer, with your back against the chair, your thighs and forearms parallel to the floor, and your wrists at a neutral angle. If you have one of those fancy desk chairs with all the adjustments, adjust it:

✔ Push your hips as far back into the chair as possible.

✔ Adjust the seat height so your feet are flat on the floor and your knees are equal to or slightly lower than your hips. (If the keyboard or mouse height is fixed, the proper chair height may leave your feet not touching the floor. In this case, you need a footrest.)

✔ Adjust the back of the chair to a 100° to 110° reclined angle.

✔ If the chair can be adjusted for back height, adjust it to follow the contour of your back.

✔ If the chair's seat pan can be adjusted, adjust to allow for a two- to four-inch gap between the back of your calf and the front edge of the seat.

✔ Adjust the armrests vertically and laterally so they do not impede typing and mouse use. Forearms and elbows should not continuously rest on the armrests.

✔ Use a footrest if your feet cannot be firmly planted on the ground.

Get your hands up

Now that your chair is adjusted, turn your focus to your keyboard:

✔ Center your keyboard in line with the monitor.

✔ Position your keyboard directly in front of your body and close to you.

✔ Adjust the keyboard height so you can type with your shoulders relaxed, elbows close to your body, forearms parallel to the floor, and wrists fairly straight. (Your upper and lower arms should form 90-degree angles.) Your keyboard height should be level with your elbows when your upper arms are resting against your body.

✔ Make sure your keyboard is flat or has a slight *negative tilt* (meaning the front, or spacebar, edge is higher than the back). Do not work with a *positive tilt* (where the back of the keyboard is higher than the front). You want to maintain a neutral straight position in your wrists, and a positively tilted keyboard forces you to work with your hands bent backward.

Consider getting a height-and-tilt-adjustable keyboard tray, which can provide optimal positioning of the keyboard.

✔ Pad hard surfaces, and use a wrist rest to help maintain neutral posture.

✔ When not using your keyboard, avoid maintaining static hand and wrist positions by moving your hands away.

Give your wrist some help

If you can help it, try using your arm and shoulder muscles a little more when maneuvering your mouse, instead of solely relying on your dainty wrist. Here are some suggestions:

✔ Place your mouse (or other pointing device) at the same elevation and as close as possible to your keyboard. Your posture for mouse use should be similar to your typing posture (meaning a neutral position).

✔ Position your mouse to avoid severely bending your wrist or turning it inward or outward.

✔ When you're not using your mouse, avoid maintaining static hand and wrist positions by moving your hand away.

Look alive

These tips can help your eyes and upper body feel better during an editing or proofreading session:

- ✔ Place your monitor directly in front of you, not angled to the left or right.

- ✔ Center your monitor so your body and neck aren't twisted when viewing the screen.

- ✔ Place your monitor at a horizontal distance where you can read the text clearly, usually 18 to 28 inches away from your eyes (approximately an arm's length). If you squint or bend forward to read text on the monitor, that means the monitor is too far away.

- ✔ Adjust the monitor height so your eyes are aligned with the top quarter of the monitor viewing area. If you wear bifocals or progressive lenses, lower and tilt back the monitor so you can view it without tilting your head back.

- ✔ Use a document holder to position printed materials in your line of vision, close to and at the same height and angle as the monitor.

Break it up

Probably the worst thing you can do for your body is work for hours on end without taking a break. Once every hour, take a three- to five-minute break. Get up off your tush, and shuffle around your area. (Maybe mush a few maca-roons in your mouth, rifle through your inbox, or call your friends to gloat about your glorious job.)

Also give your parts these mini-breaks to help you get through your work unscathed:

- ✔ **Avert those eyes:** Every 15 minutes or so, pull your peepers away from the computer screen to take in the scenery around you. Rapidly blink your eyes — kinda like a crazy person — to moisten and clear your eye surface, and try to focus on objects farther away from you before jump-ing back into your read.

- ✔ **Make like a gorilla:** When not using your mouse or keyboard, let your arms hang at your sides. Change positions frequently, and feel welcome to do your best King Kong "Oooh! Oooh! Oooh!" if you think it will help.

- ✔ **Set the mood, baby:** Lower your blinds or draw those drapes, dim all the lights, and slide that Barry White from its sleeve, because this is gonna be one . . . um, glare-minimizing night for you and your baby blues (or gleaming greens, in my case). Glare is just not good enough for you, honey — you and soft lighting were made for each other. The exception? When you need to reference hard-copy materials. You may want a desk lamp on hand so you can light things up when hard copy comes into play.

Consider a pro's advice

If you want to make sure you're not doing anything to injure yourself, consider talking to the pros. If you work at your computer two or more hours per day, repeat the same movements over and over, or hold the same posture for prolonged periods of time — in other words, if you're an editor or proofreader working electronically! — you can benefit from an ergonomic evaluation.

Ergonomic evaluations help you identify problems with your workstation layout, whether it's at your desk, in your bed, or on your ironing board. Whatever setup you've got, it could contribute to physical discomfort or the risk of repetitive stress injury. Search the Web for an expert near you.

Reading the Electronic Page

Yes, it *feels* different reading text on a screen rather than on a page you physically hold in your hands. Maybe you can't read as quickly either. Or your eyes get tired more quickly than usual.

If you aren't reading online newspapers and blogs each day, proofreading or copyediting an electronic page is likely to take some getting used to. But here's the good news: that bad habit of reading with your fingers you acquired in grade school? Well, you'll finally be forced to break it. You won't be able to put your finger on the page and follow the text line for line — at least not without leaving croissant-grease streaks on your monitor!

Retraining your eye

Not in the habit of reading online? Where have you been living?! Alas, you've nothing to worry your old-school noggin about: You can retrain yourself to read electronic copy just as easily and quickly as if you were reading it from copy in your paws. I suggest starting a daily regimen of reading a few news articles online. Start with reps of two or more articles a day, and gradually work yourself up to four sets. In no time, you'll feel a lot more comfortable and your eyes will have adjusted to the new medium. Feel the burn.

Appeasing your paper partiality

If, like me, you have a strong belief that your reading comprehension is somehow tied to the feel of paper in hand, listen up: There's no law against printing the pages. No, you will not be doing your share to save the environment, but I doubt that Greenpeace will camp out on your front lawn as a result.

Know thy software

If you're just now making your entrée into the world of computers and word processing, welcome! If you've lived in this world before but are now returning after a hiatus, welcome back! Whether you need a crash course on the gamut of computerdom or a light brush-up on the latest advances in Microsoft Word or Adobe Acrobat, you can feel like an expert in no time by flipping through any number of *For Dummies* books on computing and software.

Shameless plug? Actually, it's a prideful plug. Each *For Dummies* book is designed to show you the ins and outs of a particular subject with the consideration of a warm and trusted friend. Don't know a wingding from a ring-a-ding-ding? Check out one of the *For Dummies* books on Microsoft Office. Need something that steps back a bit more? Try one of the all-in-one desk references for PCs or Macs.

Before you rush out and pick up whatever black-and-yellow-bound book your hands land on, do some easy research first. Take a minute to reintroduce yourself to the computer you'll be using most often for editing. Write down whether your computer is a PC or a Mac, and find out both the name and version of the currently running operating system. Go deeper, and record the version of Microsoft Office currently installed. All this is important in making sure that you get the right book for your needs.

Clueless as to how to get to the guts of your computer? If you know whether you use a PC or Mac, this piece of knowledge leads right into your operating system. If you use a desktop or laptop PC, you use some version of Windows. An older PC should be running Windows 98 or higher, while a newer PC will have been preloaded with Windows XP or Vista. To find out

what you're running on, right-click My Computer, select Properties, and click the General tab. To see which version of Microsoft Word you have installed, click Help on the Word toolbar and select About Microsoft Word in the resulting drop-down menu.

If you are a Mac user, you are likely using OS 9 or OS X. To get the goods, go to Finder and click the Apple icon in the left top corner; when prompted, click About This Computer or About This Macintosh — whichever one you see — and a window will open containing what you want. Not able to find the Apple icon in Finder? Then you're using OS X. To discern which version of Microsoft Word you're using, click Word on the Microsoft Word toolbar and select About Word in the resulting drop-down menu.

With all you're capable of, it would be silly to pigeonhole yourself by purchasing a Microsoft Word–only guide. I suggest picking up either *Office 2007 All-in-One Desk Reference For Dummies* by Peter Weverka or *PCs All-in-One Desk Reference For Dummies* by Mark L. Chambers (Wiley). Each gives you the goods not only on Word, but also on Excel, PowerPoint, Outlook, Access, FrontPage, and more.

If you're still in your pajamas, don't get dressed yet; there's plenty of stuff you can find online until you get to your neighborhood bookstore. The Microsoft Office Assistance site at `http://office.microsoft.com/` is full of information on all the programs in the suite. And the best part is it's searchable! You can also browse through articles and hints like "10 tips to save time in Excel" and "Formatting made simple," and you can get answers from other Office users.

I must whisper a word of caution here: You won't make the most efficient use of your time if you edit on paper first because you still have to copy your edits to the electronic version. The extra step may add more chance for error to the process, too. Accuracy and timeliness definitely count, so your best bet in the long run is to train your eyes to read from the computer.

Hey, I did it — and I haven't purchased a new toner cartridge all month!

Touring the technology benefits

So, what's in it for you? Why should you get on board with this paperless trend in editing?

While you may be resistant at first, after you take the plunge, you'll see clearly how this medium can make your life as a proofreader or copyeditor much easier. I go into more detail later in the chapter, but bottom line is that your computer software has some great tools that save you a lot of time and help you catch errors.

Plus, like your family photo albums, publishing has gone digital. That means the entire production workflow has changed. It is becoming the norm for publishers to work with electronic copy from the beginning of the production process to the end (see Chapter 2), and you want to be sure that process doesn't pass you by.

Mastering the Electronic Process

It may seem ironic that a publisher of printed materials would go to the trouble of refashioning the traditional, paper-pushed production process into an electronic one. This change has little to do with a future-forward mindset or a granola-crunching concern about saving trees. Instead, the motivation is — shocker — money. Publishing companies have adopted electronic technologies to streamline and enhance their production processes, thereby saving steps and printing costs and increasing the all-important bottom line. Singing the copy electric also leaves more time for the editors to go to lunch, shop, and debate wide misuse of the apostrophe . . . or (more likely) to work on more projects.

Most of the skills I advocate elsewhere in this book apply to the electronic-editing process, but marking up the copy will feel a little different. If you're proofreading electronically, for example, all those squiggly proofreading marks I present in Chapter 9 won't be needed where you're going.

Saving your files (and your tuchis)

Before we go anywhere, repeat after me: I will always save a copy of the original, unblemished document *before* I begin pawing at it. Thereafter, I will always save versions so others may see the stages of editing, if they so desire. How do you do this? Before you begin editing or proofreading, save the original document with a new title, selecting Save As and writing over or modifying the existing name. For example, if the original document is titled *Ch17.doc*, save the new document to be edited as *Ch17_SueGilad.doc*. Wait, that's *my* name — use your name instead.

To save subsequent versions or editing phases, simply save the document as a new document, adding additional information — a version number or a date in shorthand — to the end of the document name: *Ch17_YourName.v2.doc,* for instance, or *Ch17_YourName.Oct1507.doc.*

Be sure to check with the publisher about naming conventions that you should follow. Some companies have very specific file-naming guidelines they want you to use.

Seeing your document clearly

Before you begin editing or proofreading, make sure you can see the text on your screen clearly. If the words are too tiny for you to take in, enhance their appearance by increasing the overall view of your document through the Zoom function. (Often this is a drop-down menu containing various view percents and is located on your general shortcut toolbar.) Using Zoom does not change the actual font size of the document; instead, it acts like a pretty precise magnifying glass atop the document itself. If you can't see a document clearly when it appears at 100 percent, for example, try changing the view to 120 percent or higher.

You can also manipulate your monitor's brightness and contrast features, making a huge difference in the appearance of the text.

It's *tres* important that you do not fudge around with the actual font size of a document to get a clearer view of the words. Instead, stick with the Zoom tool or play around with your monitor's features to get what you want without compromising the integrity of the document itself.

Tracking your changes in Word

Your publisher contact will most likely ask that you use a neat little editing feature called Track Changes, available in Microsoft Word. The designers of Microsoft Word assumed that not everybody wishes to keep tabs on each little change within a document, so you need to turn this feature on before you begin editing.

There are different ways to access the Track Changes feature depending on the age of the software and which platform you're using (Mac or PC). The simplest way to find out where your Track Changes function is located and how to enable it is to do a search for it in the Help menu. When the function is working, you'll see *TRK* on the bar at the bottom of your document. Ta-dah!

When it's enabled, the Track Changes feature records every edit you make to the text, formatting, and spacing of the document. The feature also keeps track of the fact that *you* are the one making the edits. That way, if a document is passed through several people before returning to the author or editor, that person can scroll through and see who made what changes.

Before beginning any project, you want to review the default preferences for the Track Changes feature. Though you can change the look and color of revision marks to whatever you'd like, most editors require that you track your changes in red. Lucky you, this is exactly the color that Microsoft Word defaults to for edits.

If you find the edit marks distracting while you read, you can opt for a more normal view of the document while still tracking all your edits. Again, the Help menu is your best resource for determining how to hide the edit marks in your particular software.

As with any software feature, the more you wade around in all that Track Changes has to offer, the more you'll be able to tailor its features to meet your needs. Put in some practice with the program: Create a dummy document and start making some changes; see how the software handles your additions and deletions of letters, words, and spacing.

Viewing formatting

Another tool you may want to turn on is Show Formatting. Depending on the version of your Microsoft Word, you may find a shortcut button for this feature on your toolbar; it looks like a paragraph symbol (that's a backward *P*), and clicking it once turns the tool on.

This trusty tool allows you to view paragraph symbols, spacing dots, line breaks, and the like. How does this help you? These symbols act as a cheat sheet in spotting common formatting errors, like two (or more) spaces after a period. (Quick note: The use of two spaces after a period is generally regarded as a holdover from the days of typewriters. Use one space. Another quick note: The Replace function can be your best friend when you find that a document has formatting errors. See the upcoming section "The Find, Replace, and Search functions.")

The first pass: Correcting errors

Correcting errors in an electronic document is as easy as doing what you always do with Microsoft Word. Want to delete a word? Position your cursor and backspace over it. Need to add a letter? Position your cursor and get typing. Need to delete a large amount of text? Use your mouse to highlight the chunk of words you want to banish and delete, delete, delete. Seriously, if you've ever worked with word-processing software, you've already got most of the skills to do this job.

So, ready to begin? You'll take several passes at the material, but at first, you want to take stock of the *feel* of the work. Think about the author's writing style and the publisher's format while you try to get a feel for the whole she-bang. While you work on getting into the groove, cross-check the text against the publisher's instructions and the style sheet, if one was given to you.

During the first pass, make only essential edits, such as correcting grammar, spelling, and punctuation errors. If you find that you need to undo an edit you performed, simply go to the Edit dropdown list on your toolbar and click Undo (or Undo Typing). Voilà!

The second pass: Digging deeper and adding comments

On your second editing pass, peck through the surface of spelling and gram-mar and wade a bit deeper into the mechanics of the language and the unifor-mity of the document's format. Keep in mind the author's voice, the work's audience, and the publisher's house style, just as you would during a hard-copy edit. Mark corrections when you feel certain that you've identified something inconsistent or inaccurate, and insert comments — the electronic version of queries — for the author or editor whenever you spy something a bit more complex that may need attention.

How exactly do you insert comments into an electronic document? First, a bit of visualization: On hard copy, you'd write a query on a sticky note, right? The same concept applies here: You place a virtual sticky note smack up against the word or phrase you have questions about.

When you bump up against a query-worthy spot, click the New Comment icon on your Reviewing toolbar. The highly intuitive robots that run Track Changes will add a balloon in which to place your comment. Type your query into the comment balloon, and you're done! And keep in mind that you're not limited to short comments; the balloon can stretch to be as large as you need if you've got lots of questions or concerns. (See the nearby sidebar "Keeping your comments clean" for ideas about how to comment on changes you're making or suggesting.)

As a bonus, your computer keeps track of who added the comment to the document. How is this a bonus? After a manuscript has been reviewed by a handful of editors, a proofreader, and maybe the author herself, a quick scroll through the document reveals who made what comments. Very useful, indeed. (To make sure your name or initials identify your edits or comments, use the Help tab to search for the User Information function.)

Keeping your comments clean

There's nothing wrong with making changes to an electronic document; that's what copyeditors and proofreaders are paid to do. But sometimes it's best to explain what you're doing. That way, when your author reads an edit of yours and grunts, "Why did she change the type of alcohol?" he'll see your note that says, "Since the protagonist is making a martini, consider having him pick up a bottle of *gin* or *vodka*, rather than *scotch*."

Keep in mind that a comment is not an open critique of the author's work. You should use the Comment function to politely query the use of a word or make a recommendation that will result in clearer format or meaning.

Sometimes you'll read a phrase and not have a clue what the author meant to impart; even the best authors can occasionally lapse into incomprehension. (If you don't believe me, read Faulkner's *The Sound and the Fury*.) No matter how bad the text may be, resist the urge to jokingly suggest medication. Your comments should always be legitimate and professional. Whether the comment is meant to advise of erroneous word usage, query a double meaning, or recommend a change, the best approach is to say it with a high level of respect and tact.

Keep in mind that the Comment feature isn't limited to author queries, so you should always begin a comment by identifying who you want to read it. Comments can also be addressed to the assigning editor or to the typesetter (compositor). Begin each comment with *Au:*, *Ed:*, or *Comp:* to avoid confusion.

Thinking globally: Functions you can't live without

Gather around the fire, because we've come to the most oh-so-fabulous feature of electronic editing: the glorious global. The list of reasons I love global functions is long and begins with these awesome features: global Find, global Replace, global Search, and global spell-checker.

You're going to like this aspect of electronic editing so much that I bet you'll shell out money for an I LOVE GLOBAL T-shirt. If there's any reason you should prefer to work with pixels over paper, it's this one.

The Find, Replace, and Search functions

Consider this example: You're editing a fiction story, and you're nearing the middle of the manuscript. The author describes your heroine punching out on the clock at her hospital job. Now, you're sure that earlier she was described as a cab driver, not a hospital employee. Which is it? Global Find to the rescue!

If you're working with a large electronic document, you can forget about sifting through pages in a panic for confirmation. Simply click the Edit drop-down menu on your Microsoft Word standard toolbar, and select Find. In the resulting pop-up box, type the word or phrase you wish to find in the Find What field. For the above example, you could type *cab* to see if your memory was correct. If that word doesn't produce any results, don't stop there: Type in such similar words as *taxi* or *drive* to see what comes up. A-ha! She *is* described as a cab driver, but now what? Flag the first instance for a query, then click the Find Next button in your pop-up box to see every instance where that word is used.

Now, let's say you've noticed a few instances of *teh* — the mistyped, backward cousin of *the* — peppered here and there throughout the document. Under the same Edit drop-down menu in which Find can be found, there's a selection called Replace. Clicking Replace pulls up a similar box as Find but with an additional field: Replace With. Here, you'd type *teh* in the Find What field and *the* in the Replace With field, and then you'd click the Replace button. Voila! Instant correction. If you don't want to go through the hassle of replacing the typos one by one, you can click the Replace All button, and in every single place the bastard cousin appears, its correct relative will replace it. (If only family members were so easy to replace.)

The beauty of global Find or global Replace is that you can search to your brain's content. Want to check that the author used semicolons correctly throughout the work or make sure she was not too overzealous with exclamation points? Use the Find tool, and search for semicolons or exclamation points. Need to change those errant *Moron*s into *Moran*s? Use Replace to change each instance with one click. Are you starting to appreciate how awesome these functions are?

If that's not great enough, you can use the global Search function to locate words or phrases that appear in multiple documents. Let's say that you need to change *Morons* to *Morans* in 27 individual chapter files. Instead of going through each file individually to find *Morons,* you can search an entire folder for that word. How? Right-click on the folder, and select Search. Type in the word or phrase you're looking for, and hit the Search button. You'll get a list of the files in which the word or phrase appears.

The glamorous, glorious global not only covers your *if*s and *and*s; it can also cover the tender skin of your butt. I've used it to do this very thing many, many times. For example, after proofreading one manuscript, yours truly was advised by her editor that there were a number of instances of double spaces after periods — a no-no in the publishing world. Fortunately, I was given a chance to correct this oversight on the second proof, where I relied on global replace to assist me in the search for double spaces. I simply typed two character spaces into the Find What field and typed one space into the Replace With field; clicking Replace All solved everything, and clicking it yet again confirmed that there were no more double spaces to be replaced. Perfecto!

Sit and check for a spell

You can also go global with spell-checker. Why not let the computer do some of the work while you save your eyes for more important things? As with many software tools, there is a limit to this function's usefulness, and you certainly can't sit back and let it do everything. But global spell-checker is great for catching ridiculous typos. This function — Spelling and Grammar — lives under Tools on your Microsoft Word general toolbar.

Beyond the everyday spotting of misspelled words, spell-checker is incomparable when it comes to finding subtle differences in the spelling of character names, places, and other proper nouns not in the dictionary. The Ignore All option is your pal here. For example, say you run the spell-checker and the correctly spelled *Katharine* appears. Click Ignore All, which instructs the spell-checker to remember that spelling so it will not appear as an error again, at least not in this particular spell-checker run. That way, if the spell-checker stops on a word that looks like *Katharine,* you know it must contain an error. (Perhaps you've got *Katherine* instead.)

Keyboard shortcuts

Keep these keyboard-shortcut keys handy while electronic editing, and leave the mouse to better things.

Function	Working on a PC?	Working on a Mac?
Make letters bold	CTRL+B	⌘+B
Make letters italic	CTRL+I	⌘+I
Underline letters	CTRL+U	⌘+U
Remove character or word formatting	CTRL+Spacebar	CONTROL+ Spacebar
Find	CTRL+F	⌘+F
Replace	CTRL+H	SHIFT+⌘+H
Save current document	CTRL+S	⌘+S
View document formatting	CTRL+Q	⌘+8
Run spell-check	F7 key	OPTION+⌘+L

It goes without saying, but let me say it anyway: Spell-checker is not a substitute for actual proofreading. The lists of homonyms that slip through the net are endless; then there's the occasional word that, although spelled correctly, doesn't quite fit the context. If you think *Thank you for mating with me* is bad, think about how red your face would be if you didn't catch that missing *l* in *public.*

Formatting documents

If you're asked to format an electronic document, start with the most obvious part: the margins. Your editor or publishing house should provide page-layout parameters, which you can set using the Page Setup function under File.

If you need to insert tags (the electronic version of codes) to identify design elements in a document, be sure to read Chapter 16 where I cover the subject in detail. You may be asked to work in a document template instead, which means that instead of coding you'll be formatting each text element using a set of established type styles. (Templates may come into play if you work on branded titles, for example; see Chapter 2 for an explanation of branding.)

Your other formatting responsibilities may include reviewing indents, line breaks, and spacing for uniformity.

When engaged, the Track Changes feature records any changes you make to the format of a document, just as it does for your changes to the text.

Adding page numbers, running heads, feet, and footnotes

Microsoft Word makes these functions fairly simple; if you can locate them, you can easily use them to achieve whatever the publisher requests. If you have any trouble locating them based on what I've written here (because functions can vary from one version of software to the next), visit your Help menu and search for the function in question. Here are the basics:

- **Page numbers:** Click on the Insert drop-down menu on your Microsoft Word general toolbar and search for Page Numbers. Select their position and alignment based on the publisher's specifications. Easy!

- **Running heads and/or feet:** If the publisher wants you to add running heads and/or feet to the document (see Chapter 13 if you don't know what these terms mean), go to the View drop-down menu and select Header and Footer. You can insert a chapter name, book title . . . whatever the publisher requests.

- **Footnotes:** If the work you're plugging through contains footnotes (see Chapter 5 for a full discussion), go to the Insert drop-down menu and look for the Footnote function (which may be tucked under Reference).

Proofreading and copyediting PDFs

So far in this chapter, I've focused on editing and proofreading in Word. However, there's a whole other world out there in terms of electronic workflow, and it revolves around the PDF.

PDF stands for *Portable Document File* and refers to a file that has been converted from any other document type (such as Word) and can be reviewed using any of the Adobe software programs. PDFs are often used for documents that contain graphics and complex layouts because they preserve the look of the document better than Word files can. That means that if you work on magazines, newsletters, corporate communications, and other graphics-heavy publications, you are likely to be proofreading PDFs after the text has been through copyediting and has been set in the layout. And even though the editing functions in PDFs are pretty limited, copyeditors are increasingly finding themselves having to deal with PDFs too.

You're probably aware that the Adobe Reader program is available online and can be downloaded for free. Unless you work primarily on PDFs, you can get away with not plunking down the money for Adobe Acrobat Professional or Adobe InDesign (each of which allows much more complex markup and manipulation of graphics). A production editor who creates a PDF in one of these programs can, as an administrator, set the document to allow markup. Then you can use the basic functions to add or delete text and add comments.

As I write this, Adobe has just released version 8 of its Reader software, but versions 6 and 7 are still being widely used. The location of the tools has changed in the new version, so I recommend that you use the Help drop-down menu to locate the tools I mention here. Also, only versions 7 and higher of Reader will allow markup.

There is a multitude of ways to mark corrections on a PDF if you have a full version of Acrobat or InDesign, and you'll want to ask your hiring editor what tools he prefers that you use. But if all you have is Reader, these are the three main ones you will use:

- **The Text Edits tool:** The icon for this tool is a capital letter T with a red line through it and an insertion mark (caret) next to it. Use it to add or delete text. Click on the icon, then click your cursor into the text and start typing. A note window will appear that shows your edits.

- **The Highlighter tool:** Just like it sounds, this tool is an electronic highlighter that you can use to highlight a word or phrase. The icon has a stylized letter T with a yellow highlighter drawing a line through it. Click on it, then click your cursor into the text and drag it across whatever you want to highlight.

- **The Note tool:** Use this to put a note anywhere in the document. The icon is a yellow comment bubble; click on it, then click into the spot in the document where you want to insert the note. A note window will appear; just type your note in there. You can drag and drop the note anywhere in the document after you have created it. After you write a note or query, you can reduce the notepad by clicking on the "X" in the corner. (And if you see a little yellow balloon on a page of the document that's sent to you, double-click on it to expand the notebook so you can see what's been written.)

Electronic Pros (e) and Cons

The pros of electronic editing abound. Now that laptops are no longer the stuff of dreams, copyeditors and proofreaders don't have to be chained to desks or desktop computers. Hooray for the freedom of mobility! Plus, the ease and expediency of electronic editing, thanks to tools like Track Changes and global Find and Replace functions, frees up precious time, making an editor all the more productive.

Another beauty of this electrobusiness is that you can immediately view the results of your labors. By changing the view of your document to hide the edits you've tracked, you can see the results of your work. Don't be ashamed — your oohs and aahs are absolutely appropriate.

So, are there any cons to consider? Problems with electronic editing commonly have less to do with the beefiness of its features and more to do with the way in which a user wields them. Yes, you read that correctly: Some of those software "glitches" you may complain about can be traced back to the, ahem, user. But how do you avoid them if you're not a software expert? Stay alert, and keep control. Don't let the robot do all the thinking for you, and keep a cool head about the grammar or spelling suggestions the robot tries to feed you. If Mr. Silicon Face tells you something's right, but your gut growls that it's wrong, it's probably wrong.

So keep your head in the game, but embrace the technology. It wasn't long ago that writers were using manual typewriters to create manuscripts. When editors made changes, the whole thing had to be retyped. Fun job that must have been. And when it came time to bind the book, they did it with saber-toothed cat teeth and a club. Believe me, we've got it easy. So embrace the work that your microprocessor is able to do for you. Soon you won't be doing much of anything except asking your toaster to order new batteries for your slippers and telling your lawnmower what kind of beer you want it to bring you. So wrap your arms around your computer and kiss it until the cooling fan kicks on. And keep telling yourself that you're the pilot, and the computer is the copilot. Open the pod bay doors, Hal.

Part V
Turning Your Skills into Paychecks

The 5th Wave   By Rich Tennant

PRONOUNS   AMATEURNOUNS

YOU   YOUS
THEY   YAWL
HE   WHOZITS
SHE
IT

In this part . . .

Let's show you the money, honey! In this part, I walk you through the steps you need to take to turn your fierce skills into some even fiercer paychecks. The first chapter is chock-full of advice for your job hunt. Then I turn my attention to freelancing: I share some success stories from established freelancers and show you how to turn your first freelance job into a steady stream of work.

Chapter 18

Hunting for Work

In This Chapter

▶ Putting your skills into action

▶ Constructing a résumé and cover letter

▶ Identifying and contacting potential employers

▶ Keeping yourself organized

*N*ot that the rest of the book isn't fun, but this chapter deals with the most fun topic of all: getting a job. And not just any job — a job that fulfills as much of your publishing dream as possible while also filling your wallet.

I can't pretend to know what your dream is: Maybe it involves wearing a suit every day and working a steady Monday through Friday schedule, or maybe it involves wearing pajamas until 3 p.m. and doing the bulk of your work in the wee hours of the morning. (If the latter scenario sounds most appealing, be sure to check out the next two chapters, in which I detail how to establish yourself as a freelancer and build a thriving freelance career.) Maybe the work on your dream desk is a science fiction manuscript being published by one of the major houses, or maybe it's an electronic article on a recent medical breakthrough to be posted on a Web site with a full-time staff of one.

The great thing about copyediting and proofreading is that after you develop the skills and understand common work practices, you can apply what you know to any situation in which you're asked to improve copy. You may need to invest some time doing not-so-dreamy jobs in order to build a résumé that gets you noticed by your ideal employer, but don't fret: As I state in Chapter 1, patience and persistence are essential qualities in a copyeditor or proofreader. They carry you through when you're poring over a tough assignment, and they will carry you through when you're developing your skills and résumé.

So let's talk about how to move from dream to reality — and paychecks.

Getting Some Practice

You knew I was going to say this, right? Before you start shopping for paying work, you should invest some time putting your new-found knowledge about copyediting or proofreading to the test — possibly for free. If you've already been doing this (if you're the person all your friends turn to whenever there's a résumé, thesis, or letter to the editor that needs finessing), don't stop now. The next time someone asks you to "just take a quick look" at whatever piece of writing needs help, feel free to use the proofreading symbols I present in Chapter 9 to communicate corrections, and write a query or two just to see how it feels. You may be giving the writer more than he expected, but that's okay: You both get what you need.

If you haven't yet had opportunities to put your skills into action, start now. Reading about how to copyedit and proofread is great, but you also have to do the work to fully understand what's involved — and to convince potential employers that you understand it. Following are a few ways you can get some practice:

- ✔ **It's a family affair:** Ask your loved ones about any projects they need your help with. Network with friends and ask if you can proofread their brochures, correspondence, or menus. Ask college students you know if they need someone to look over their theses or dissertations. And if you know somebody in publishing, by all means let her know that you're interested in moving along with a copyediting or proofreading career.

- ✔ **Think global, start local:** Get involved in your community. Is there a hometown newsletter whose writing makes you cringe? Offer to help the staff out for free. Involved in a community center? See if it needs its Web site copyedited. What about your local library? The staff may appreciate your offer to take a look at their brochures and press releases.

Here are some other organizations that you may want to approach with an offer to edit or proofread their publications:

- Churches
- Historical societies
- Museums
- Neighborhood groups
- Police and fire associations
- Recreation centers
- Sporting leagues
- Theaters

Make a phone call or stop by in person to see what you can drum up. Let the staff know that *you know* how important their publications really are.

Everywhere you patronize, anywhere you eat — these are also places to get the experience you need, while lending a hand to people you like. And who knows, maybe you'll get a free coffee out of it next time you drop by.

✔ **Dear Publisher, I genuflect at your feet:** Even if your goal is copyediting, get your hands on as many proofreading tests as you can. How do you do this? Inquire directly to your favorite publishers about freelance proofreading opportunities. Most likely, they will send you a letter thanking you for your interest and enclose a proofreading test for you to complete and return. If freelancing is actually your goal, complete and return each test, but also make copies that you can reference for study later. And don't forget to ask for feedback on how you did — you're bound to learn something new.

✔ **Billions of friendly strangers:** Most Internet communications occur through writing, which has two great benefits: All that writing translates into lots of copyediting and proofreading opportunities, and you may feel more comfortable approaching unfamiliar people online (in writing) to ask about getting some practice.

There is an endless number of writers' Web sites, Web rings, and online writing classes supporting (mostly unpublished) authors. Go to your favorite search engine (that begins with "Go" and ends with "ogle") and type in "writer" plus other keywords like "Web site" or "Web ring." Sift through your search results for sites that let you post to bulletin boards. Then post a simple message such as this:

I am a copyeditor/proofreader in the process of expanding my résumé. I would like to add (fiction/nonfiction/whatever you're interested in) to my experience. I will proofread a chapter of anything you are writing at no charge. Materials should be no shorter than ten pages and not longer than 30. I will return pages to you with corrections in Microsoft Word, tracking changes. In exchange, I ask that you allow me to add your name and the title of your work to my résumé. I will not plagiarize your work or share it with anyone else.

When you get the word out that you're giving your skills and time away for free, you will be astounded at the responses you receive. Struggling writers need people to review their work. And having a stranger look it over is much less threatening to them (and their poor, battered egos) than having a friend or professional colleague review it. Much of what you work on may be awful, but tough it out — the experience will be priceless.

When trolling the Web for writers who need your help, the big fish to land is the published author. If you get bites from one of those, offer to copyedit or proofread any forthcoming projects. Then act bored.

In addition to taking these steps to gain experience, you may also want to seek out free or low-cost courses and other training opportunities offered through community centers or career-building networks. If you live in a bigger city, take a look at the courses and seminars section of www.mediabistro.com (see the sidebar in this chapter titled "Get to the bistro"), or do an Internet search on free editing or proofreading courses in your city.

Generating Documents That Get You Noticed

If you want to make money editing or proofreading words on paper, the first thing you have to do is put *yourself* on paper. After proclaiming that you are, in fact, a copyeditor or proofreader, you have to trust a résumé to do some of your talking. So let's figure out how to make it really sing your praises.

Don't let lack of experience get you off-key. Everyone starts a new career with little in the experience department, at least as far as paid work goes. The trick is identifying unpaid or indirect experience you've collected through other work projects and life pursuits. (If you follow my suggestions in the previous section, you'll soon have a lot of related experience to include on your résumé.)

Good editing and proofreading skill-builders are nestled into many other activities. In this section, I show you how to read between your own lines, repurposing anything noteworthy you've done into real-world credentials.

Reconsidering your résumé

The right résumé — one that highlights your skills and shows your enthusiasm and eagerness — may convince a publisher to give you a chance even if you lack substantial experience. Whether you start by scanning a past résumé or by jotting ideas on a blank page, your key task here is the same: Think about your previous jobs, volunteer positions, and even personal experiences, and run down the following list of questions:

> ✔ Where was the editing or proofreading in these activities?
>
> ✔ Where did I review, correct, improve, or rework someone else's words?
>
> ✔ Where was paperwork involved, and what aspects involved specific, exacting follow-through skills?

Of course, be sure to list any freelance jobs you've done, as well as any related courses you've taken. Until you methodically reconsider your work history and your life history, you can never really know what valuable credentials lie buried just beneath the title of another job or hobby.

In Figure 18-1, I present a sample resume that demonstrates how to work related experience, skills, and interests into your overall presentation.

Crafting your cover letter

Even as your résumé starts to take shape, you want to work on your cover letter. It may seem a bit premature, but you want to be ready when opportunity knocks, and now that you're working with words, you can't just rush through business correspondence. Your cover letter has to be polished, proofread, and perfect. There's nothing like a typo-riddled introduction to say to editors that you either don't care or aren't capable.

As a caring and capable copyeditor or proofreader, you want a simple cover letter template that you can customize for each potential employer or client. Your cover letter shouldn't be more than three or four paragraphs long, with two or three sentences per paragraph and line spaces between each paragraph. This format makes for a gratefully quick read for busy editors looking to hire you. If you mail your cover letter instead of e-mailing it, I recommend using the same impressive stock as your résumé paper.

In Figure 18-2, I offer one example of a cover letter template, which is geared toward finding freelance work.

Working with temp agencies

If you're interested in proofreading, consider contacting a temporary agency near you. Temporary agencies can often keep a proofreader busy enough to be working full-time or near full-time. And proofreading as a temp gives you the advantage of working in a variety of shops. You may be able to gain some incredible (and incredibly diverse) experience, make contacts that lead to consistent freelance work and/or a full-time staff position, and work with other proofreaders who can share their tricks of the trade.

100 Proof

Professional Editing Services

Angel Werber, President

☎Cell: 646.555.0179   🏠 364 Kiwi Street

☎Home: 646.555.8540   Brooklyn, NY 11215

☎Fax: 646.555.1234   ✉100Proof@gmail.com

EMPLOYMENT OBJECTIVE

To add value to your literary works, utilizing exceptional proofreading and copyediting skills

PUBLISHING EXPERIENCE

Freelance proofreading projects completed for:

- **Bob Barlow,** *Oral Presentations Made Easy*

- **Precious Williamson,** *Princess Daughter*

- **Bob Hack,** *Quiet Aruba*

- **Elaine Freed,** *Uncle Sal's Apple*

RELATED EXPERIENCE

- Student Teacher, William O. Schaefer Elementary School, Tappan, NY. Progressive classroom setting for at-risk third- and fourth-graders promoted research-validated practices to maximize student self-confidence and celebration of learning

- Private Tutor: ESL (English as a Second Language), 2005–present: Designed curricula for students' specific needs

EDUCATION

- **MS**, University of Iowa, Chemistry

- **BA**, University of Texas at Austin, Spanish

- Paid to Proofread School, NYC

SKILLS

- Conversant in a broad range of fields, especially those of a business nature

- Outstanding performance with multitasking and deadlines

- Top-notch organizational and communication skills

INTERESTS INCLUDE

Sports ▪ Fiction ▪ Biographies ▪ Gardening ▪ Astronomy

Figure 18-1:
A sample
résumé.

```
┌─────────────────────────────────────────────────────┐
│              Suzy Q. Proofreader                      │
│                   Proofreader                         │
│                                                       │
│              12 Reader Street, #1, Willcox, AZ 85643  │
│                          520-384-1234 (phone)         │
│                            520-384-5678 (fax)         │
│                        SuzyQ@proofreader.com          │
│                                                       │
│  [CONTACT NAME]                                       │
│  [COMPANY NAME]                                       │
│  [ADDRESS]                                            │
│  [ADDRESS]                                            │
│                                                       │
│  Dear [CONTACT],                                      │
│                                                       │
│  [OPENER]                                             │
│                                                       │
│  I have experience proofreading for many companies on a freelance basis. I'm │
│  comfortable reading both general and specialized publications and have       │
│  completed work in the full gamut of subjects, from fiction and art to academic │
│  texts and children's books.                          │
│                                                       │
│  My schedule is flexible enough that I can accommodate projects on very little │
│  notice, and I can complete them on rush turnarounds. I'm proud to say that I've │
│  never missed a deadline (references available on request!). │
│                                                       │
│  [CLOSER]                                             │
│                                                       │
│  Sincerely,                                           │
│                                                       │
│  Suzy Q. Proofreader                                  │
└─────────────────────────────────────────────────────┘
```

Figure 18-2:
A sample cover letter template.

The first paragraph provides a little background on your experience. The second paragraph gives your potential employer a glimpse at the good life your dependability would secure for him or her. Here's what you really want to convey (without actually saying it): I'm your go-to person in a pinch, and I'm going make you look great to your boss. If you're hoping to freelance, offering quick turnaround times endears you to potential clients, so offer away — one-week completions, an entire job over the weekend, whatever it takes to open the opportunity door and march on through as a hero.

Breaking into Books or Magazines

When you're ready to take your skills to the paid professional level — whether as a staffer or freelancer — you've got two best friends: *Writer's Market* and the Web.

You don't need to enjoy what you're reading as a copyeditor or proofreader, but wouldn't life be more fun if you did? Target the publishers of books and magazines you like; then you'll be able to work on copy you would read even if you weren't being paid.

Finding contacts in Writer's Market

In Chapters 2 and 3, I list the big players in book and magazine publishing, but how do you figure out whom to contact within these huge conglomerations? Or, if you'd rather focus your efforts on smaller publishing houses or only those that are located near your hometown, how do you find them and determine if the titles they publish interest you?

You definitely need a go-to guide on the guts of the publishing industry, and luckily for you, one is available as close as the shelf of your local library.

Writer's Market (F&W Publications, Inc.) is your one-stop shopping bazaar for information on the wicked world of words. It gives you names, phone numbers, Web sites . . . everything you need to start spreading the news of your professional intentions. And it also gives you information to help you whittle down your list of dream employers, such as how many books or periodicals each publisher produces each year and what categories of fiction and nonfiction writing the publisher deals with.

Everything you need to know as you prepare to contact publishers is contained within this bulky tome. But don't think of it as bulky; embrace it as your best friend, through thick and thin.

Are you saying to yourself, "But I don't necessarily want to *write* anything, so why would I consult a resource for writers?" Of *course* you don't want to write. (Wait, or do you? If so, check out *Writing Copy For Dummies* by Jonathan Kranz, *Writing a Romance Novel For Dummies* by Leslie Wainger, *Writing Children's Books For Dummies* by Lisa Rojany Buccieri, or any other Wiley books I can shamelessly plug here.) But the writers and publishers who use this industry bible are the people who will one day scribble their John Hancocks on your paychecks. This book guarantees that the hard part — the taking of names and recording of contact information — has been done for you.

If you're always on the go, you could opt for the online version of *Writer's Market*. Yup, this baby's gone big time with www.writersmarket.com. For an annual fee of $29.99, you get access to up-to-the-minute publishing contacts, and you can search the databases by publishing house, by imprint name — however you want. The Web site also offers advice, newsletters, and daily updates, keeping you at the heart of all things published.

Literary Market Place (Information Today) is another great resource for information about book and magazine publishers, and it also includes information on newspapers. Talk about bulky: This one is roughly the size of a phone book. But if you want to supplement your *Writer's Market* research, look for *Literary Market Place* in the reference section of your local bookstore or library.

Get to the bistro

There's one Web site I can't say enough about, especially if you live near a big city: www.mediabistro.com. Proudly declaring a dedication to "anyone who creates or works with content," mediabistro.com is the place to find work within book and magazine publishing, share tips, meet others like you, improve your skills, and advertise your work.

The site features a job board, forums, and a freelance marketplace. Its periodic mingling parties give you a chance to actually talk to people who do what you want to do for a living. While a lot of the content is free, the premium content is definitely worth paying for. It's a great place to get — and remain — involved in the publishing industry.

Taking your aspirations online

The Web sites you visit to find jobs are the same places to post your résumé and let the strangers who matter know you're trolling for work. Web sites like www.monster.com, http://hotjobs.yahoo.com/, and www.careerbuilder.com are great, but there are also editing- and proofreading-specific Web sites you can try, such as the following:

- ✔ **www.copyeditor.com:** The newsletter *Copy Editor* has a job board just for in-house and freelance copyeditors and proofreaders.

- ✔ **www.editorandpublisher.com:** The journal *Editor & Publisher*'s classified board includes all types of publishing (including newspaper work).

- ✔ **www.magazine.org:** The Magazine Publishers of America host a job bank for the consumer magazine publishing industry.

- ✔ **www.mediabistro.com:** One of my favorites, mediabistro.com has both job listings and a résumé database in which you can advertise your skills. (See the sidebar "Get to the bistro.")

- ✔ **www.publishersmarketplace.com:** This Web site's job board advertises the span of publishing jobs, from sales representatives to editorial assistants, and you can search by job title, city, or state.

- ✔ **www.writejobs.com:** Though you can't post your résumé at The Write Jobs, you can search for freelance positions, magazine jobs, publishing-industry jobs, and technical-editing jobs.

And don't forget the Web sites of publishing houses themselves. These days, most every publisher Web site includes a job board — just look for a <u>Careers</u> or <u>Jobs</u> link on the homepage.

Knock, knock: Contacting publishers

What's the best way to get through the door to publishers without having to wield a chainsaw? Try picking up the phone and calling the publisher of interest. Depending on the size and type of publisher (book or magazine), and your professional goal (staff position or freelance work), you need to tailor your request for information. Here are some suggestions:

✔ If you're cold-calling a large book or magazine publisher to ask about staff positions (meaning you haven't seen a position advertised that fits your skills), and you don't have the contact name of a managing editor in a division that interests you, you'll have to ask for the human resources division. You'll get a receptionist, and you may not get much further. But while you've got a human being on the phone, ask whether you can submit a résumé for future consideration, and whether you should send it to the human resources department (ask for a name) or to the managing editor of a particular division. Do your homework: Know in advance which divisions publish the kinds of books or magazines you want to work on so you can mention them specifically; then you're more likely to be given the name and title of the person who should receive your résumé.

✔ If you're contacting a large book publisher about freelance opportunities, ask to speak to an editorial assistant in whatever division interests you. Then ask the assistant if she can put you in contact with the production editor or managing editor for the imprint that is of greatest interest to you within that division. A production editor or managing editor is usually responsible for hiring freelance copyeditors and proofreaders to work on individual manuscripts (see Chapter 2), and every imprint will have at least one production editor.

If the assistant (or whomever you initially speak with) resists patching you through to the production editor or managing editor, explain your purpose for calling. ("My name is Word Smith, and I am a freelance copyeditor. I'm very interested in working on Knopf books, and I'm wondering if you can give me the name of the person in the division who is responsible for hiring freelance copyeditors.")

You may not actually get the production editor or managing editor on the phone, but at least try to get the name. With a name, you can create correspondence that can spell out your skills and intentions.

If you do actually get to speak to a hiring editor, above all be polite. ("My name is Word Smith, and I am a freelance copyeditor. I'm very interested in working on Knopf books, and I'm wondering if you're looking to expand your pool of available freelancers.") Depending on the response, you may need to simply say, "Thanks for your time. May I send you a résumé to have on file"? Or you may find yourself describing your experience to this person so she knows whether you're worth considering for a manuscript on her desk right at that moment.

✔ If you're contacting publishers of consumer magazines (those that are marketed to the general public), keep in mind that you probably want to inquire about a staff position rather than freelance work. Consumer magazines use fewer freelance copyeditors and proofreaders because the deadlines come fast and furious as the publication date draws near. Your best bet may be to simply ask the person who answers the phone for the name and title of the person responsible for hiring. If you're feeling bold, ask if that person is available to take your call. (Chances are the answer will be no.) Otherwise, simply use the information you receive to get your résumé and cover letter into the right hands.

It may be a long shot, but you can also check the masthead of a particular magazine of interest, note the name of the credited copyeditor, and make a cold call to that person. What would you say? Ask whether the magazine ever hires freelance copyeditors or proofreaders. Even though you know the answer will probably be no, the question may open the door to a conversation with someone who knows the ins and outs of that organization and can tell you how to get noticed when submitting your written materials for consideration. That person may also tell you whom to contact about a staff position.

✔ If you're contacting trade magazines or other periodicals (such as the scholarly sort), my best advice is to pore through past issues before getting on the phone. The staffs of these pubs may be fairly small, and you may have a decent chance of being connected to the person responsible for hiring in-house staff or freelance copyeditors and proofreaders. If you get that person on the line, you want to be sure to sound knowledgeable about the subject matter and the publication. And if you get the brush-off from the person answering the phone, at least aim for getting the name and title of someone who should receive your résumé.

Selling Your Services to Web Sites

Generating work with Web sites may be easier than you think. As I explain in Chapter 3, a great way to start is by scouring your favorite Web sites for errors. When you encounter one, send an e-mail to the site's Webmaster, whose contact information is usually at the bottom of the homepage or included in an "About Us" page. Your e-mail should note the error but also introduce who you are and why you care enough to point out the need for correction.

Here's an example:

Dear Webmaster Jason:

As I was browsing your Web site this afternoon, I was surprised to stumble upon an error: In the second paragraph, line two, the word *the* appears twice in a row. By the way, I'm a proofreader. I find errors professionally. This one's for free, but if you'd like help with the rest of your site, let me know. My résumé is attached.

I look forward to helping you have a perfect Web site.

Best regards,

Polly Proofreader

Of course, the tone of this note may be too lighthearted for a Web site like `www.fortune.com`, but you can change your language to reflect that of the site itself. Your approach to a site like `www.luckymag.com` should be very different from your approach to a site like `www.entrepreneur.com`. The first should be more lighthearted, while the second should be professional and reflect some knowledge of the company and its business.

Breaking into consumer magazines

I'll be honest: Getting work on a consumer magazine is a bit more difficult than getting work with a book publisher. There's a time-honored tradition of hiring interns (who may not even see a blue pencil for the better part of a semester). If you're willing to start as an intern, how do you make it happen? Oftentimes, magazines hire journalism students who start as fact-checkers, researching and verifying factual statements within the magazine's articles, charts, graphs, and the like. (The job may feel a bit like hazing, but that's just how the industry tends to work.) If you haven't studied journalism, do your best to present yourself as an organized, fact-obsessed person willing to play whatever role the magazine wants you to play. If you don't live in New York or another city home to lots of consumer magazine publishers, you need to be willing to move, and you also need to be willing to do the internship for free — or close to free — with the goal of proving your worth.

What if you don't want to move? Or what if you need to get more experience before trying to land a consumer magazine job that actually pays and involves something other than fact-checking? You may be able to find work locally with a regional consumer publication. If you live in a fairly large city, you may discover that there's a tourism and travel magazine about the city that gets placed in hotel rooms and other touristy spots. Or if you look through the magazines at your grocery store or local newsstand, you may notice a regional consumer magazine whose readership is city residents.

You can search online for magazines that publish in your region or state, and I encourage you to visit the membership directory at the City and Regional Magazine Association Web site at `www.citymag.org`, which also boasts a job board.

Before you take the time to send an e-mail of this sort, first qualify the Web site's owner as a potential client. You may not want to query sites that update their information constantly; if the copy changes every hour, chances are the site owner won't invest in editing or proofreading services because the product just doesn't exist long enough to warrant the expense. (If the copy stays put for a few days or weeks, however, you may be in business.) Also, sites that require security clearance, including news, government, and banking sites, may not be your best bets. But retailers, restaurants, and other companies have a lot at stake in their online copy because that copy can build (or break) their reputations for a long period of time.

If you can become the official editor or proofreader for one Web site, you should be able to leverage that position to land similar work for other sites. See Chapter 3 for additional tips for working with online content, and be sure to check out Chapter 17 for a crash course on copyediting and proofreading electronic documents. When you edit Web content, chances are you'll never touch a piece of paper.

Organizing Your Efforts

Sometimes the search for work can take time, and you may find that you contact a whole lot of people at a whole lot of companies before landing the job(s) you want.

Here's what you don't want to happen: You're hanging out at home one day, surfing channels and wondering why no one has called to offer you a job. Then the phone rings. Some professional-sounding person asks to speak to you and proceeds to ask you some questions about the nicely crafted résumé you submitted several weeks ago. Problem is, you don't recognize this person's name, and he didn't identify the company he's calling from. Time to panic? That depends.

As long as you organize your job-search efforts, no panic is required. That's because you're going to keep a journal (written or typed — doesn't matter to me!) of every phone call you make, every person you speak to, every contact name you receive, and every résumé you submit. You're going to note the dates associated with each piece of information ("Spoke with editorial assistant Jay Brown on 4/19"). And when you hear back from a potential employer — with good news or bad — you're going to update that entry to reflect its status.

With this journal in hand (or on screen), you can quickly sift through entries as soon as your professional-sounding caller states his name, so you have no doubt that he's calling from XYZ company that received your résumé three weeks ago in response to a posting on the *Copy Editor* online job board.

You can even take this organizing process a step further to include information about the publisher so your mind doesn't go blank during just such a conversation.

Here are some suggestions for types of info to include in each journal entry:

- Company name, address, phone number, and Web site.
- Contact name, phone number, and e-mail address.
- How you found out about the company.
- What types of publications the company produces.
- Recent mergers or other significant changes to the company structure.
- What you know about whether the company is hiring full-time staff members or freelancers.
- Notes on any phone conversations you've had: Who answered? What information did you get?
- The date you sent a résumé and cover letter.
- Any information you may know about the person you sent the résumé to. For example, if you know that he used to work for a different publisher and is new at this company, write it down. After you have an initial conversation with him, write down anything you find out, including whether he's married, has kids, enjoys gardening, recently traveled to Scotland . . . anything that may be a good starting point for a future conversation.

Chapter 19

Preparing for a Freelance Career

$\bullet$ $\bullet$

In This Chapter

▶ Hearing from successful freelancers

▶ Figuring out how much to charge

▶ Finding your first jobs

$\bullet$ $\bullet$

*F*reelance editing or proofreading doesn't require six diplomas and five more years of residency. The start-up cost of launching your freelance career? The price of one computer with Internet access, a good printer, some nice stationery for your invoices, and business cards. You don't need much luck either — just good resources (like this book) and a strong work ethic. And you don't even have to be initiated into some geeky grammar club.

The truth is, you start by simply saying "I am a freelance copyeditor (or proofreader)" and meaning it. Can you then discuss freelancing for ten minutes with a straight face? Presto chango: Your transformation is complete. You've acquired all the credentials you need to start baby-stepping toward your first paycheck.

The journey may be a lot quicker than you think. In this chapter, I offer a bit of inspiration in case you're wavering about whether freelancing is right for you, and then I explain how to lay some groundwork to get your first jobs.

So, jump right into this newborn career path, and watch how fast it grows up!

Succeeding As You Go: Reasons to Consider Freelancing

You're not the first person to pursue a career as a freelance copyeditor or proofreader, so don't isolate yourself. Support is everywhere. See my recommended list of resources in Appendix C, and sit back and relax while I take you through a few inspiring success stories and their accompanying insights.

Freedom and flexibility

As an aspiring actor, I have to drop everything whenever an audition comes a'callin' — this one could be my big break and there's no telling when I'll get my next opportunity. Needless to say, my actor's schedule wasn't so conducive to finding employment in the 9–5 world. My prospects were bleak, and then: Enter Proofreading — and its full-time paycheck with the flexibility of setting my own hours. I have firm deadlines, but I decide how and where I meet them. I can and frequently do read during downtime on the set — no matter where that set is located. Proofreading will always be a star in my book.

Amy Marshall

Picture a schedule as pliable as you need it to be. If you're a night owl who works best from midnight to 4 a.m., don't bother justifying it; your proofreading hours have been approved — by you. Do you need Monday through Friday off to paint your *oeuvre*, write your novel, earn your Master's, launch your start-up company? No problem. Get your freelance copyediting done on the weekends to tide your income over until the big IPO.

When my daughter was born, I really didn't want to return to my full-time job. I wanted to be at home with her. I was always good at writing so I figured I would try freelance copyediting. I contacted some publishing companies I knew of, took some editing tests and now am able to work at home, be with my daughter, and still earn a decent salary around my schedule.

Marjorie Rilms

Let's not forget mobility. Proofreading and copyediting can be done from any place on the planet, and a few places off the planet, too. During your morning train commute, on sleepy Sunday mornings at home, between beach naps — wherever and whenever you can read is wherever and whenever you can work.

A no-fee education

I'm a freelance writer who loves to learn, not just about my craft and my career, but about everything — because each new lesson opens the door to another article I can write as "an expert." Which is why my proofreading career has been such an unexpected boon to my writing career. Every book I proofread is like having a one-on-one class with the author, who's more often than not an established expert in his or her field. Although I request — and receive — many how-to books about writing, my tutelage actually spans from the history of the London Tube to the intimate tribulations of modern-day teens. Proofreading has been even better than a free education. I'm getting paid to learn!

Jessica Salmons

One thing's for sure: Higher education is not cheap. College tuition is sky high, and even the cost of books for college can be prohibitive.

What if you could get a brilliant education for free? Without spending a penny, you could be introduced to completely new subjects, new ideas, new everythings that could inspire you to think, do, and succeed at new anythings. With such eclectic knowledge, I'm sure you'd be the most fascinating person at parties, too.

Now, what if you could actually get paid for that brilliant and eclectic knowledge? I earned more than $1,000 for proofreading — and positively relishing — *The Da Vinci Code*. Sure, without this profession, I could've purchased the book for $24.95 instead. But you don't need a degree in mathematics to figure out which deal worked out better for me — and which deal can work out better for you.

I've also been paid to read *Oh, Yuck!: The Encyclopedia of Everything Nasty; Sugarbusters!; The Little Strength Training Book;* and *Sex for the Clueless* — all books I probably wouldn't have picked up on my own. All books that taught me something, that gave me a better understanding of the people and world around me, which in turn helped me to recognize and nurture untapped aspects of myself. You too could find some unknown topic that truly lights you up. Sometimes the proofreading paycheck is second fiddle to the epiphanies that come from the work.

Plus a hefty paycheck!

I started proofreading to supplement my writing income, but, in little over a year, I ended up surpassing it altogether. A few modest jobs turned into a few glowing recommendations, and next thing you know it's my third year working for Time *magazine as a freelance proofreader — earning $75/hour! And lately I've been earning nearly double that rate, proofreading and copyediting for corporations and ad agencies. I can't wait to see what caliber of income is waiting just around the corner!*

Anthony Tedesco

How much money can you earn from freelance copyediting or proofreading? I know that "sky's the limit" is a weary cliché, but the earning potential is really that limitless. My proofreading income quickly soared up to six figures, and with each new project I get more efficient and savvier about how to increase profits. A full-time freelance editor or proofreader can definitely survive — and thrive — without any other source of income. Part-time freelancers can really benefit, too, generating a significant amount of supplemental income through even just a few projects a month.

The number of simultaneous projects (and paychecks) you accept is completely up to you. Why would one publisher give you more than you could handle? One publisher wouldn't. But you don't work with one publisher. You're a fearless freelancer who works with any and every publisher you choose — and no single publisher has to know. Some freelancers juggle five projects on their desk at once. (Recommended for hyper-organized and wholly manic people only.)

The point is, so long as you're making deadlines and sleeping occasionally, you can take on as much or as little work as you want. It's really important to know yourself and how much you can handle.

Covering your duff and other key stuff

When you accept a staff job, the important things, like how much you'll be paid, are pretty clear. But when you're freelancing, sometimes clarity is hard to come by. Here are a few ways to protect yourself and nurture business:

✔ **Don't start a job without a contract.** If you are not presented with a contract before you start the work, create one yourself that specifies your project, pay rate, deadline, and any limits you wish to include for protection. Which leads us to . . .

✔ **Don't feel uncomfortable asking for limits.** As a freelancer, you are the only person looking out for you. You can ask for a clause in your contract that specifies a maximum number of revisions, total-hour limits, and hourly rates, should any of the limits be expended.

✔ **Create a niche for yourself.** Is there something you enjoy that you'd love to read about? Specialize as a copyeditor or proofreader for a specific field, subject, or hobby.

✔ **Track your time.** Even if you're working for a flat fee, keep track of your total hours to determine exactly how much you're getting paid. This is useful information for later, when you can decide whether a particular project or publisher is worth the effort expended.

✔ **Make some friends in the field.** Get out there and schmooze at workshops and conferences. (Book Expo America is a good conference, and it is held each spring, usually rotating between New York, Chicago, and Washington, D.C.) Buy industry-related books and magazines. Join a professional association such as the Editorial Freelancers Association (www.the-efa.org) or The Bookbinders' Guild of New York (www. bookbindersguild.org). Take a few classes, even online. The more people you know, the more real information you'll have to go by. And venting with people who understand what you're going through is never a bad thing.

Considering the Cash: How Much to Charge

Let's talk turkey — here's where we get into the glorious details on getting paid. Before you accept your first job, think about what you want to earn. You may or may not have the opportunity to set your own rate, but you can at least identify if someone is offering you way too little for your time.

Knowing the industry standards

The proofreading field operates mostly on hourly rates, beginning around $12 per hour for smaller publishers in smaller towns and climbing to roughly $25 per hour for standard publishing houses. However, if you start working consistently for a publisher or let your interests develop into specialized expertise of certain genres, your pay can double these rates.

Copyediting starts off with basic rates of $30 to $35 per hour, rising to $40 per hour with experience. Heavy copyediting and technical copyediting can demand $40 to $50 per hour.

If you work for clients that you know are rich in resources, such as corporations or advertising agencies, you may be able to earn double or even triple these rates. Within the book field, after you establish yourself as a hot freelance commodity, you can demand increased rates for rush projects.

Consulting firms and other independent companies often contact publishers to get the names of their top proofreaders. You can make a quick fortune when you work for big businesses — they pay big business rates!

Charging per hour or per page

While most clients pay by the hour, some pay by the page. And some may ask you to determine which method to use when tallying your final paycheck. Here are some considerations:

✔ **Per-hour rates:** Billing hourly sounds easy enough until you try to track how long you worked between loads of laundry or while sitting outside the elementary school waiting to pick up your kids. It's nearly impossible to accurately assess your time (was I concentrating fully? Half-concentrating?) and precisely record it. If you bill this way, keep careful notes of the time you spend on the job, but know that you're likely to be making some guesses.

✔ **Per-page rates:** If you're asked to name your per-page rate, or if a client offers this kind of rate, you want to be sure it translates into adequate compensation for your time. Therefore, you need to calculate how the per-page rate translates into a per-hour rate.

If you're working with a publisher or anyone else who's used to hiring copyeditors and proofreaders, ask this question: "How many pages per hour do you expect from your (copyeditors or proofreaders)?" The answer will depend on the document's layout, font, lines per page, level of edit requested, and genre of content (standard or technical in nature), but you can probably expect to hear up to six pages for copyediting and ten to twelve pages for proofreading.

Use the answer, plus your desired hourly rate, to calculate how much you should charge per page. If you're proofreading and want to earn $20 per hour, for example, you probably want to charge $2 per page.

Here's a nice benefit of being paid per page: As you gain experience and can do your job faster, your hourly rate goes up. For example, if you charge $2 per page and can eventually read 18 pages per hour, you earn $36 per hour. Improving your skills can really pay off!

However, before you commit to a per-page rate, I strongly recommend that you ask to see the project. You need to edit at least ten pages and time yourself so you have a feel for the job and how much time and work will be involved.

Creating an invoice template

Invoicing is easy. Some projects arrive with an invoice form that you just fill out. If you don't get one of those, put together a one-page document that contains the following info:

✔ Your name and company name (if applicable)

✔ You contact info: address, phone, and e-mail

✔ Your Social Security or federal tax ID number

✔ The name and contact info of the company you're billing

✔ An invoice number (if the client requires it)

✔ The name of the project

✔ The date you began and completed work

✔ Your hourly rate and how long the project took, or the per-page rate and the number of pages involved

✔ The grand total

✔ The words *Payable Upon Receipt* (which simply indicate that the client can't let the invoice sit on a desk for three months before giving it some attention)

See Figure 19-1 for an example.

Figure 19-1: A sample invoice.

Suzy Q. Proofreader
Proofreader

12 Reader Street, #1, Willcox, AZ 85643
520-384-1234 (phone)
520-384-5678 (fax)
SuzyQ@proofreader.com

John Squire

Sample Publisher

150 Publisher Street

New York, NY 10003

INVOICE

#11 of Year 2008

RE: Proofreading services rendered

DATE: April 4, 2008

JOBS: 60 Seconds by Talia Green

24 hours @ $20/hour

BALANCE DUE: $480

SS #: 123-45-4321

Payable upon receipt.

Beating a Path to Clients

Generating opportunities is the first step toward freelance editing and proofreading success. After you're a seasoned pro, the work will find you, but initially you need to find prospects for yourself. The key to success is an eclectic search: Use both traditional and alternative means, and look for work from as many different angles as possible.

Considering the usual suspects

My first suggestion is to take a look at Chapter 18, if you haven't already done so. The advice I offer there about researching potential employers applies here as well. Here's the scoop, in a nutshell:

- ✔ **Books:** If you want to work in book publishing, start by considering publishers whose titles you already read, and make *Writer's Market* your new best friend.

- ✔ **Magazines:** If you're interested in magazine work, you may find it difficult to get freelance opportunities with print magazines. Because magazines publish so frequently, they often have in-house copyeditors and proofreaders. (Exceptions exist, as Anthony Tedesco's testimonial earlier in this chapter proves.)

  If you're hooked on periodicals, you may want to target each magazine's online counterpart. Copyediting and proofreading are crucial to these online pubs because the copy can be read (and its typos ridiculed) forever. Yet, lucky for you, their budgets are usually more limited than those of their print counterparts so they may not employ full-time copyeditors or proofreaders. Freelancers to the rescue!

- ✔ **Corporate publications:** If you're considering corporate work, you've got some networking to do. Start by letting friends, family members, and even casual acquaintances who work in big companies know that you're in the market for freelance work. Put yourself into networking situations whenever you can, and always carry business cards with you, just in case.

- ✔ **Online publications:** Mine the Internet for mistakes. Look at Web sites that you'd be interested in reading anyway, and when you run across typos, send the Webmaster a polite letter that points out the problems and offers your services.

Checking the classifieds, more closely than you think

Ah, Sunday morning: the perfect (albeit only) time to pick up the Sunday edition of any city's major newspaper and start leisurely perusing its classified ads. You may occasionally find freelance jobs in those listings, in which case, have a ball! But if you don't find what you're looking for in that particular edition, take a bird's-eye view.

Expand your vision to include listings for *Editor, Production Editor,* and *Publishing*. Within these sections, take particular interest in the job listings for production editor positions. (If you're looking for proofreading work, also pay close attention to listings calling for full-time copyeditors.) These people may become your clients — the in-house folks who make your freelancing career. Scan the job responsibilities in the listing. See any requirement that resembles "work with freelancers"?

Write down the publisher's contact information, and put it under your metaphorical pillow for about three weeks. That's usually how long it takes for the publisher to fill the position — and for the Freelance Fairy to turn that phone number into a shiny new job lead for you. Pick up the phone, call, and ask for the name of the new person hired in the advertised position. Then, reap the following benefits:

- ✔ Because your contact hasn't yet begun soliciting copyeditors or proofreaders, you may be the only one sending in materials for consideration.
- ✔ You'll establish a relationship with a brand-new employee before anyone else begins the process.

Taking your search online

Here are two more resources overflowing with job listings, which may offer you direct employment opportunities (through freelance listings) or indirect opportunities (through listings for full-time production editors or copyeditors, with whom you can establish relationships as soon as they're hired):

- ✔ **Publishers' Web sites:** Go to the sites of book or magazine publishers, and find a section labeled "Careers" or "Employment," often located within the "About Us" heading or at the bottom of the home page.
- ✔ **Career Web sites:** Don't forget about www.monster.com, www.career builder.com, http://hotjobs.yahoo.com/, www.mediabistro.com, and the job board at www.copyeditor.com, all of which I tout in Chapter 18.

Dealing with a client's process

Having pizza for dinner is fast and easy, right? Only if you get it delivered hot. Pick up a pizza-making kit, with the flour and the sauce and the doctoring to be done, and dinner gets a bit more complicated. If you have to start from scratch by making your own dough . . . well, it may be a while before you sit down and chew.

Different clients also deliver your work in different ways — some neatly assembled, some messier than a counter full of mixing bowls.

Some clients are like your buddy Carmine at the pizza joint around the corner. They give you ample turnaround time for each project, mail everything with a style guide and individual style sheet, and throw in tons of comfy, huge rubber bands to boot. Sometimes you even find an invoice complete but for the few blanks you need to fill in. And best of all, they pay you within two weeks of receipt of the project and invoice! And can you say FedEx?

Then there's the next-tier crowd — the pizza kits of the publishing world. They send you the project and sometimes include a style sheet or style guide. You write your own invoice, but they give you the guidelines. (Don't forget to include your name and address and invoice number and title and author and rate per hour and page count and amount due, thank you.) Sure, they

pay you . . . within a month or two or so. They're reliable, but occasionally a pain in the arse.

Then there are the stinkers — the ones that force you to make the pizza from scratch. Sometimes you have to pick up projects or at least pay for the shipping yourself. You write your own invoices and have to stay on top of them, lest they forget to pay you. The pages may come marked up, smudged, or even torn. And you need to get working on that style sheet, because you definitely won't be getting one.

Obviously, I'm generalizing here, but you'll notice some significant differences between clients. Some contact you by e-mail for a project, while others call. You may have to take a proofreading test for a few, while others send you a first-time trial project to make sure you're up to snuff. In the book industry, bigger publishers have huge longevity with their production editors — five or ten years or more — which is great because you can develop a steady trickle of work. Other publishers have production editors who last no more than two years. This can sometimes be great as well, because when those production editors move, you have an opportunity to work with yet another pub house!

Chapter 20

Keeping the Freelance Jobs Coming

In This Chapter

▶ Walking through your first project

▶ Caring for your connections

▶ Letting the jobs find you

▶ Being the boss you've always wanted

*P*ut your party hat on! This chapter celebrates (and walks you through) your first job and the many splendid ways you can keep your next jobs rolling in. It's your official transition from green freelancer to expert freelancer making mucho green.

Expertise will grow your opportunities exponentially. Publishers will start seeking out your services, and with all that freelance income, you may decide to keep more of it by setting up your own corporation or LLC. Or maybe you'll want to capitalize on your freelance connections to catch the perfect full-time job at the company of your dreams.

No matter which benefits you decide to reap, the good life begins with landing that first freelance gig and delivering it like your editor's very own Fourth-of-July fireworks. I start the chapter by showing you how.

Handling Your First Project

Woohoo! Your hard work — on your résumé, your experience, your networking (see Chapter 18) — has paid off, and you've received your first project. Don't panic. The whole process will be as easy as your first day of school — that is, after you stopped worrying and enjoyed your first day of school. In this section, I take you step-by-step until you're at the top of the entire class.

Celebrating the grand opening

If you receive your first project in a Jiffy bag, you'll be tempted to treat it like the gift that it is — by tearing it open in a frenzy of glee. Resist the temptation, or else you'll be covered in cardboard fluffies. If your project is delivered in a box, feel free to tear it open like it's your eighth birthday. (But you may want to save the box, as you can probably cover the address labels and use it to return your work.)

If you happen to be proofreading a book, here's what you may find inside your package:

- ✔ The latest pass of galleys
- ✔ A *dead* (or *foul*) manuscript, if you're doing a comparison read
- ✔ A cover letter to you detailing all the trials and tribulations the book has survived thus far, as well as your deadline (see Figure 20-1)
- ✔ A blank invoice
- ✔ A style sheet

Figure 20-1:
A sample cover letter accompanying a book project.

Dear Suzy:

Enclosed are the second-pass pages of BEDTIME TRYSTS for you to proofread. The first-pass pages are included. This is a good romance, and I think you'll enjoy the story. Unfortunately, the copyeditor was a little too focused on the mechanical task of correcting punctuation to really "read" the manuscript—and the first proofreader missed quite a number of corrections. Keep an eye out for formatting problems, and double-check that the line and letter spacings are consistent.

Please review the proofreader's guidelines before beginning each job. Also, please flag all queries on Post-Its instead of writing them on the proof pages.

Please return this by **Tuesday, 22 March**, and feel free to call before then if you encounter any problems with this project.

Thanks a bunch,

Melanie Wells

Production Editor

If you're copyediting, or if you're working on a project other than a book — an article, an annual report, a Web site — you may not receive a package at all. Instead, you're likely to get an e-mail with a Microsoft Word document or PDF file attached. (PDFs are accessible through Adobe Reader, which comes bundled into most computers. You can download a free copy of Adobe Reader from www.adobe.com/products/acrobat/readstep2.html.) You'll miss the joy of unwrapping your present, but you'll savor the benefits of working electronically (see Chapter 17).

Beating the deadline

Deadlines are aptly named because, if you miss one, it'll most likely be the end of your copyediting or proofreading life — with that publisher anyway. The deadline is everything. I repeat, in flashing neon giant billboard capital letters:

THE DEADLINE IS EVERYTHING.

It's everything to you and to the editor who's waiting on you, and to the compositor who's waiting on the editor, and to the company or publisher who's waiting on the compositor. Missing your deadline has an unfortunate domino effect, knocking down the punctuality of everyone who follows you. Don't miss your deadline.

But don't miss sleep worrying about it, either. Copyediting and proofreading deadlines are usually reasonable, especially if you're working for a company or publisher that hires freelancers on a regular basis. If you have three weeks to complete a 400-page book, just divide 400 into 20 days (so your editor will receive your project on the 21st day). Your daily editing or proofing schedule? Twenty pages a day. If you want to be an MVP, try adding a few extra pages a day and returning your project early. Editors love team players. As an MVP, you can be sure your editor will want you back up to bat on the very next project.

If there's (gulp) any chance that you can't make your deadline, be sure to call up front instead of after the deadline has passed. There's nothing your editor can do post-deadline except be late. Give him — and your career — a fighting chance by sending notification and apologies as early as possible.

When your project is officially en route back to the editor, call him to say so, and also to slip in a "Hey, need me for any other projects?" It can't hurt to ask, and it may land your next job. Now, that's instant-turnaround business.

Doing the work

You'll develop your own sensible process that works for your lifestyle and for the type of project at hand, but I want to offer some insights into the methods I find effective. Check out the chapters in Parts II and III for lots more details about how to approach the work itself.

Copyediting or proofreading on hard copy

Here's how I suggest approaching an edit or proofread on hard copy: If it's a cold read, just plunk it down in the center of your tidy editing desk. If it's a comparison read, place the most recent copy on the right side of your desk and the marked-up copy on the left side. (If you're a southpaw, reverse that. The crux is that you want to be able to write on the newest copy comfortably with your dominant hand.) You want to have your dictionary and style guide within reach too.

Before you make any marks, read the instructions that came with the project, as well as the house style sheet and anything else sent to you. Use your prerequisite red colored pencil, and write clearly, neatly, and nicely. (You never want to risk insulting anyone in your queries.) Then it's just about catching all the errors you can.

Your project is probably enveloped in a slew of rubber bands. Save that slew in the delivery box or bag under your desk. (Editors choose their own rubber bands, so you score big points if you return a project with all those rubber bands you received enclosed. Quirky, but true.)

Copyediting or proofreading electronically

If you're going to work on an electronic document, read through Chapter 17 for my suggestions on preparing your workspace for optimal output and minimal discomfort. You want to have your reference materials nearby, of course, and spend just as much time getting familiar with the house style and the project instruction sheet as you would if you were working on hard copy. (Sure, it's easier to undo your edits in electronic files than on hard copy, but why waste your time?)

Wrapping the project

You're done with the project! Nice work. Now it's time to send it back to the person who hired you and take some next steps to make sure you get hired again.

Returning a hard copy edit or proofread

If you've been editing or proofreading a project on hard copy, write a short cover letter to the editor (which I explain in the upcoming section "Thanking your client: The all-important cover letter"), create or complete an invoice, and put those two pieces on top of the finished manuscript. Wrap rubber bands around the whole shebang, and that's what you're going to ship back.

Most likely, you'll return it using the same method by which it arrived: FedEx, UPS, DHL, U.S. mail, or (if you live fairly close to the company) a messenger. Shipping services should be paid for by the company that hired you; you may get a prepaid or account-billed shipping label with the project manuscript, or you may be asked to include the shipping costs in your invoice. (If the publisher asks you to incur any other costs, such as photocopying the marked-up manuscript, include them on separate lines in your invoice as well.)

If the shipment goes through FedEx, UPS, DHL, or a messenger, the company will give you a tracking or reference number that you should hold onto until you know the package has been delivered. If you ship through the post office, request a tracking number and receipt. The last thing you want is for a package to disappear, but it does happen occasionally, and a tracking number is essential in that situation.

If you work with clients who favor FedEx, UPS, or DHL, you may want to open online accounts at www.fedex.com, www.ups.com, and www.dhl.com. With your contact info stored, you'll never waste time repeating your address, and you'll be immediately identified by your phone number when you call for a pickup. Plus, it's free. You can register online and have the courier at your door the same day with only a few clicks. Quite convenient, especially if you're still in your kangaroo pajamas at 3 p.m.

Returning an electronic edit or proofread

When you complete an electronic copyedit or proofread, you may need to e-mail the document(s) back to the assigning editor, or you may need to go online to the publisher's FTP (*File Transfer Protocol*) site, which is essentially a big online filing cabinet that allows you to transfer documents. Your client will undoubtedly tell you how you should return the finished product, but if that doesn't happen, be sure to ask. If you need to use an FTP site, the assigning editor will provide the URL and any password or other security information you need to access it.

Don't delete your completed files as soon as you e-mail or transfer them. No one should trust technology quite that much! Hold onto them at least until you confirm that they've made it into the editor's hands. Even then, you may want to keep them around; until the document is actually printed, you never know if you may need to revisit the work you've done.

After you transfer files onto an FTP site, or at the same time that you e-mail the files back to the assigning editor (if that's the preference), write a short e-mail telling the editor anything she needs to know about the job. Attach a completed invoice for the job (and keep a copy for your records), and be sure to thank the editor for the opportunity. (Much more on that topic in the next section.)

Thanking your client: The all-important cover letter

Miss Manners may not require that you write a thank-you note to the person who hired you, but doing so will help ensure that you get another project — soon.

Enclose a cover letter (or e-mail, if you're working electronically) with every single project you return. No exceptions. Especially if you're new to the industry, the person who hired you is taking a chance by putting so much responsibility into your hands. Telling this person that you appreciate the opportunity to work together is appropriate, considerate, and business-savvy.

Try to add something personal in the letter, if you can. If you know that this person has a vacation coming up, has been caring for a spouse with the flu, or has been stressed about difficult deadlines, write a few words that show you were listening. Do whatever you can to conscientiously build the relationship.

And never disparage even the most dreadful of projects — not in your cover letter, not anywhere in your business world. It's tempting, especially if you think this person would agree with you, but don't do it. There's always the chance that the project was written by this person's best friend. When asked, just say that you found the writing really "interesting."

In Figure 20-2, I present a sample cover letter for your consideration. Obviously, yours needs to be written from scratch to address the specifics of your work situation. But this example offers a sense of the tone you should aim for.

Asking for feedback and following up

Whenever you complete your first freelancing project with a new client, you should close your cover letter with a request for feedback, clarifying that you want it so you can meet this person's needs even more effectively on future projects.

Asking for feedback shows dedication and initiative. You're more than a flash in the freelancer's job pan — you'll be constantly improving, so this person constantly has more reasons to hire you.

Dear Lynn:

Thanks for another favorite. I really enjoy those feel-good romances.

Other than modifying some punctuation to make the second story a little less exclamation-point heavy (noted in the manuscript), this cold read was fairly straightforward.

My schedule includes a lot more time devoted to freelance work, so I can say a big YES to anything you want to send on over. Also, if you know other editors/publishers in need of freelancers, I would greatly appreciate any referrals.

Thanks so much for keeping me busy!

Sincerely,

Suzy Q. Proofreader

Figure 20-2:
An example of a thank-you cover letter.

Here's the schedule: Return your first project, wait two weeks, and then call the person who hired you — but only on a Wednesday or Thursday between 3 and 4 p.m. When she answers, respond in your most calm, cozy, and baggage-free voice: "Hi, it's Suzy Q. Proofreader. I wanted to check in with you on the proofread I returned to you a few weeks ago, *The Clandestine Holiday.* I'd love to hear your feedback, since it was our first time working together."

Then pause. This person may respond a few different ways. Here are your response notes for each situation:

✔ **She's too busy:** "Sorry, Suzy Q, work has been so hectic that I haven't reviewed it yet." Your response: an empathetic laugh and an offer to help. "If you're completely bogged down, I'm more than happy to take on some more work." Whether she offers you work on the spot or thanks you but declines, you're now on the forefront of this person's mind as available and considerate.

✔ **She gives great feedback:** She offers not just positive feedback but helpful tips, too. You thank her and say that you'll be sure to keep those points in mind for any future projects.

✔ **She gives negative feedback:** "Well, Suzy, since you asked, I was a little disappointed in your work because I identified about 40 more corrections than you did." Breathe. It's all right. You're learning, and this is part of the natural process of getting great at this. Your response: "I'm sorry about that, and I'm doubly glad I called, because I'm very committed to a career as a copyeditor/proofreader. If I missed errors, I'd like to know what they are so I can improve my skills and catch them in the future. I'd really appreciate it if you could get me the pages that I missed corrections on or just send me the corrected manuscript once the compositor finishes, so I can review it and be truly prepared for upcoming proofs." Offer to pay for postage if the work is happening on hard copy.

When you get the corrected pages or document, really study the errors you missed. Grammar, punctuation, and spelling problems are finite — you'll quickly figure out the common ones because they come up over and over again. (See Chapter 12 for lots of hints.)

Don't forget to send this person a note or an e-mail after you review the errors. Take responsibility for your mistakes, and assure her that your future work will be improved. Let her know that you really appreciate her help with your improvement. You'd be surprised how a glitch like this can even create a stronger bond with a client; she'll respect the commitment, effort, and professionalism you showed by transforming a potentially problematic situation into a positive interaction.

What if the payment never arrives?

It happens occasionally — though never to the same person twice because it's a lesson you need to learn only once. I hope I can save you from learning it the hard way with the help of this unfortunate story:

I used to love working with Carol Publishing — one of my very first clients. Editors would send me such interesting books: on the most magical honeymoon spots, where to find the best ice cream, how to learn foreign languages. All fluff and fun, so I didn't really mind that the company took over 60 days to pay outstanding invoices. Truth be told, I was new and just grateful they had hired me at all. Year Two working for them was a different story. I had many of their editors sending me projects, and my outstanding balance totaled over $7,000. My

concern finally kicked in but it was too late: Out of the blue, the company went bankrupt. "Substantial creditors" would get paid first — if funds were available. Proofreaders and the rest of the freelancers were at the bottom of that barrel. That $7,000 was never paid to me.

The moral to that irksome, real-life account? Bill promptly. Don't let bills pile up, and don't take one more project from a company unless you've already been paid for the last project, or unless you know the company is credible and flush. Some proofreaders keep projects in hock until they get back pay, but this method of extortion is ill-advised. You did the work, and you deserve to get paid.

Caring for Your Connections

With so many capable copyeditors and proofreaders out there, how can you set yourself ahead of the pack? By building relationships with editors, other clients, and, in some cases, authors. Nurturing these connections takes know-how. As someone who knows how, I'm proud to share a few critical secrets I've discovered along my way.

Monday morning check-in

The best way to check in with an editor or other client is through an e-mail sent Monday morning before 8:45. Please note: that's e-mail, not phone. Ever heard of the song "I Don't Like Mondays"? The Boomtown Rats may have recorded it, but lots of people empathize with it every Monday when they show up for work and are immediately mired in a swampful of back-logged work. If you bother someone with a phone call during this time, there's a good chance you'll be singing "I Don't Like Mondays" for the rest of your week.

Show you're in the know by sending an e-mail instead. Your contact will know you're available and show his thanks by keeping you in mind while doling out projects for the coming week.

Don't over-think the content of your e-mail. You can try to be clever in the e-mail's subject line — *Your manuscripts miss me!* or *Copyediting for sale* — but don't get too flip. Then just follow with two or three sentences, such as

> *Good morning, David,*
>
> *I'm available for any and all proofreading you have coming up this week. My schedule is flexible, and I can deliver on standard or rush deadlines. Thanks very much,*
>
> *Suzy*

Or if you've built up some rapport, and you know that this person trusts your professionalism,

> *Hi Jane,*
>
> *Got any torrid romances for a dependable copyeditor? Or a thriller or a biography or, heck, even a textbook?*
>
> *Looking forward,*
>
> *Suzy*

A little something special

You can show your appreciation in many ways to someone who has helped launch and/or nurture your freelance editing career, but the best way is always with your words. Say thank you. Editors and other clients don't get to hear it as often as you'd think.

You can also resurrect the lost art of the thank-you note, which doesn't have to be formal. Even a few casual words of gratitude seem substantial when they're handwritten on a card and sent the old-fashioned way — with stamps and steps to a mailbox.

As you develop ongoing relationships with your contacts and the projects are coming in on a regular basis, you should consider elevating your thank-yous to include a gift around Thanksgiving — because you've got a lot to be thankful for. No need for a spending spree. Thoughtful goes a lot further than expensive. And don't forget the note!

Gifts that give back to you

Food is always a fabulous gift, especially delivered into an office of overworked editors who are often too busy for real lunch breaks. Feed them and your career in one fell swoop, with the help of these satiating recommendations. Remember: Forsake the fruitcakes, and think fresh.

✔ The Manhattan Fruitier Company, www.manhattanfruitier.com, has an exotic fruit basket with fruits most people can't even pronounce. Thankfully, it comes with a darling little booklet that details each fruit's finer points. It's such the perfect gift because no one's allergic to it, and the whole office can *ooh* and *aah* while thumbing through the booklet trying to figure out what place/planet the pepino and carambola fruits are from. The company ships all across the United States.

✔ Harry & David, www.harryanddavid.com, is always a regal way to say thanks.

And its Royal Riviera Pears are the juiciest things this side of juice.

✔ Organic Bouquet, www.organicbouquet.com, offers gorgeous fresh organic and green label flowers, gourmet organic gift baskets, and fresh organic gift-packed fruits. Prices are reasonable, especially considering that you're showcasing how socially and environmentally responsible you are.

✔ Ithaca Fine Chocolates, www.ithacafinechocolates.com, luxuriously combines fine art and exquisite chocolate by offering gifts like Art Bars — delectable, organic, Fair Trade chocolate bars that feature work by a regional adult artist or an international child artist on a collectible card inside the wrapper. Just imagine, you can support artists, art education, *and* your freelance editing career in a single sweet gift.

Taking Your Business to the Next Level

With your first job behind you, you may be ready to pump up the volume on your freelancing career. In this section, I show you how to generate even more work and, if you choose, become your own corporation.

Creating your own Web site

The days of only techies having Web sites are long gone. Now you can promote your services, your résumé, your portfolio — with no HTML experience and no money spent. If you can point and click, you can design the Web site you want. Peruse the many free hosting providers and blogging services until you find the right one for your needs. Regardless of which service you use, consider springing for the $10 annual fee for your own domain name (suzyQproofreader.com), which can forward seamlessly to your free Web site. Don't forget your contact information!

Here are some prominent and proven free hosting providers:

- http://geocities.yahoo.com/
- www.free.prohosting.com
- www.50megs.com

Also, the URL is long, but so is this list of free providers within Yahoo's directory. Take a deep breath, and type in dir.yahoo.com/Business_and_ Economy/Business_to_Business/Communications_and_Networking/ Internet_and_World_Wide_Web/Network_Service_Providers/Hosti ng/Web_Site_Hosting/Free_Hosting/.

Another option is to use the free sites offered to you by blogging services. (A *blog* is really just a Web site geared toward journal entries that can be easily archived, searched, and commented on by interested readers.) Blogs are super easy to set up and design — again, no HTML needed. And, in my uncompensated opinion, these free providers are the best (even better than many of their fee-charging competitors):

- www.wordpress.com
- www.blogger.com
- www.livejournal.com

One fee-charging Web site worth considering is www.publishersmarket place.com. For $20 per month, you get a daily news feed about the publishing industry and access to a fantastic Web site that offers tons of resources. You can also advertise your services on the site and get help creating your own Web site.

Stepping up your networking

The long-term benefits of networking are well worth the potentially delayed gratification. This is your chance to be Johnny Appleseed, sowing your freelance credentials worldwide, patiently waiting for your business crop to grow. Your eventual prize: unlimited harvest year-round.

And you never know: Sometimes networking can show immediate returns. You meet someone who knows someone in need of a rush job, which you complete with flying colors, and suddenly you're the sole freelancer for Big Rich Corporation.

Here are a few options for getting that fruitful network of yours underway:

✔ **Editorial Freelancers Association:** It touts itself as "the largest and oldest national professional organization dedicated to supporting freelance career choices and opportunities." You can join whether you're a full- or part-time freelancer, and whether or not you live in its hometown of New York City. Dues vary depending on your location. See www.the-efa.org for more information.

✔ **Copyediting-L:** This online community describes itself as "a list for copy editors and other defenders of the English language who want to discuss anything related to editing." It's got more than a couple thousand subscribers who are part-time, full-time, any-time copyeditors. The subscription is free and comes with the free option to add your service profile to its directory of freelancers. For more information about this community, see www.copyediting-l.info.

✔ **Bay Area Editors' Forum:** This is a not-for-profit association of in-house and freelance editors from all walks and all locales. Membership is open to anyone with an active interest in editing. Annual dues are $40 and include member service Web portfolios, promotion, discussion lists, and additional support for us editorial types. See www.editorsforum.org for more information.

✔ **The Slot:** "A Spot for Copy Editors" is the tagline of this community of posting readers devoted to the ins and outs of the copyediting field. Bill Walsh, the national desk copy chief at *The Washington Post* by night, is the site's writer by day. See www.theslot.com for more information.

Promoting yourself in other ways

You may want to promote yourself through posting a résumé on the same job search Web sites you use to identify potential clients. Any client searching `http://hotjobs.yahoo.com/`, `www.careerbuilder.com`, or `www.monster.com` for your particular skills will be en route in no time. Added bonus: Posting is free; all you have to do is register with a username and password.

Don't forget your keywords! Enter as many terms as you're allowed, including *proofreader, copyeditor, editor,* and *publishing.* When a prospective client searches under these keywords, voilà! — your impeccable résumé will appear.

And don't forget to search the smaller but more specialized sites for posting opportunities. For example, `www.copyeditor.com` allows freelancers to post résumés and portfolios for free, and then it promotes job seekers to publishers seeking freelance services.

Another idea is to join *Web rings*: hundreds and even thousands of Web sites bound together based on kindred content. You can use search engines to find and join ones that even indirectly reach your clients, looking beyond publishers and magazines to communities that connect proofreaders and editors. Start at `www.webring.com`; it has a searchable directory featuring such Web rings as The Write Way Ring, which "wishes to bring together writers, authors and publishers for the mutual benefits of networking and traffic-sharing. For beginning writers, published authors, independent publishers, traditional publishers, and literary professionals (editors, proofreaders, agents, and ghostwriters) who wish to increase their client lists. Welcome aboard!"

Finally, within just about every blogger's site, whether it's written by someone in publishing, copyediting, or rock climbing, there are opportunities for you to get noticed — and networked. Each post or journal entry made has a tool that lets readers add comments, which in turn get read by all the same readers. Making blog comments is a great way to introduce yourself and bond with other people in your field. It's also a way to embarrass yourself to those same people, so be sure your comment is contextual and beneficial to the topic at hand, as opposed to blatantly promotional. One of the most popular and insightful blogs in the copyediting world is Deanna Hoak's at `http://deannahoak.com/`.

Incorporating or creating an LLC

When your freelancing business really starts booming, you may want to consider becoming a bona fide business. Depending on where you live, the cost of incorporating through an online service can run between $70 and $600. Is it worth the money? If the jobs are starting to come in, yes, because creating a corporation not only saves you money in taxes; it can actually make a lot more potential jobs come in and stay in. It legitimizes you in so many ways. More credentials, more professionalism, more business.

Think about it: Instead of being a lone freelance copyeditor or proofreader, you're now the president of a company that provides freelance editing or proofreading services. Plus, who can resist inventing her very own company name?

There are many online incorporation companies, including `www.bizfilings.com` — a friendly site that also provides its services through Yahoo as a trusted partner. BizFilings has a great Q&A section, too.

A newer entity, the limited liability corporation (LLC), doesn't require as much formality as a corporation and has become very popular among small businesses that want to incorporate. The site `www.lectlaw.com` defines an LLC as "a business structure that is a hybrid of a partnership and a corporation. Its owners are shielded from personal liability and all profits and losses pass directly to the owners without taxation of the entity itself." The site also notes an additional benefit: "You don't need an attorney to set up an LLC." (In other words, it's pretty easy.)

Whether you opt for becoming an LLC or a full corporation, you'll reap the following benefits:

✔ **Averting a tax implication:** As owner of a corporation, you're lifted out of the "self-employed/work from home" red flag that the IRS so often scrutinizes. As a corporation, you file corporate returns instead of individual tax returns, and you compete for the IRS's attention alongside showstoppers such as GE and Microsoft.

✔ **Charging your expenses against the income flowing through your business:** When you incorporate or open an LLC, you qualify to open a matching bank account in your company's name. (Remember to have your payments made out to your corporation or LLC name.) Next step: Acquire a business credit card to save you the trouble of itemizing your expenses. American Express is especially open to working with small businesses.

Is it time to go full-time?

As you further endear yourself to editors and other clients, they may start keeping an eye out for full-time positions for you at their places of employment. If you get an offer, you may not have much time to respond, so I recommend that you periodically check in with yourself to ask the question, "Would I rather be working full-time?"

There may be lots of background factors, but on center stage are Money and Time. If you're not yet earning in the upper echelons of freelance pay rates or you aren't yet securing a steady flow of freelance work, you may want to go full-time. After all, you get stable income, health benefits, paid vacation and sick days, and probably a 401(k). But if you've got droves of satisfied repeat clients and are already getting what's jokingly referred to as "the friendship

rate" (a high rate due to your proven reliability and track record, but also due to the fact that you've been making the editor happy for a long time), the freelance life may be too sweet to trade in.

Your schedule, of course, is a key factor. Are stability and benefits worth working rigid hours, often more than 50 per week? Will you have enough time for family commitments, creative pursuits, and other business ventures?

I encourage you to make your decision meticulously, as opposed to basing it on your mood on a given day. That's why considering the question before a job offer arises can be so helpful. And when you find yourself facing a great job offer and uncertain about what to do, remember: It's a happy problem to have!

Whether you're incorporated or not, business meals can be tax deductible when you're a freelancer. So can business supplies, travel expenses, and any other expenses that help support your freelance career. If you work from home, you can calculate what percentage of your home is taken up by your work space and deduct that percentage of all your utility bills. I strongly recommend making nice with a CPA or tax attorney at the start of your freelance journey so you can take full advantage of all the tax savings you can get.

Benevolent Dictatorship: How to Be Your Own Boss

I know, being your own boss is supposed to be all about giving yourself the day off — and a raise. Eat another bon-bon, and then let's both get back to reality.

Being an effective boss, especially when you're trying to manage yourself, takes a mastery of the delicate balance between Good Boss and Bad Boss.

Good boss: Taking care of yourself

Your Good Boss is the one who sets boundaries and recognizes that you're finite, and finite freelancers can't work more than 24 hours in a day or 15 hours 20 days straight. Good Boss takes care of you by limiting the number of projects you take on, the number of hours you work in a day, the number of days you work in a row.

Thanks to Good Boss, you not only work more effectively and efficiently, you also keep your sanity and your family intact. Workers are happiest when their families see them often enough to recognize them.

Oh, and one other thing: Good Boss ain't gonna let ya take on another project from a company that hasn't paid you for the last job. (See the sidebar "What if the payment never arrives?" earlier in this chapter.)

Bad boss: Meeting the deadline, no matter what

Tough love is still love. Bad Boss knows what's best and takes responsibility for the difficult decision to skip today's Steelers game — or even your daughter's soccer game — if that's what it's going to take to finish your project on time. Bad Boss closes the door to your home office, even when neighbors are still visiting. Do you have to actually pull an all-nighter to meet your deadline tomorrow? Do you really have to ask Bad Boss?

The key to a long and prosperous freelance career is listening to both of those bosses in you. They're both smart.

And right now they're both saying you deserve another bon-bon for completing Chapter 20. Enjoy.

Part VI
The Part of Tens

The 5th Wave   By Rich Tennant

"Your buddy says the two of you were peripheral to the incident in question. You just said you were superficial to the incident. Now which is it, peripheral or superficial?!"

In this part . . .

Every *For Dummies* book ends with top-ten gems, and this book has the two Hope Diamonds: secrets to success as a copyeditor and secrets to success as a proofreader.

Chapter 21

Ten Keys to Success as a Copyeditor

As a copyeditor, you have power. You can shape up a dismal book and make it reader-worthy or award-worthy. You can rearrange titles, paragraphs, and sometimes entire chapters. You can rewrite whatever you want! You can ignite your lightsaber and . . .

Whoa, young Padawan. Before reveling in the power that your pen (or keyboard) wields, let's jump back and examine, with a cool head, how a copyeditor creates and maintains that fine balance between running an absolute copyeditor monarchy and kowtowing to the creative team.

Figure Out Your Employer or Client

Occasionally you'll have an opportunity to get to know the author of a project you're working on. More likely, though, she'll remain simply a name on the title page.

Whom *do* you have the chance to know? Your editor, or whoever else is managing the project. You have an obligation to know this person, whether you're a permanent member of his staff or a freelancer accepting your first assignment from him. Pay attention to his instructions, his preferences, his pet peeves, even his editorial weaknesses so you can jump in and do a slam-bang copyedit that makes him look good. If he looks good to his higher-ups, you will look very good to him.

If you're a staff copyeditor, you should have lots of opportunities to get to know the people managing your projects. Pay close attention at staff meetings, ask coworkers for insights, and read every e-mail or memo that comes your way so you're aware of changes to policies, procedures, or house style.

As a freelancer, you may not have much personal contact with your clients. You may get an occasional phone call, but even that's not a guarantee; some clients communicate solely through e-mail. How do you figure out what a client wants when your access to this person is so limited? When you receive a project, you usually receive a cover letter or e-mail that details concerns specific to the project. This document contains clues that will help you figure out your client's needs.

Read the cover letter or e-mail word for word. Sometimes you won't even understand a given direction until you're immersed in the manuscript, so keep the cover letter or e-mail in full view as you proceed through the copyedit.

The cover letter may note modifications that cropped up recently in the editorial process. (For example, "Please note that the protagonist's sister is named Melvina, not Melinda" or "Remove 'www.' from URLs that work without it.") Obviously, you want to keep your eyes peeled for those issues; your client expects you to locate and correct every instance.

Here's why this cover letter business is so crucial: I once received a job from my publisher that had a tight deadline. I began working on it, got a few pages in, and noticed that sometimes the author used a serial comma and sometimes not. I decided to implement the serial comma and began adding caret and comma wherever I found one missing. Before long, I had a bloodbath on my hands. I became obsessed with these commas, and when I got to the end of the manuscript, I was confident that I hadn't missed a single one.

While packaging the book for shipment, I happened to glance at the cover letter. There, in the third paragraph, were these words: *Please note that per author request, serial comma should remain inconsistent. You may notice that it is attached to some characters' voices and not others.*

I looked at the red ink dripping from the pages and had to sit down to absorb the valuable lesson.

Meet the Deadline Every Time

Before you start a project, make sure you're clear about its deadline, and make sure you can meet it. If you have any doubts, say so up front. As a staffer, that may mean you need to ask whether another project on your plate can be given to someone else so you can focus on meeting this deadline. Or it may even mean that you need to ask for this project to be divided between you and another copyeditor. Communicate your concerns clearly to the person managing your time or the project in question, and be willing to work with whatever solutions are offered.

As a freelancer, the solution is pretty simple: If you have doubts about whether you can meet a deadline, don't accept the project. Better to turn down a project, even for a new client, than fail to deliver it on time.

Your employer or client may say something like "Ideally, I would like this project back on my desk Friday, August 7th, but you can take until Monday the 10th if need be." When should you return the project? On the 7th. Always hit the ideal date instead of the last-minute one.

And be sure to acknowledge your speediness (in your return cover letter, if you're a freelancer): "I wanted to get this project back to you before your requested deadline so that you could really take your time reviewing it." A copyeditor who makes deadlines gets a big thumbs-up (and a freelancer gets repeat business).

Review the Manuscript Before You Start Editing

When Ikea recently delivered an entertainment center to me, I panicked. This was because when my husband and I put together our Ikea bed a month earlier, our happy-go-lucky puttering and tinkering almost turned into a full-blown hex-key fight. I can't remember exactly what went wrong, but let's just say that mistakes were made. I was as close as I've ever been to sleeping in the kitchen. So this time, I called my upstairs neighbor, Matthew, for assistance. The first thing he did amazed me. He found the directions and read them from start to finish. This meant that he knew in advance how the initial steps would tie into the later steps. After that, putting everything together was a breeze. And the most shocking part was that we didn't have any widgets left over (except the hex-key).

Going through a manuscript is no different. Page through initially, and you are likely to find any leftover widgets . . . before you begin to build your style sheet or make executive decisions about grammatical and syntactical inconsistencies.

Getting your hands on a raw manuscript for the first time can be a heady sensation, but take my advice: Don't plunge into the reading immediately. Put down your pencil, or push back from the keyboard, and spend some time getting your bearings. Go through the front matter — everything that precedes the text — for an introduction to the project. Opening sections, such as a preface written by the author, a foreword written by someone else, or even a dedication page, can furnish info as to intent, style, and general condition of the manuscript. Take care of preliminaries; for example, perhaps you need to paginate (or repaginate) at the outset. Then skim the text for an overview of content and a sense of author voice. Do all this before you begin a page-by-page read, and your projects will turn out even better than Ikea's floor models.

Respect the Author (Even When You Don't)

Have you any idea what percentage of submitted book manuscripts get accepted for publication? It's a minuscule number, with lots of zeroes after the decimal point. When a publishing house sees enough merit and/or marketability in a particular stack of loose sheets to want to convert them into a bound book, you have to give credit where credit is due — to the person who wrote it. The same is true if you're working on a magazine article, a Web site, a corporation's annual report . . . someone with more authority than you trusted this writer to create something workable. You've got to respect that decision.

Okay, so the author is ignorant, self-satisfied, boring, condescending, trite, and a laundry list of other negatives, in your opinion. The point is, it's *your* opinion. Never assume that your employer or client agrees with your assessment, and keep your opinion to yourself even if he does.

Although your project may be your baby, don't get too attached. The author's voice and opinions trump yours. If the author sends his protagonist to the "theatre," that's his choice. You can suggest sending her to the "theater" instead, but don't stress if the author says no.

If you want to get attached to something, turn your focus to making your author happy and fulfilled. Then you'll be happy too because your employer or client will have fewer author issues to resolve. As a staffer, this approach will help you earn trust and, perhaps, receive better and better assignments. As a freelancer, this approach will help ensure that the client — and maybe even the author himself — will have more work for you in the future. Just remember who's signing your paycheck.

Look It Up

Running spell-check is one way to start rooting out errors in a document, but don't swear by it — not when the English language is a strange amalgam of homonyms and inconsistencies. Just because a conglomeration of letters forms a bona fide word doesn't mean it's the word you want. For example, I can type the word *miniscule,* and my spell-check program won't notice that it's misspelled. That's because it's an alternate spelling of *minuscule,* which is what *Merriam-Webster's Collegiate Dictionary,* 11th Edition (*Web 11*) prefers.

 If you have an iota of doubt about anything you read, look it up. Don't be intimated by an apparently erudite, meticulous author; everybody can and does make mistakes — that's why you have a job. The more careful the author, the more grateful she'll be for any corrections or improvements you make.

If you haven't already read it, turn to Chapter 5 for suggestions on how to fact-check any document.

Google It

When I wrote my first book report (on Betamax versus VHS), I had to go to the library. The librarian looked into a daunting cabinet of cards, and then she handed me a scrap of paper. I had to decipher the Dewey Decimal System and find the book on a shelf too high for me to reach.

Nowadays, if an author has not provided adequate info on a given item — enough to clarify the text and satisfy the reader — I can ask for help from Google (or Yahoo or any other Internet search engine).

Google is a goody of a search engine. If you're in the mood for some fun, type into the search box whatever you're looking for, then hit the "I'm feeling lucky" button on the bottom right. You can have hours of fun at www.google.com.

 Even Google can't cure every manuscript ill. If you need clarification and don't feel confident suggesting changes that provide it, go back to the source: the author. Write a query that clearly states the problem. Sometimes the author knows the topic so well that he simply forgets to include a vital fact; other times he may need to rewrite.

Write It Down, Write It All Down

Remember the advice of your favorite teachers back in school: take good notes. As you read through a manuscript, take notes on what you come across. The longer the document you're working on, the more vital these notes are so you can ensure consistency throughout.

For instance, if the author starts out using serial commas, make a note of it. If she abbreviates state names, make a note of it. If you read that a character's wedding ring "tapped against her pencil" as she wrote a goodbye note, jot down that she's probably left-handed. And keep an eye out for dialects in dialogue. (I don't know why, but sometimes authors switch them up mid-manuscript.)

These notes can be huge time-savers, and ultimately, you give many of them to the editor or other person managing the project in the form of a style sheet (see Chapter 14). Or, if you have conflicting notes, they form the basis of queries to the editor or author.

Proofread Your Own Work

You're telling me I need to do *one more* read-through? Awww . . . Well, read this.

There's a big wedding in the family. Within the elegant invitation mailing will be a card perfectly worded to direct guests to the ceremony and reception. The mother of the bride creates the card and proofs it before printing. When she picks it up, the very first heading jumps out at her: *To the Congregrational Church.* Granted, it's a small, ornate font where the letters seem to meld into each other, but still, how on earth did that extra "r" sneak its way in?

True story. And here's the kicker: This was no ordinary civilian mom but a seasoned copyeditor. So what happened? Enmeshed in her topic, she read not the words but the intent.

Moral 1: Read what they write, not what they mean.

Moral 2: Do one more read-through.

Moral 3: Work on manuscripts you're not emotionally involved with.

So when Great Aunt Clara is getting her memoirs published and insists that you copyedit them, resist! Surgeons don't operate on their own family members, and even the most skilled authors need objective copyeditors.

(P.S. Happy ending: The printer redid the direction cards at minimal cost. Had it been a book, we know whose head would be rolling on the carpet.)

Even though there may be a whole chain of checks and rechecks on the conveyor belt to publication, don't assume the next person in line will catch what you miss. Act as if you are the final checkpoint before publication, and you will be a great copyeditor.

Read (and Then Read Some More)

Read everything that crosses your line of vision — from the daily papers to billboards to television ads to incoming mail. If you're a file-it person, start a folder of items that range from the scholarly to the everyday. Were you taken with a turn of phrase — concise yet charming — in a friend's thank-you note? Save it, to inspire you in those instances when a line of text needs gentle doctoring. Above all, have a love affair with the English language. It's the most incorrigible, incredible, and incisive language out there. A good dictionary — like *Web 11* — is the ultimate page-turner, juicy as any mystery. Prove it to yourself: Pick a page, any page, and start reading. You'll be amazed at how much you learn.

Begin to carry reading materials around with you. Lightweight paperbacks are perfect for perusing in your doctors' and dentists' waiting rooms. If your back is suffering under the weight of your messenger bag and you have access to a photocopier, copy a chapter of your latest summer thriller, and stash it in your pocket.

Do you take public transportation to work? If so, you're in for some wicked fun. I don't know why this is, but the people who put advertisements on buses and subways don't seem to pay the slightest attention to spelling or punctuation. Challenge yourself to find an error in each ad. Believe me, this is a game where you can rack up some points. Give yourself bonus points for misused quotation mark's "or" apostrophes. (For fantastic examples of misused quotation marks, go to www.juvalamu.com/qmarks/.)

Stay on Top of Changes in Your Profession

The copyediting world is changing quickly, and we wordsmiths have to zip to keep up. As I explain in Chapter 17, copyeditors don't often work on hard copy anymore; electronic editing is the norm. If you want to work at home, that means you accept responsibility for maintaining your computer. (If your operating system is Windows 98, you've got some updating to do!) And make sure your skills keep pace with the technology of the field; that means you may want to take courses on editing in PDFs or on the desktop publishing applications Quark or Adobe InDesign, both used by a lot of magazines. If you're drawn to Web editing, you may also want to know some HTML. You may be able to get by without it, but having that knowledge definitely increases your value.

Changes in the profession aren't always related to technology, though. Believe it or not, new editions of style guides often feature significant changes. Be sure to check out the latest edition of your preferred style guide and hunt for the amendments.

And finally, make a concerted effort to be a part of the copyediting community. It's pretty easy to do so these days, thanks to the Copyediting-L Listserv (Google it, then join it) and some great Web sites devoted to copyediting such as www.copydesk.org, run by the American Copy Editors Society, and the subscription newsletter *Copy Editor* available at www.copyeditor.com. Checking a favorite copyediting Web site periodically can help ensure that you're in the know when new work processes and technologies emerge.

Chapter 22

Ten Keys to Success as a Proofreader

*I*t may be difficult to imagine that the writer of that hot new best-seller could require the services of a proofreader like you. But rest assured that authors are not infallible, and the runaway success you see on the shelf at your local bookstore is flourishing in large part due to the work of behind-the-scenes proofreaders and editors.

If you want to be on the top of the list to get proofreading jobs that are future best-sellers (or the cream of whatever crop of writing you fancy), here are ten tips to up your game.

Know That Once Is Not Enough

Well, okay, sometimes it is. Especially after you've been proofing a while. But if you're looking to be a Halle Berry or George Clooney — you know, a superstar — you want to work it a bit. They say a good actor approaches a role the way you peel an onion: a layer at a time. Likewise, a proofreading project sometimes needs to be looked at again and again — peeled and repealed, if you will. Oops! I mean re-peeled. But you knew that.

The first pass or read-through of the material is somewhat superficial; you just want to correct obvious errors and get a broad sense of the concepts. Then, when you take your second pass, you gain deeper comprehension and familiarity with the material. You may need a third pass to reach the core.

By taking a quick superficial pass, you gain familiarity with the subject matter or storyline, the writing style, and any peculiarities of usage particular to the author. On the next pass, you're sure to catch a high percentage of errors. Familiarity with the document makes the process so much easier because after you *know* the author, you can proactively proofread — intuiting where problem areas will arise.

Proofreading has been around for centuries — since the first monk printed that weighty tome. I'm sure the first proofreader's job was tough because no one had ever edited a book before. He was finding errors for the first time. But guess what? The errors have all been found. There is no little man sitting in the corner inventing new ones. If you've seen one transposition of *from/form,* you've seen 'em all.

So, the good news is that although authors do make mistakes, there are a finite number of them. Also, you can usually notice a pattern of mistakes; it emerges quickly if you're paying close attention. After you identify the author's unique pattern of usage errors, you're over the first set of hurdles. You can bet your paycheck that the same errors will reappear time and again throughout the text.

Jot down brief notations — for your own purposes — of any usage patterns you notice as you make your way through the text. Review your list before each pass to remind yourself of the most common and habitual errors. This list also comes in handy if you are working on an electronic version of the manuscript: You can cross-check your proofreading accuracy using the incredible global Find function (see Chapter 17).

Hold on to this list when you're done with the project, too. If you're lucky enough to proofread for the same author again, it can reduce the time you spend on that next document.

Give the ToC Some TLC

The table of contents is just a bunch of short lines listing chapter or section headings and their corresponding page numbers. Compiling a ToC must be pretty easy, right? What could possibly go wrong? Well, now that you mention it . . .

The ToC is very important but frequently overlooked. Especially if you're working on an educational text, you want to give this section a thorough proofread. Even if your document is not overly complex, a well-reviewed ToC will help you stand out from the proofreader pack.

Certainly, the ToC is easy to proof. It's a flip job: Look at the ToC. Look at Chapter 1. Check the title. Check the page number. Look at the ToC. Look at Chapter 2. Rinse. Repeat.

But ToCs can be more complex depending on the type of project. Other elements, such as illustrations or maps, may be included in the ToC, and you need to note whether all levels of subheadings are included or only the top tier or two.

In magazines, proofing the ToC can get a little hairy. It's got to be done at the last minute, and the layout usually distinguishes between departments, features, and "other stuff." You have to be sure that each item in the magazine is accounted for in the right section.

In titles and headings, pay attention to the little words. The treatment of articles and prepositions should be consistent — same spelling and same case as per the publisher's style guidelines. You'd be surprised how big a deal the prepositions *about* and *because of* can be in the realm of the ToC. Prepositions of five letters or more are sometimes capitalized and sometimes lowercased in titles and headings. Just be sure that what you're seeing is consistent throughout the project.

Speaking of titles, don't forget the kingpin and queen bee of them all: the title of the book, article, or project itself. Suppose you're proofing a book with the title *Ring Around the Rosie* and the subtitle *Just Between Us Girls*. If "around," "between," or any other prepositions of comparable length or longer are capitalized in the book title, they must also be capitalized if they appear in chapter titles or headings in the text.

Don't Forget the Headings

This one takes a little practice and a discerning eye for typeface and size to master. In addition to checking headings and subheadings for the accuracy of grammar and spelling, you also check them for formatting uniformity.

Your editor should give you specific guidelines on typeface and size to use as a reference. If you are doing an electronic edit, checking these is a fairly straightforward process. If your eyes aren't certain if a heading is correctly formatted, you can click your cursor on the words of the header and look to see what the user-friendly toolbar at the top tells you about the font and size.

If you are working from a hard copy manuscript, you can manually compare the latest header to ones on previous pages (assuming those previous ones are correct).

If you make any changes to chapter headings *other than* formatting corrections, those changes need to be reflected in the ToC. You always want the ToC to match exactly how the headings appear in the document itself.

Don't Forget the Running Heads and Feet, Either

The term *running heads* refers to text that appears in the space at the very top of the page. Running heads typically include the title of a book, chapter, article, annual report . . . whatever type of document you're working on. The term *feet* refers to text placed in the space below the last line of body text on each page.

Each publisher and organization has a particular style, so you have to find out what information should appear in the running heads or feet of your particular document. If you're working on a book, you'll probably find that the book title is placed on the left side and either the chapter title or the author's name appears on the right side.

Some documents include the page numbers in the header, and some put them in the feet. Make sure the pages are numbered consecutively, that the numbers appear in the exact same spot on every page, and that the typeface and size are uniform. Also, pay close attention to the numbering system for any introductory pages, glossary pages, and appendix pages. You may find that you need to bone up on Roman numerals for some of these elements. In the event that you find errors in the numbering of the pages, update your ToC.

Give the heads and feet a thorough proof. Seasoned proofreaders and editors will tell you that errors are often missed in these little elements. As painful as it may be to read the same line again and again, you must do so to ensure that each head appears correctly.

This part of the proofread is a lot easier on an electronic edit. But be careful not to become overly reliant on the software's (or typist's) accuracy. Even in this digital age, information can still be omitted, reversed, or inserted in the wrong place.

Look Out for Graphics

Not to worry, this section is not rated R. I'm talking graphs and images here, not graphic images.

The first thing you look for is proper layout of the graphic elements. If graphics appear in the body of the text you're proofreading, you want to ensure that the text wraps around the image in an aesthetically pleasing way. Obviously, images should not overlap with text and vice versa, unless that's the deliberate style (as we see in some magazines).

Graphics and images usually need captions. The house style of the publisher or other organization you're working for should indicate whether captions are required and how they are formatted. In the captions of group pictures, people are usually named left to right, bottom row to top. If house style doesn't call for captions, a description of the image needs to appear in the body of the text.

If you don't understand the relevance of a graphic or picture, flag it. Chances are that if the graphic is left as is, the reader will be just as baffled as you are.

Sometimes graphics are numbered; for example, within a chapter, the author may refer to Image 1.1, 1.2, and so on. Make sure that this reference number also appears with the actual image. Plus, cross-check the order of the references to confirm that each number is placed with the correct image.

Here's a crucial thing to know: Many photographic images are copyrighted. This means that images should never just be copied from a Web site and reprinted somewhere else. At the very minimum, there needs to be a credit somewhere that identifies the photographer or copyright holder. With news photography, it is typical to credit both the photographer and the news agency. If the photo is a picture of artwork, often the museum that owns the art is credited. As proofreader, you don't need to know the finer details. Just be on the lookout for graphics and pictures that don't seem to be credited anywhere in the book.

If you have any doubts whether the author has sought permission for the reprint of an image, voice those doubts to the editor. The improper use of copyrighted material, or even incorrect notation of a credit, can lead to legal trouble. No point in chancing that.

Keep It Neat

We all know how important first impressions are. If you work on hard copy, one of the first things the editor sees on the manuscript is your proofreading marks. You don't want all those conscientious hours spent proofreading to go unnoticed over something as easy to manage as neatness, right? If your markup is sloppy (or worse, unintelligible), it reflects badly on your abilities as a proofreader and hurts your chances of being hired again. Take the time to draw those proofreading marks correctly and legibly. Your extra effort will go far to show the editor what an organized, detailed, and conscientious proofreader you are.

I was a grubby kid, so how did I get so neat?

It makes no difference to me how long you go before cleaning your bathtub. I don't care how many pairs of underwear you have hanging from the TV. Just remember that in editing, neatness counts.

In my personal life, there's little I hate more than tackling dishes after a relaxing meal. But when I proofread and copyedit, I'm a neat girl. And my editors appreciate it. Here's how I do it.

I keep my workspace clean. While it's not like a shrine or anything, it is an area that contains only my proofreading. I find that if my table or desk is clean, my project stays clean. Even if I'm using the kitchen table, I clear it of sharp knives, avocado rinds, and stray children before setting out my work.

I work with sharp implements. (They also come in handy if someone comes in to bother me while I'm reading a salacious scene.) I use a finely sharpened pencil with an eraser that doesn't leave tracks. When writing, I make distinct, non-smearable marks. (Here's where electronic projects have the edge: When I'm editing an electronic document, the lousiest handwriting in the world means nothing — no one will see it.)

I don't write anything in indelible ink. I've made my share of mistakes. Even when I notice the mistake mere seconds after making it, with permanent ink it's too late to do anything but write "stet."

I bask in fantastic lighting. And — since this isn't a dress rehearsal but the real deal — so should you. Lighting is key for me. The better my lighting, the less tired I get, and the more likely errors pop out at me. I use a strong overhead light for hard-copy editing, as well as a directional lamp that I can pull very close to the page. But I have known many a well-placed floor lamp that can do the trick. Glare-minimizing soft lighting works well for electronic editing.

I tend not to bleed on the projects. Nor do I spill pie filling on them. On the rare occasion that I eat and read, I make sure it's white, dry food — like paint chips.

I don't let people smoke near my work (or my kids). Paper absorbs the odor of cigarettes. I know a production editor who had to take some pages home and air them out on her deck before being able to read them. Needless to say, she was not amused. No one came out ahead — except Big Tobacco. Certainly not the freelancer, who was never called again.

Basically, I keep the project in the condition in which I received it. I don't re-collate it, staple it, paper-clip it, or make colorful magic marker exclamations on it.

Keep your projects neat in whatever way works for you. But keep them neat.

Never write anything critical of an author unless you are absolutely, completely positive she will not see it. Even stickies sent to your editor could find themselves in the hands of a very angry and insulted writer. (Believe you me, these folks are sensitive.) The rare suggestion on content, if you must make it, should be jotted briefly and tactfully on a sticky note affixed to the page. (Of course, if a sentence on page 32 is repeated on page 107, the editor needs to know this.)

Don't think that you are off the hook for neatness just because you happen to be working on an electronic document. While you won't have to worry about writing legibly, the same concept holds true. Put some thought and strategy into your electronic edits. They should be clear and easy to follow. If the pages start to look more like a Jackson Pollock work than a manuscript, you may have a problem getting your point across to the editor. Comments need to be concise, comprehensible, and, most of all, tactful (see Chapter 17).

Mind Your PEs (and AAs)

In addition to finding errors, in the book publishing world you also get to assign blame to the error-missers! Blame is assigned in the form of PEs (*printer's errors*) or AAs (*author's alterations*). You may also come across the term EAs, which stands for *editor's alteration* or *editorial adjustment,* but AAs is generally used to indicate any change that the printer can charge the publisher for (because it wasn't the printer's error).

When you proofread against dead copy, the errors that you find that were missed or introduced by the compositor (or typesetter) are PEs — printer's errors. We love PEs because no one on "our side" needs to pay for them.

When you find errors that were missed by the copyeditor, production editor, or author, you mark those as AAs. These AAs cost the publisher — sometimes a dollar or more per correction. So there's a bittersweet feeling accompanying the AA: First, "Yes! My eyes were sharper than all the pros who came before me!" and then, "Aw. The people who hired me need to pay to fix this."

As the editorial process becomes more and more electronic, PEs and AAs will become less of an issue. For example, proofreaders of *For Dummies* books do their work on-screen only, so corrections are made before a manuscript is even sent to a printer.

In the land of magazines, PEs and AAs rarely apply.

Never Reedit

Let's say a document you're proofreading has several sentences ending in not one, not three, but a series of eight exclamation points. You and I both know that's not necessary, and you may be tempted to cross out anything above three. There's a proofreader out there — a very good one, in fact — who did just that and was crossed off the publisher's freelance list for keeps. Moral: Resist temptation!!!

Your corrections and queries are not your soap box, your podium, your platform, or your best friend Jane. Use them cautiously, and don't vent or otherwise dramatize whatever dire mistake you feel the author has made.

You can be sure that the author has run his work by more than a few other readers, and that he currently values it and will vehemently defend it if attacked. Instead of going into battle over something you're uncomfortable seeing in print, opt instead for a polite query to your editor on a sticky note or in an electronic comment box — either of which can be removed before the document reaches the author.

Make your queries polite for two reasons: Every once in a while, a sticky note or electronic comment isn't removed en route to an author; and you don't know your editor's relationship to the author. Make humble suggestions and requests instead of incensed demands or gloating error catches.

Read (And Then, Read Some More)

When not working on a proofreading project, keep those special skills you honed sharp by reading everything within your sight. At home? Read the newspaper, cookbooks, coupons, and so on. In your car? Read billboards, bumper stickers, whatever. Create fun games for yourself like seeing how many grammatical errors or misspellings you can catch each day, or keep a tally of which local restaurant has the most typos on its menu. Who knows, maybe you can get a part-time gig as its preferred menu proofreader!

Dig the Deadline

Repeat after me: *The deadline is key.* I've heard stories of second-rate proofreaders who get more work than first-rate ones simply because the second-raters always meet their deadlines.

The deadline is there for a reason: Whatever you're working on must move to the next level of production in order to get published on time. So treat your deadline with the utmost responsibility and respect.

Here's how I like to work the deadline: I act as if the project is due 24 hours before its deadline, so that even if I'm running a bit behind, my behind is not on the line. Save your behind: Make your deadline.

Part VII
Appendixes

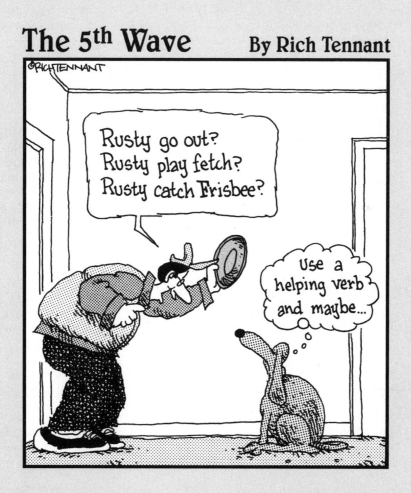

In this part . . .

1 give you three resources that may make your professional life a wee bit easier. First is a list of some of the
most commonly misspelled words (including the word
misspelled). Next is a glossary of terms that can help
you navigate the book and magazine publishing world.
And finally is a list of online resources that can help you
do everything from confirm trademarked names to convert metric measurements. You're welcome!

Appendix A

Commonly Misspelled Words

· ·

*A*s you plug away at proofreading or catch mistakes while copyediting, you'll see all sorts of ways people misspell words. Writing down the wiliest of the lot is not only extremely entertaining, but it also trains your brain to recognize the wonky spelling when it comes up the next time. Here's a list to get you started.

absence	believe	deceive
abundance	benefit	defendant
accessible	broccoli	definitely
accommodate	business	desiccate
achievement	calendar	desperate
ad nauseam	camouflage	dictionary
alcohol	carburetor	disastrous
a lot	Caribbean	dumbbell
amateur	cemetery	ecstasy
apology	characteristic	eighth
apparent	chili	eligible
arctic	committee	embarrass
argument	conceive	environment
ascend	condescend	exceed
atheist	congratulations	exercise
auxiliary	conscious	exhaust
balloon	controversial	facsimile
barbecue	courteous	Fahrenheit
beggar	daiquiri	familiar
beginning	Dalmatian	February

fiery	irresistible	missile
fluorescent	island	misspell
forfeit	jealousy	mortgage
forty	jewelry	muscle
friend	judicial	nauseous
fulfill	Juilliard	necessary
Gandhi	knight	neighbor
gauge	knowledge	neutron
genius	laboratory	newsstand
government	legitimate	ninety
grammar	length	ninth
guarantee	leprechaun	noticeable
guerrilla	liaise	nuisance
guttural	liaison	obedience
handkerchief	license	obstacle
harass	lieutenant	occasionally
height	lightning	occurred
hemorrhage	liquefy	occurrence
heroes	luxury	official
hierarchy	maintenance	omission
hors d'oeuvre	maneuver	omit
hypocrisy	marriage	omitted
idiosyncrasy	marshmallow	opinion
ignorance	medicine	opportunity
immediately	memento	oppression
implement	millennium	optimism
independence	miniature	optimistic
independent	minuscule	orchestra
inoculate	miscellaneous	ordinarily
introduce	mischievous	outrageous

overrun

pamphlets

parallel

particular

pastime

pavilion

peaceable

peculiar

penetrate

perceive

performance

permanent

permissible

permitted

perseverance

persistence

personnel

perspiration

pharaoh

physical

physician

piece

pleasant

portray

possession

possibility

practically

practice

precede

precedence

preceding

preference

preferred

prejudice

preparation

presence

prevalent

principal

principle

privilege

probably

proceed

professor

pronunciation

propaganda

psychology

publicly

puerile

pursue

quantity

quarantine

questionnaire

quizzes

raspberry

realistically

realize

recede

receipt

receive

recommend

reference

referring

relevant

relieving

religious

remembrance

reminiscence

renowned

reservoir

resistance

restaurant

restaurateur

rhyme

rhythm

ridiculous

roommate

sacrifice

sacrilegious

safety

salary

sandals

schedule

secede

secretary

seize

seizure

sentence

separate

sergeant

simile

simultaneous

sincerely

sophomore

souvenir

specimen

sponsor

spontaneous

strategy

strength

stubbornness

subpoena

subtle

succeed

sufficient

supersede

suppress

surprise

susceptible

syllable

symmetrical

synonymous

technical

technique

temperamental

temperature

tendency

theories

therefore

though

threshold

through

tomorrow

tournament

twelfth

tyranny

unanimous

unforgettable

unfortunately

unique

unnecessary

until

usage

usually

utilization

vacuum

valuable

vehicle

vengeance

village

villain

vinaigrette

violence

visible

vision

warrant

weather

Wednesday

weird

wholly

withdrawal

withhold

yacht

yield

young

Appendix B

Glossary

● ●

Acquisitions editor: The person who is responsible for finding and buying a publishable book manuscript.

All caps: The use of all capital letters, for example in a title.

Alley: The space between columns of type on a page.

Author's alteration (AA): An author's change or other alteration to laid-out text that is not a *printer's error* (*PE*).

Backbone: The bound edge of a magazine or a book.

Back of (the) book (BoB): The back pages of a magazine that contain follow-up information (like "where to buy it" or story credits), and often some columns and *departments*. Also used for books, but *back matter* is more common.

Back matter: The back pages of a book that contain supplemental information such as endnotes, appendixes, indexes — even ads for the author's next book.

Bad break (BB): An incorrectly hyphenated word at the end of a typeset line.

Blow-in cards: Those "subscribe now" or "smell me" cards literally blown between the pages of a bound magazine. (If they're bound into the magazine, they're called "bind-in cards.")

Bluelines: Also referred to as "blues," these are proofs of the final book or magazine that are printed, folded, and bound. Bluelines represent the editor's last chance to catch any errors before the presses start rolling. (Blues can actually be more than one color, or not blue at all; they are a cheaper way of checking layout and type issues than paying for full-color proofs.)

Bound book: The finished product, ready to be sold.

Callout: A few sentences pulled from an article, blown up, and placed prominently on the page to break up copy; intended to "call out" the reader's attention and entice further reading.

Camera-ready: A term you will still hear used instead of *print-ready* to describe files that have gone through final approval for printing, even when the process is entirely digital.

Caps: Short for "capital letters." Used in the terms *all caps, initial caps,* and *small caps.*

Center spread: An article, image, or ad that covers the two center pages of a magazine or newsletter.

CMYK: The abbreviation for the colors used in *four-color process* printing: Cyan, Magenta, Yellow, and Key color (which is black).

Cold read: The process of reading a piece of copy straight through, with nothing to compare it against.

Column inch: A measurement of space for copy that is one column wide and one inch deep.

Column read: Copy that is set one column wide and one inch deep.

Comparison read: The process of comparing two pieces of copy to ensure that they are identical; also called *slugging.*

Compositor: A person who converts electronic manuscript files into page proofs that conform to the design *specs*; also known as a *typesetter.*

Content: Anything within a magazine that is not advertising.

Continuity: The overall logic and consistency of a story's internal world.

Copy: The actual words of a manuscript, article, caption, and so on.

Coverlines: Sometimes referred to as "cutlines," short lines of copy placed on the cover of a publication to tempt potential buyers.

CQ: Scribbled next to a word, it's magazine talk for "This word is spelled correctly, capiche?"

Dead copy: The edited version of the original manuscript, with the corrections implemented, that is compared against the first typeset proofs.

Deck: The short text under an article title and before the lead paragraph that is meant to get the reader interested in the story.

Department: A regular feature of a magazine such as letters, beauty, health, and so on.

Designer: The person responsible for the physical appearance of a book or other publication, including layout and graphics.

Editorial inventory: A magazine's reserve of unpublished articles for possible future use.

F&Gs: A set of galleys that may be sent to the *production editor* after a book is fully printed and before it is bound, to make sure no major errors have crept in. (The term F&G — "folded and gathered" — is from the days when books were all printed on large sheets of paper, then folded and cut to size; these days, many sheet-fed printers cut the paper beforehand.)

Fact-checker: A person who confirms the accuracy of the information presented in a book or magazine, and brings any inconsistency or error to the author's attention.

Filler: A short article or editorial used to fill blank space.

First pass: The first set of *page proofs* that are proofread against the *dead copy*. These are nearly always in separate sheets, often blown up for easier markup.

Fixed elements: Elements within a magazine whose positions remain constant from issue to issue, including the magazine title and editorial page. This term is also used for books (for the placement of the copyright page, for example, or for elements that remain the same across a series of books).

Foul manuscript: A *dead copy,* or the proof pages of a previous pass that are no longer used because an updated, corrected set of proofs has been produced. Often called "foul matter" or "the fouls."

Four-color process: The process used to produce the full range of *CMYK* for a full-color image appearance.

Front of (the) book (FoB): The beginning pages of a magazine, usually including editorials, the masthead, and some departments and columns. Also used for books, but *front matter* is more common.

Front matter: The beginning pages of a book that include the title page, copyright page, acknowledgements, table of contents, and other introductory material that is not part of the main text.

Galleys: In book publishing, another term for a set of *page proofs,* often reserved for the first set of proofs that is oversized for easier editing. In magazine publishing, galleys are produced of the text only, for review before the final page makeup.

Gatefold: A fold-out advertisement or article printed on a larger piece of paper and folded to the size of the magazine.

Graf: Short for "paragraph."

Head: Short for "headline." Also used for magazine article titles. In books, it means a break in the manuscript that is treated differently type- and design-wise to indicate a new section.

Imprint: A set (or line) of books that usually share a common look and feel (or brand) and are marketed to the same segments of the population.

Initial caps: The use of a capital letter to begin each significant word, following a particular style's guidelines for headlines, titles, and so on.

Kerning: The amount of space between characters on a line, which can be adjusted to make a line or word look better.

Leading: The white space between lines on a typeset page.

Lead time: The time it takes from planning a publication to getting it on the newsstand.

Lede: An insiders' spelling of "lead" — the introductory paragraph of an article that is meant to lead the reader further into the story.

Manuscript: A book in loose pages or an electronic file submitted to a publishing house for evaluation and/or publication.

Masthead: The section of a periodical that details the publication's ownership and staff members, as well as contact information.

Orphan: A single word or piece of a word on its own line at the end of a laid-out paragraph, or the first line of a paragraph on its own at the bottom of a column or page.

Out of house: A term applied to any work that takes place outside of the publishing offices.

Page proofs: A set of pages that are composed according to the design *specs* for review to ensure that the type is correctly set and that art and other display elements are correctly placed. Page proofs are produced for each new pass after corrections are implemented. Also called *galleys* or *typeset pages*.

Perfect binding: A binding method for magazines and paperback books in which the folded and gathered signatures are cut and then glued to a cover. This binding is convenient for inserts but doesn't allow the text to lie open flat and is more expensive than *saddle stitching*.

Printer's error (PE): An error made by the typesetter or printer in production.

Print-ready: Used to describe electronic files that have final approval for printing. In the case of a book, there are often separate files for the jacket, the cover, and the composed pages. Compare *camera-ready*.

Print run: The number of copies of a publication that are to be printed.

Production editor: A person at a book publisher who coordinates all the steps in the publishing process after the editor transmits the manuscript, from copyediting to bound books.

Production manager: A person at a book publisher who assigns projects to the *production editor* and deals with printers and manufacturing costs. At a magazine, the production manager is responsible for relationships with outside vendors involved in the manufacturing process, such as printers, compositors, and ad agencies.

Proof: A sample of typeset and/or laid-out material that is checked against an original or earlier version. Proofs are made of typeset manuscripts, laid-out pages, book jackets, *blow-in cards* — whatever needs to be printed.

Proofreader's marks: Shorthand symbols used to indicate alterations or corrections in the copy. The symbols are standard throughout the U.S. printing industry (see Chapter 9).

Query: A question concerning the copy by the copyeditor or proofreader to the editor, author, or *typesetter*.

Roman: The standard unformatted typeface for the document, which can be either serif or sans serif. (This term is also often used to describe serif type.)

Run in: To set type with no paragraph breaks or to insert new copy without creating a new paragraph.

Running head: A book title or chapter head repeated at the top of every page in a book.

Saddle stitching: A binding method often used for smaller magazines, newsletters, and pamphlets, in which gathered sheets are stapled or stitched through the fold.

Sans serif: A font like Arial that literally has no serifs — those little lines that cross the strokes that make letters and numbers.

Second pass: The second version of *page proofs* from a manuscript, with implemented corrections from the *first pass*.

Serif: A font like Times New Roman that has little lines (serifs) that cross the ends of the strokes that make letters and numbers.

Side stitching: A binding method used especially for hardcover books in which signatures are stacked and then stitched through the side, near the spine, before the case is attached.

Slugging: Reading the *galleys* against the original manuscript, looking for errors either by the typesetter or the copyeditor.

Slush pile: A backlog of manuscripts sent to a book publisher that have not yet been evaluated by an editor. These are usually "over the transom" submissions — manuscripts sent by authors who don't have agents.

Small caps: The use of capital letters that are shorter than standard upper-case letters, usually the height of the lowercase letter *x* in a font.

Specs: Short for "specifications." The designer's instructions about what the final pages will look like — fonts and their point sizes, margins, leading between the lines, and so on.

Spine: The bound edge of a magazine or book that has printing on it (title, issue date, logo, and so on).

Style sheet: A guide that defines a book's style elements, created by the copyeditor.

TK: Editorial shorthand for "information to come."

Transposition: A common typographic error in which letters or words are not correctly placed.

Typeface: The way letters and numbers are formatted on a page — roman, bold, italic, strikethrough, shadow, and so on.

Typeset pages: In book publishing, a set of *page proofs,* usually loose-leaf, that are composed according to the design *specs* for review to ensure that the type is correctly set. Also called "composed pages."

Typesetter: A person who converts electronic manuscript files into *page proofs* that conform to the design *specs.* In these days of electronic page layout and composition, this person is often known as a *compositor,* especially because typesetting, strictly speaking, deals only with copy, not with display elements.

Well: The main middle section of a magazine where the feature articles appear.

Widow: The final word or line of a paragraph that appears alone at the top of a laid-out page or column.

Word break: The division of a word on a syllable at the end of one line, with its continuation on the following line.

Wrong font (WF): A type character set in a face, style, or size other than that specified.

Appendix C

Online Resources

Reference

All Words (www.allwords.com): This site can help you with those Dutch, French, German, Italian, and Spanish words you may run across.

***The American Heritage Book of English Usage* (www.bartleby.com/64):** "A Practical and Authoritative Guide to Contemporary English," or so they say.

CIA World Factbook (www.cia.gov/cia/publications/factbook/ index.html): Maps, profiles, geographic and demographic data, and other interesting information for every country from some very spooky people.

Merriam-Webster OnLine (www.m-w.com): This site features the 10th edition of the *Merriam-Webster's Collegiate Dictionary,* including definitions, abbreviations, illustrations, and tables. If you pay a subscription fee, you can get online access to the 11th edition. (If you buy a print version of the 11th edition, you get a year's subscription to the online version for free.)

***Roget's New Millennium Thesaurus* (www.thesaurus.com):** Use this online thesaurus to find synonyms for just about any word.

Fact-Checking

Abbreviations.com (www.abbreviations.com): You can search this database for acronyms and abbreviations in a number of ways. Not sure what a federal agency acronym stands for? What about that Internet-chat shorthand? With more than 411,000 entries, it's bound to be found here.

alt.usage.english (http://groups.google.com/group/alt.usage. english): This group has grown so popular that it has moved to a more easily accessible site at Google groups. Visit it to read about all things English.

Amazon.com (www.amazon.com): This site is a great starting point for verifying the names of authors, book titles, albums, and artists. But keep in mind that publishers often submit book information to this site long before a title is actually published, and they may not always update that info after publication. Your best bet is to use amazon.com to identify a book's publisher, and then visit the publisher's Web site to confirm the details.

Bible Gateway (www.biblegateway.com): Look up passages, search by keyword, or play in the topical index. This is a great place to confirm biblical references.

Biographical Dictionary (www.s9.com): Use the search feature to find out about more than 33,000 famous people.

***Columbia Journalism Review*'s Language Corner (www.cjr.org/tools/lc):** Look up specific words and general stuff on language, including articles, archives, and author responses in plain language.

Convert-me.com (www.convert-me.com): Need to convert Euros to dollars? Kilometers to miles? Celsius to Fahrenheit? Convert pretty much anything here.

Encyclopedia Britannica (www.britannica.com): The online version of your old favorite. Nonpaying visitors get stripped-down information.

Encyclopedia Mythica (www.pantheon.org): An amazing Web site encyclopedia of mythology, folklore, and religion. This is a great place to verify the spelling of those Greek (Roman, Norse, Christian) gods and heroes. It's divided by geographical region, as well as many other subdivisions.

The Encyclopedia of Television (www.museum.tv/archives/etv/index.html): The Museum of Broadcast Communication's Web site makes up for all those television shows you missed because you were studying.

Epicurious (www.epicurious.com): This extensive cooking site includes a food and wine dictionary of advanced cooking terminology.

Go Daddy (www.godaddy.com): Confirm domain names through this domain-name registry site.

The Holy Qu'ran (www.wright-house.com/religions/islam/Quran.html): Access the entire Koran, section by section.

Infoplease (www.infoplease.com): Biographies, businesses, and the ways of the world — all searchable here.

International Trademark Association's Trademark Checklist (www.inta.org): Click on <u>Information & Publishing</u>, and then on <u>Trademark Checklist</u>. This is the International Trademark Association's attempt to stop brand abuse, with nearly 3,000 registered trademarks and service marks searchable in alphabetical order.

Internet Movie Database (www.imdb.com): Get the scoop on Hollywood with this enormous movie database. Take this one with a grain of salt; there are some inconsistencies and inaccuracies.

Library of Congress (www.memory.loc.gov/ammem/help/constRedir. html): Peruse the primary documents in U.S. history: Declaration of Independence, U.S. Constitution, and many others you studied in high school.

MapQuest (www.mapquest.com): Useful for determining directions and distances between places. You can also use it to navigate your way to your next interview.

Newsroom Navigator (www.nytimes.com/navigator/): This is *The New York Times*'s fact-checking launchpad for its reporters.

QuoteWorld (www.quoteworld.org): In cahoots with www.amazon.com, this site boasts more than 15,000 quotations, with links to whole documents in which the quotes are found.

RxList (www.rxlist.com): Keep tabs on the latest drug names and other pharmaceutical information.

U.S. Census Bureau (www.census.gov): Find the latest census statistics, including regional surveys, a population finder, and the U.S. Population Clock.

United States Copyright Office (www.copyright.gov): The basics on copyrights, with access to the details, for anybody interested in researching this sort of thing.

United States Postal Service ZIP Code Lookup (www.usps.com/zip4): Enter an address — even partial — to verify a U.S. zip code.

WhatIs.com (www.whatis.com): Calling all nerds. This site defines thousands of the most current IT-related words.

Usage and Style

***Associated Press Stylebook* (www.apstylebook.com):** Search the "Ask the Editor" database for niggling questions. (The main section of this site requires an online subscription.)

The Chicago Manual of Style Online (`www.chicagomanualofstyle.org`): Search the Q&A section of this site to tackle the difficult nuances of grammar. (The main section of this site requires an online subscription.)

The Elements of Style **by William Strunk, Jr.** (`www.bartleby.com/141`): Classic reference work, now online.

Other Stuff

ACES: American Copy Editors Society (`www.copydesk.org`): Professional organization with an online discussion board, job bank, and resource links.

The Atlantic Monthly's **Word Police** (`www.theatlantic.com/unbound/wordpolice`): The official site of *The Atlantic Monthly*'s column, run by Barbara Wallraff, self-proclaimed Word Police commissioner. From this URL, you can read recent "Word Court" columns and a forum full of questions and advice.

Cliché Finder (`www.westegg.com/cliche`): Search by cliché, or enter your own keyword to find a cliché it occurs in.

Confusing Words (`www.confusingwords.com`): A collection of more than 3,200 words that are often confused or misused.

A Dictionary of Slang (`www.peevish.co.uk/slang`): Heavy on the Briticisms, but still rollicking fun to peruse.

The Gallery of "Misused" Quotation Marks (`www.juvalamu.com/qmarks`): This site tracks those strange places quotes end up. You'll "love" it.

HowStuffWorks (`www.howstuffworks.com`): Complete explanations, including diagrams and tables, on such topics as science, health, travel, electronics, and automotives.

Regret the Error (`www.regrettheerror.com`): A site of media errors that also includes an annual best-of media errors and plagiarism roundup.

RhymeZone (`www.rhymezone.com`): Find rhymes, synonyms, definitions, and more.

The Slot (`www.theslot.com`): Run by Bill Walsh, national desk copy chief at *The Washington Post* and author of *Lapsing Into a Comma: A Curmudgeon's Guide to the Many Things That Can Go Wrong in Print — and How to Avoid Them* (McGraw-Hill), this blog includes periodic articles called "Sharp Points." It's a good place for friendly advice.

Testy Copy Editors (`www.testycopyeditors.org`): Topical and general discussion board, with such threads as "Nightmare Job of the Week" and "British English."

Index

• C •

• R •

BUSINESS, CAREERS & PERSONAL FINANCE

0-7645-9847-3

0-7645-2431-3

Also available:
- Business Plans Kit For Dummies
  0-7645-9794-9
- Economics For Dummies
  0-7645-5726-2
- Grant Writing For Dummies
  0-7645-8416-2
- Home Buying For Dummies
  0-7645-5331-3
- Managing For Dummies
  0-7645-1771-6
- Marketing For Dummies
  0-7645-5600-2

- Personal Finance For Dummies
  0-7645-2590-5*
- Resumes For Dummies
  0-7645-5471-9
- Selling For Dummies
  0-7645-5363-1
- Six Sigma For Dummies
  0-7645-6798-5
- Small Business Kit For Dummies
  0-7645-5984-2
- Starting an eBay Business For Dummies
  0-7645-6924-4
- Your Dream Career For Dummies
  0-7645-9795-7

HOME & BUSINESS COMPUTER BASICS

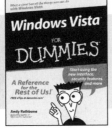

0-470-05432-8

0-471-75421-8

Also available:
- Cleaning Windows Vista For Dummies
  0-471-78293-9
- Excel 2007 For Dummies
  0-470-03737-7
- Mac OS X Tiger For Dummies
  0-7645-7675-5
- MacBook For Dummies
  0-470-04859-X
- Macs For Dummies
  0-470-04849-2
- Office 2007 For Dummies
  0-470-00923-3

- Outlook 2007 For Dummies
  0-470-03830-6
- PCs For Dummies
  0-7645-8958-X
- Salesforce.com For Dummies
  0-470-04893-X
- Upgrading & Fixing Laptops For Dummies
  0-7645-8959-8
- Word 2007 For Dummies
  0-470-03658-3
- Quicken 2007 For Dummies
  0-470-04600-7

FOOD, HOME, GARDEN, HOBBIES, MUSIC & PETS

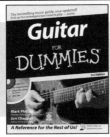

0-7645-8404-9

0-7645-9904-6

Also available:
- Candy Making For Dummies
  0-7645-9734-5
- Card Games For Dummies
  0-7645-9910-0
- Crocheting For Dummies
  0-7645-4151-X
- Dog Training For Dummies
  0-7645-8418-9
- Healthy Carb Cookbook For Dummies
  0-7645-8476-6
- Home Maintenance For Dummies
  0-7645-5215-5

- Horses For Dummies
  0-7645-9797-3
- Jewelry Making & Beading For Dummies
  0-7645-2571-9
- Orchids For Dummies
  0-7645-6759-4
- Puppies For Dummies
  0-7645-5255-4
- Rock Guitar For Dummies
  0-7645-5356-9
- Sewing For Dummies
  0-7645-6847-7
- Singing For Dummies
  0-7645-2475-5

INTERNET & DIGITAL MEDIA

0-470-04529-9

0-470-04894-8

Also available:
- Blogging For Dummies
  0-471-77084-1
- Digital Photography For Dummies
  0-7645-9802-3
- Digital Photography All-in-One Desk Reference For Dummies
  0-470-03743-1
- Digital SLR Cameras and Photography For Dummies
  0-7645-9803-1
- eBay Business All-in-One Desk Reference For Dummies
  0-7645-8438-3
- HDTV For Dummies
  0-470-09673-X

- Home Entertainment PCs For Dummies
  0-470-05523-5
- MySpace For Dummies
  0-470-09529-6
- Search Engine Optimization For Dummies
  0-471-97998-8
- Skype For Dummies
  0-470-04891-3
- The Internet For Dummies
  0-7645-8996-2
- Wiring Your Digital Home For Dummies
  0-471-91830-X

* Separate Canadian edition also available
† Separate U.K. edition also available

Available wherever books are sold. For more information or to order direct: U.S. customers visit www.dummies.com or call 1-877-762-2974.
U.K. customers visit www.wileyeurope.com or call 0800 243407. Canadian customers visit www.wiley.ca or call 1-800-567-4797.

 WILEY

SPORTS, FITNESS, PARENTING, RELIGION & SPIRITUALITY

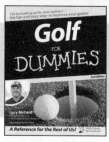

0-471-76871-5

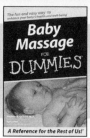

0-7645-7841-3

Also available:
- Catholicism For Dummies
  0-7645-5391-7
- Exercise Balls For Dummies
  0-7645-5623-1
- Fitness For Dummies
  0-7645-7851-0
- Football For Dummies
  0-7645-3936-1
- Judaism For Dummies
  0-7645-5299-6
- Potty Training For Dummies
  0-7645-5417-4
- Buddhism For Dummies
  0-7645-5359-3

- Pregnancy For Dummies
  0-7645-4483-7 †
- Ten Minute Tone-Ups For Dummies
  0-7645-7207-5
- NASCAR For Dummies
  0-7645-7681-X
- Religion For Dummies
  0-7645-5264-3
- Soccer For Dummies
  0-7645-5229-5
- Women in the Bible For Dummies
  0-7645-8475-8

TRAVEL

0-7645-7749-2

0-7645-6945-7

Also available:
- Alaska For Dummies
  0-7645-7746-8
- Cruise Vacations For Dummies
  0-7645-6941-4
- England For Dummies
  0-7645-4276-1
- Europe For Dummies
  0-7645-7529-5
- Germany For Dummies
  0-7645-7823-5
- Hawaii For Dummies
  0-7645-7402-7

- Italy For Dummies
  0-7645-7386-1
- Las Vegas For Dummies
  0-7645-7382-9
- London For Dummies
  0-7645-4277-X
- Paris For Dummies
  0-7645-7630-5
- RV Vacations For Dummies
  0-7645-4442-X
- Walt Disney World & Orlando
  For Dummies
  0-7645-9660-8

GRAPHICS, DESIGN & WEB DEVELOPMENT

0-7645-8815-X

0-7645-9571-7

Also available:
- 3D Game Animation For Dummies
  0-7645-8789-7
- AutoCAD 2006 For Dummies
  0-7645-8925-3
- Building a Web Site For Dummies
  0-7645-7144-3
- Creating Web Pages For Dummies
  0-470-08030-2
- Creating Web Pages All-in-One Desk
  Reference For Dummies
  0-7645-4345-8
- Dreamweaver 8 For Dummies
  0-7645-9649-7

- InDesign CS2 For Dummies
  0-7645-9572-5
- Macromedia Flash 8 For Dummies
  0-7645-9691-8
- Photoshop CS2 and Digital
  Photography For Dummies
  0-7645-9580-6
- Photoshop Elements 4 For Dummies
  0-471-77483-9
- Syndicating Web Sites with RSS Feeds
  For Dummies
  0-7645-8848-6
- Yahoo! SiteBuilder For Dummies
  0-7645-9800-7

NETWORKING, SECURITY, PROGRAMMING & DATABASES

0-7645-7728-X

0-471-74940-0

Also available:
- Access 2007 For Dummies
  0-470-04612-0
- ASP.NET 2 For Dummies
  0-7645-7907-X
- C# 2005 For Dummies
  0-7645-9704-3
- Hacking For Dummies
  0-470-05235-X
- Hacking Wireless Networks
  For Dummies
  0-7645-9730-2
- Java For Dummies
  0-470-08716-1

- Microsoft SQL Server 2005 For Dummies
  0-7645-7755-7
- Networking All-in-One Desk Reference
  For Dummies
  0-7645-9939-9
- Preventing Identity Theft For Dummies
  0-7645-7336-5
- Telecom For Dummies
  0-471-77085-X
- Visual Studio 2005 All-in-One Desk
  Reference For Dummies
  0-7645-9775-2
- XML For Dummies
  0-7645-8845-1